Communication Across Cultures

Mutual understanding in a global world

Second edition

The study of intercultural communication continues to grow in importance in response to greater population mobility, migration and globalisation.

Communication Across Cultures explores how cultural context affects the use and (mis)interpretation of language. It provides an accessible and interdisciplinary introduction to language and language variation in intercultural communication. This is done by drawing on both classic and cutting-edge research from pragmatics, discourse analysis, sociolinguistics, linguistic anthropology and politeness studies.

This new edition has been comprehensively updated to incorporate recent research, with an emphasis on the fluid and emergent practice of intercultural communication. It provides increased coverage of variation in language within and between cultures, drawing on real-world examples of spoken and written communication. The authors review classic concepts like 'face', 'politeness' and 'speech acts', but also critique these concepts and introduce more recent approaches.

Each chapter provides a set of suggested readings, questions and exercises to enable the student to work through concepts and con-solidate their understanding of intercultural communication. The culmination of each chapter is a simple project, which encour-ages students to conduct their own research. Further resources are available to instructors online at www.cambridge.edu.au/academic/communication2e.

Communication Across Cultures remains an excellent resource for students of linguistics and related disciplines, including anthropology, sociology and education. It is also valuable resource for professionals concerned with language and intercultural communication in this global era.

Communication Across Cultures

Mutual understanding in a global world

Second edition

Heather Bowe, Kylie Martin and
Howard Manns

CAMBRIDGE
UNIVERSITY PRESS

CAMBRIDGE
UNIVERSITY PRESS

477 Williamstown Road, Port Melbourne, VIC 3207, Australia

Cambridge University Press is part of the University of Cambridge.

It furthers the University's mission by disseminating knowledge in the pursuit of education, learning and research at the highest international levels of excellence.

www.cambridge.org
Information on this title: www.cambridge.org/9781107685147

© Heather Bowe, Kylie Martin, Howard Manns 2014

First published 2007
Reprinted 2009, 2012, 2013 (twice)
Second edition 2014

Cover designed by Kerry Cooke, Eggplant Communications
Typeset by Aptara Corp.
Printed in Singapore by C.O.S Printers Pte Ltd

A catalogue record for this publication is available from the British Library

A Cataloguing-in-Publication entry is available from the catalogue of the National Library of Australia at www.nla.gov.au

ISBN 978-1-107-68514-7 Paperback

Additional resources for this publication at
www.cambridge.edu.au/academic/communication2e

Please be aware that this publication may contain several variations of Aboriginal and Torres Strait Islander terms and spellings; no disrespect is intended. Please note that the terms 'Indigenous Australians' and 'Aboriginal and Torres Strait Islander peoples' may be used interchangeably in this publication.

Contents

List of tables and figures

Transcription conventions

T HIS BOOK has dialogue examples drawn from a variety of works. We have sought wherever possible to maintain the original transcription conventions of these works. Consequently, the reader will notice slight variations in the transcription conventions used in this book. Transcription conventions and variations in these conventions are outlined here.

. or \	final pitch contour, falling intonation
!	exclamatory or animated intonation
> <(e.g. >actually<)	marks emphasis of word(s)
? *or* / *or* ↑	rising intonation
xxxxx	inaudible or incomprehensible talk
<X word X>	uncertain hearing; the most likely text
+ *or* (.)	slight pause
+n+ *or* (n)	pause of n (number) seconds length
: *or* double consonants	an extension of the syllable or sound indicated (e.g. a:ah *or* mmm . . .)
[ ] *or* * *	speakers' utterances overlap
= *or* (0) (0)	latching, indicates no interval between contiguous utterances such that the second latches immediately onto the first without overlapping with it
~ ~	speaker breaks off before completion of word
(( ))	depending on context, used to mark omitted names or relevant body movement

Preface and acknowledgements

THE STUDY of intercultural communication continues to grow in importance in response to greater population mobility, migration and globalisation. Howard Manns has joined Heather Bowe and Kylie Martin in this revision of *Communication Across Cultures: Mutual Understanding in a Global World* to incorporate insights from research in the field since the publication of the first edition in 2007.

The first edition sought to present relevant research approaches in the field of linguistic aspects of intercultural communication, including pragmatics, discourse analysis, studies of politeness and cross-cultural communication, and to explain and exemplify these for beginning researchers, drawing on material from a variety of languages and cultures. It has been adopted as a required or recommended text for students of intercultural communication, language culture and communication, cross-cultural pragmatics and related fields at undergraduate and postgraduate level in Australia and elsewhere, and has also been adopted as a resource for university students of non-English-speaking background exploring issues in using English as a global language.

This second edition incorporates recent research in the field, which now includes research from more global and pluralised perspectives, including hybrid or mixed language practices, and takes account of cultural and linguistic diversity within groups as well as between groups. More recent research involving actual intercultural communication complements the cross-cultural comparative nature of much early research, which, though crucial to an understanding of some of the issues involved, fails to take account of the creative strategies that speakers can use when communicating across cultures.

Heather Bowe's interest in the multifaceted nature of language and the way the components of vocabulary, grammar, metaphor, style, politeness and inference are shaped by sociocultural practices was kindled when she was a student at the University of Southern California. Here, she observed the interaction of the work of Bernard Comrie, Edward Finegan, Elaine Anderson, Elinor Ochs and Robert Kaplan, and fellow students Doug Biber, Bill Eggington, Tsukao Kawahigashi, Keiji Matsumoto and Charles Randriamasimanana.

In addition to her research in the area of Australian Aboriginal languages, Heather responded to the interest of students in the applications of linguistics to intercultural communication in business and global contexts through a focus on language form and the interpretation of similar forms in different cultural contexts. She developed units in intercultural communication at Monash University at the Monash campuses in the Melbourne area for students at both undergraduate and graduate level from the Faculties of Arts and Business, and also at the Monash campuses in Malaysia and South Africa.

Heather's interest in intercultural communication was informed by the work of Michael Clyne and other colleagues in the areas of languages and linguistics at Monash, particularly Marissa Cordella, Georgina Heydon, Helen Marriott, Kylie Martin and Farzad Sharifian, as well as past and present students from a rich variety of cultures, including Margaret à Beckett, Zosia Golebiowski, Angelina Kioko, Kei Miyazawa Reid, Deborah Neil and Mingjian Zhang. Heather also wishes to acknowledge her parents for encouraging her interest in cultures beyond her own, and her husband, Robin, for his ongoing support of her work.

Kylie Martin's interest in intercultural and international communication began at the University of Adelaide where she was a student of Peter Mühlhäusler, and where she worked on a research project concerning the development of pidgins and creoles in the Pacific region. It was also at this university that she began to develop a research focus on understanding the diverse communication styles adopted by first-language (L1) and second-language (L2) speakers of Australian English in emerging intercultural settings.

Kylie's interest in intercultural communication continued into her postgraduate studies at Monash University, with her MA focusing on the convergence and divergence of Bahasa Malaysia and Bahasa Indonesia language norms used by Malaysian and Indonesian international students undertaking their studies at Australian universities. Her PhD thesis has focused on new innovative and emerging ways of language usage among the Indigenous Ainu people in the urban metropolis of Tokyo, Japan. Her research examines the influences of globalisation processes on the functions and values of Ainu, a severely endangered language, to better understand the relationship between this language and identity maintenance within the urban Kanto Ainu diaspora.

Kylie has worked at universities in both Japan and Australia in the areas of sociolinguistics, intercultural communication and English for academic purposes. She is currently based in the Research Faculty of Media and Communication at Hokkaido University in the northernmost island of Japan.

Howard Manns had his first encounter with intercultural communication as a student at the Defense Language Institute in Monterey, California. Howard worked for three years as a specialist in Iranian languages and cultures for the US Navy, travelling throughout the Persian Gulf region. He subsequently earned a BA in linguistics at the University of Pittsburgh. A love of language, culture, volcanoes and surf led him to spend the next three years travelling throughout Latin America and Asia.

Howard's PhD thesis explored how Indonesian youth and media negotiate linguistic and social change on the island of Java. Howard works in the Linguistics Program at Monash University, which is a vibrant, convivial and intellectually stimulating place to be. At Monash, he would like to thank Julie Bradshaw and Louisa Willoughby, whose materials and ideas have certainly informed the revisions incorporated in this edition. He would also like to thank Kate Burridge, Anna Margetts, Simon Musgrave and Farzad Sharifian who have all helped in their own ways. Howard is also grateful to many hundreds of students who have inspired, engaged with and challenged the ideas contained herein.

Howard would also like to thank Heather and Kylie who have been enthusiastically supportive of this edition's revisions, and David Jackson at Cambridge University Press (CUP) who has been both supportive and patient while awaiting them. He would also like to thank Isabella Mead at CUP, who oversaw the final stages of this project, and Angela Damis, whose keen editorial eye was invaluable in the project's closing weeks.

Howard acknowledges that any factual infelicities and typos in this revised edition are his own. One or two of these might belong to Howard's son, Oisín, who sat on his lap during its writing. Howard couldn't do much of what he does without Oisín's and his wife Ali's support.

Heather Bowe and Howard Manns
School of Languages, Literatures, Cultures and Linguistics
Monash University, Clayton, Australia

Kylie Martin
Research Faculty of Media and Communication
Hokkaido University, Sapporo, Japan

April 2014

1 Culture, communication and context

1.1 INTRODUCTION

THIS BOOK is intended as an academic reference for under-graduate and graduate students and interdisciplinary researchers who do not have specialised knowledge of linguistics. Key concepts relevant to an understanding of language issues in intercultural communication are drawn from the research areas of pragmatics, discourse analysis, politeness and intercultural communication. Relevant academic literature and recent research conducted by the authors is exemplified and explained throughout the book so that students can become familiar with the way research in this field is reported and can follow up on the ideas presented.

An understanding of intercultural communication is crucially related to an understanding of the ways in which the spoken and written word may be interpreted differentially, depending on the context. The message received is not always the one intended by the speaker or the writer. This book systematically examines sociocultural and pragmatic aspects of the language context, and discusses a wide range of factors that contribute to the interpretation of language in context. The authors argue that an understanding of how these principles interact in a given language, and in intercultural communication, is crucial to the development of mutual understanding in the global world.

Speakers engaged in intercultural communication in this increasingly globalised world may choose one or more languages in which to com-municate. However, regardless of whether it is their first, second or third language, individuals typically bring their own sociocultural expectations of language to the encounter. Speakers' expectations shape the interpreta-tion of meaning in a variety of ways. To manage intercultural interaction

1

effectively, speakers need to be aware of the inherent norms of their own speech practices, the ways in which norms vary depending on situational factors and the ways in which speakers from other language backgrounds may have different expectations of language usage and behaviour.

Representative research methodologies are exemplified throughout the book, although there is no single chapter devoted to methodology. This book endeavours to show how a variety of methodologies may be drawn on to uncover the nuances of language use in intercultural contexts. These nuanced linguistic behaviours are linked to wider non-linguistic socio-cultural and pragmatic processes. We outline these processes throughout the remainder of this chapter. These, in turn, lay the foundation for a more nuanced discussion of language, meaning and (mis)interpretation throughout the remainder of this book.

1.2 CULTURE, SELF AND OTHER

This section provides an overview of sociocultural concepts essential to the study of intercultural communication. Notions of culture, cultural heterogeneity and cultural difference are introduced and critiqued. We then discuss how individuals perceive and categorise the sociocultural practices of the self and the other.

CULTURE

The term culture as we will be using it, refers to the customs, symbols and expectations of a particular group of people, particularly as they affect their language use.

The term **culture** has a wide range of meanings today, because it has actually changed in meaning over time. Goddard (2005, pp. 53) provides an excellent account of some of these changes. In its earliest English uses, *culture* was a noun of process, referring to the tending of crops or animals. This meaning (roughly, 'cultivating') is found in words such as *agriculture, horticulture* and *viviculture*. In the sixteenth century *culture* began to be used to mean 'cultivating' the human body through training, and later 'cultivating' the non-physical aspects of a person. In the nineteenth century the meaning was broadened to include the general state of human intellectual, spiritual and aesthetic development (roughly comparable to 'civilisation'), giving rise to the 'artistic works and practices' meaning that is associated with music, literature, painting, theatre and film.

Goddard reports that the 'anthropological' usage of culture was introduced into English by Tylor in the late nineteenth century, in his book *Primitive Culture*. Tylor defined *culture* as 'that complex whole which includes knowledge, belief, art, morals, law, custom and other capabilities and habits acquired by man as a member of a society' (Tylor 1871, p. 1).

Goddard (2005, p. 58) makes the point that the 'anthropological' use typically related to people living in 'other places'; however, in contemporary expressions such as *youth culture, gay culture* and *kid culture* the principle of differentiation has shifted entirely to the notion of different 'kinds of people'. It is perhaps unsurprising then that growing numbers of anthropologists are choosing to work for corporations rather than heading off to exotic lands (Ferraro 2002).

We believe Tylor's definition of culture, albeit dated, provides a starting point for discussing intercultural communication. Tylor's anthropological approach implicates the relevance of processes that are cognitive (e.g. knowledge, belief) as well as practical (e.g. art, habits). We engage with both cognitive and practical processes in this book.

Yet, this book's focus on meaning and the (mis)interpretation of meaning in social contexts entails by necessity favouring a focus on practical processes. This means adopting a more **relativist perspective** on culture and the view that 'Cultural meanings are public meanings encoded in shared symbols, not-self-contained private understandings' (Foley 1997, p. 16). Public meanings are, by their very nature, learned meanings. Clifford Geertz (1973) discusses culture in terms of symbolic practices handed down from generation to generation.

A meaning- and symbol-driven approach entails deconstructing essentialist notions of culture (Hall 1997). Research on intercultural communication has historically discussed cultural groups at the essentialist level of nations and national languages. In other words, for instance, an Indonesian was presumed to speak Indonesian and behave in accordance with Indonesian cultural norms. These behaviours, in turn, could be contrasted with those of a US American who was presumed to speak American English and behave in US American ways.

These understandings of culture and language are often, and, in some ways always oversimplistic. For instance, young Indonesians engage in ethnic, national and religious cultural practices (Manns 2012). Furthermore, they vary these practices from moment to moment to construct heterogeneous selves. An essentialist view of a US American doesn't take into account intracultural variation (e.g. African American, Southern American). It also doesn't consider that more than 20 per cent of US

Americans speak a language other than English at home (Ryan 2013). Spanish speakers account for more than half of this number and often mix Spanish and English to express hybrid cultural identities (e.g. Sánchez-Muñoz 2013).

In short, essentialist views of culture and language can be limiting and less relevant in the late modern era (Hall 1995). Yet, it is our view that scholars of culture should not throw the baby out with the bathwater. There is a rich body of research that discusses culture in nationalistic terms. Ignoring this research implies that there aren't differences between, for instance, Indonesians and US Americans, or that such differences are not relevant. These macro-cultural labels are useful to a degree, but they should also be critiqued. This is perhaps clearest in a review of the traditional models for understanding cultural difference.

CULTURAL DIFFERENCE

Many models have been posited for understanding cultural difference. The two most frequently cited models are those proposed by Geert Hofstede and Edward T. Hall respectively. Both models, however, have been criticised for being essentialist and anachronistic and for having problematic methodologies.

Hofstede's work (1980, 1983, 1998, 2010) has been highly influential in the study of **national cultural differences**. Hofstede's research is based on information gained from studies of a multinational corporation (IBM) in 64 countries. He has also conducted subsequent studies concerning students in over 20 countries and 'elites' in 19 countries (Hofstede 1998, p. 11). Hofstede originally proposed four independent dimensions of national cultural differences. He then added a fifth in response to criticisms of Western bias (Samovar et al. 2013).[1]

1. **Power distance** relates to the degree to which members of a culture accept institutions and organisations having power. Hofstede classes 'Latin', Asian and African countries as accepting of power asymmetries. Conversely, he cites Anglo and Germanic countries as being less accepting of such asymmetries.
2. **Uncertainty avoidance** refers to the degree to which members feel uncomfortable with ambiguity and uncertainty and thus the degree to which they avoid these. Latin countries and Japan are among those prone to avoid uncertainty and Anglo, Nordic and

---

[1] Hoftstede (2013) subsequently posited a sixth dimension, indulgence/restraint, but this has not yet gained currency in academic discourse and is not dealt with here.

Chinese culture countries are those more likely to engage in such 'risky' behaviour.

3. The **individualism/collectivism** dimension marks a distinction between those cultures that place a higher emphasis on individual goals (individualism) in comparison to group achievements (collectivism). Anglo, European and 'developed' countries tend to be individualistic whereas Asian, African and less developed countries tend to value collectivism. It is worth noting that Japan falls between these two poles in Hofstede's scale (Hoftstede & Hofstede 2013).

4. The **masculinity/femininity** dimension presents a masculine culture as having a 'preference for achievement, heroism, assertiveness, and material success' and a feminine culture as having a 'preference for relationships, modesty, caring for the weak, and the quality of life' (Hofstede 1983, pp. 336–7). Therefore, we see that **masculinity** is more achievement-oriented and **femininity** has a greater focus on relationships and maintaining a balance among people. Masculinity, as such, is linked to Japan and Germanic countries and femininity to Nordic countries. Anglo countries are moderately masculine and many Asian countries moderately feminine.

5. The subsequently added, fifth dimension, **long-term/short-term orientation** (originally known as 'Confucian dynamism'), posits that some societies (long-term-oriented) emphasise future reward, and pursue these through persistence, savings and flexible adaptation. Other societies (short-term-oriented) align more towards the past and present, and do so through national pride, respect for traditions and the perseverance of 'face'. China and East Asian nations have rated highly as long-term-oriented nations whereas Anglo, African and South Asian nations tend to rate as short-term-oriented.

The qualities Hofstede identifies seem to be of value in understanding potentially different patterns of thinking, feeling and acting. However, there are weaknesses in his formulations. For instance, Wierzbicka (1991) draws attention to the extreme polarities inherent in Hofstede's framework. Also, Hofstede has been accused of Western bias, both in his selection of labels and collection of data (Gudykunst 2001). Clyne (1994, pp. 179–86) finds some of the features of Hofstede's model to be useful in understanding the cultural varieties in his corpus of intercultural workplace interaction. Yet, Clyne largely avoids using the labels 'masculinity' and 'femininity', which we ourselves find overgeneralise and perpetuate gender stereotypes. He instead uses such words as *harmony* and *degrees of negotiation* as well as *assertiveness* and *weakness*.

In spite of the limitations of Hofstede's model, it does contain a useful inventory of parameters along which cultural value systems and the relations within cultures can be analysed. However, it needs to be understood that such categorisations, while useful, are based on general national cultural differences and such simplifications were shown above to have significant limitations.

The second most-cited model for categorising cultural difference is also one of the oldest. This model was devised by Edward T. Hall, considered by many to be the originator of the field of intercultural communication (Sorrells 2013). Hall worked for the US Foreign Service Institute and sought to devise training courses for Foreign Service Officers heading to overseas assignments. Not unlike the authors of this book, Hall (1959, 1966, 1976) was primarily concerned with micro-communicative contexts and the ways in which differing expectations might lead to misunderstanding.

Hall (1976) categorises cultures according to whether they are high-context or low-context. **High-context cultures** are those in which much of the meaning exchanged in a context is done so without or with relatively few words. The messages communicated in such societies are more subtle, indirect and often non-verbal. Furthermore, roles in such societies are more defined and hierarchical. These societies are normally more 'traditional' and more attuned to their environments and one another. Cultures considered high-context include many Asian cultures and the African American and Native American cultures.

Low-context cultures, conversely, are those in which detailed verbal messages are favoured. Individuals from these cultures share less background information and intimate information about one another and consequently can rely less on non-verbal contextual cues. The messages conveyed in these cultures tend to be direct and verbose and these cultures value people who 'speak up' and 'say what's on their mind' (Samovar et al. 2013). These societies are typically less 'traditional' and include North American, German and Scandinavian cultures.

Miscommunications may occur when those from a low-context culture communicate with those from a high-context culture. Hall (1959) proposes cultural distance as a major factor in determining whether miscommunication will take place. For example, communication between a Japanese individual (among Hall's highest-context cultures) and a German (among the lowest-context cultures) would be expected to be particularly problematic.

This problematic communication, for instance, might take place along lines of credibility (Samovar et al. 2013). When meeting a high-context Japanese individual, our low-context German might find the Japanese silence to be an indication that he or she is hiding something and thus being dishonest. Conversely, the Japanese individual might find the talkativeness of the German off-putting or even meaningless, and, thus, untrustworthy.

As with Hofstede's framework, there are pros and cons in drawing on Hall's observations. Cultural distance has been found to be less of a predictor of communication problems than intergroup history, especially histories beset with social inequality or intergroup rivalry (Brabant, Watson & Gallois 2007). Further, Hall's discussions of context have received less academic scrutiny and works that have drawn on this model have generally accepted it without question (Cardon 2008). This lack of scrutiny has led to problems in intercultural classrooms where students have found Hall's observations to be dated or inaccurate (Hastings, Musambira & Ayoub 2011).

Hofstede's and Hall's are but two of many frames for illustrating similarities and differences of cultural value systems. There are many other models that emphasise, among other things, cultural adaptation (Kim 1977, 1988) and the negotiation of cultural anxiety and uncertainty (Gudykunst 1995). A full discussion of intercultural models is beyond the scope of this language-focused book. However, they are addressed in any number of general introductory texts (e.g. Martin & Nakayama 2004; Samovar et al. 2013; Sorrells 2013).

The ways in which individuals interpret culture, cultural practices, contexts and meanings are influenced by their view of the self and the other. Self and other categorisation are dealt with in the following section.

CATEGORISING SELF AND OTHER

The categorisation of the self and the other are critical in how we create and interpret meanings within contexts. This section introduces traditional and contemporary frameworks for understanding how individuals categorise the self and the other.

Social psychologist Henri Tajfel (1982) suggests that people often categorise themselves positively at the centre (**in-group**) to create and promote self-esteem and pride and classify others negatively on the outside (**out-group**). Positive in-group stereotypes are utilised to develop self-esteem and mark oneself as being different from the out-group (see also the 'in-group favouritism principle': Ting-Toomey & Chung 2005).

Tajfel's notions of the in-group and the out-group overlap with the concept of ethnocentrism. Sociologist William Sumner (1906, p. 13) defined **ethnocentrism** as 'the technical name for this view of things in which one's own group is the center of everything, and all others are scaled and rated with reference to it'. Sumner adds: 'Each group nourishes its own pride and vanity, boasts itself superior, exalts its own divinities, and looks with contempt on outsiders.' This positive valuation of the in-group, often at the expense of the out-group, is perhaps the most potent impediment to successful intercultural communication (Cargile & Bolkan 2013).

Ethnocentrism can be a complex affair as we have multiple selves, or rather social identities, and these vary from moment to moment (see Onorato & Turner 2002; Djenar 2008). These multiple selves are the product of our varied and complex backgrounds and experiences. For instance, as noted above, a US American may also align with Latino culture. This might be because the individual grew up in a Latino country or within a Latino community in the United States. In conversations, the individual may choose to emphasise his or her US American identity in one context, the Latina/o in another or indeed reduce both in favour of any number of other social identities relevant to the immediate context.

Implicit in the categorisation of the self is the othering of the out-group. While linking certain characteristics to different cultures serves as a useful guide in understanding relations and linguistic communication, such categorisations may lead to some level of stereotyping and overgeneralisation. El-Dash and Busnardo (2001) point out any categorisation of a group results in some level of stereotyping. **Stereotypes** are the generalised and ideological beliefs that any two cultures or social groups are opposites (Scollon, Scollon & Jones 2012).

Scollon, Scollon and Jones (2012) discuss stereotyping in 'positive' and 'negative' terms. **Negative stereotyping** is seen as a method of reiterating a binaristic contrast as a negative group difference. Scollon, Scollon and Jones (2012, pp. 273–4) identify four major steps in negative stereotyping. First, one might contrast two cultures or two groups on the basis of a single dimension, like finding migrant shopkeepers of a particular culture curt and uninterested in their customers. Second, rather than working towards mutual understanding, an individual might focus on this difference as a problem for communication. Third, one might assign a positive value to one strategy or one group and a negative value to the other strategy or group. For example, an individual in Australia, the United Kingdom or the United States might view Anglo shopkeepers in a positive light (e.g. they always say *please* and *thank you* and make small talk) and view shopkeepers from other cultures negatively (e.g. shopkeepers from culture x focus only on the transaction at hand). Lastly, the fourth step entails re-generalising this process to the entire group. For instance, the individual might decide all people from culture x are curt and rude because of an interaction with shopkeepers (or even a single shopkeeper) from culture x.

Such binary contrasts are used both within a society and between different societies. For example, the in-group may be Westerners (taken from their perspective) and the out-group Asians. Of course, placing all people of 'Western' nations in one category and 'Asian' nations in another creates a stereotype already. However, here all Westerners may contrast themselves with all Asians and state that the out-group 'refuse(s) to introduce their topics so that we [the Westerners] can understand them' (Scollon, Scollon & Jones 2012, p. 274). Scollon, Scollon and Jones emphasise that such negative stereotyping 'leads to the idea that somehow members of the other group are actively trying to make it difficult to understand them' (2012, p. 274).

Positive stereotyping, in contrast, can be divided into two main strategies: the solidarity fallacy and the lumping fallacy. The **solidarity fallacy** relates to falsely combining one's own group with some other group in order to establish common ground on one single dimension (Scollon, Scollon & Jones 2012). Scollon, Scollon and Jones review Tannen's (1994) observations about the conversational norms of North American men and women and Chinese men and women. Tannen observes that US American men have a tendency to stress information over relationship, while US American women favour relationship over information (see also Hofstede's dimensions). The solidarity fallacy develops when US American women group themselves with Chinese people in general in contrast to US American men to emphasise both the similarities between themselves and the Chinese, and the difference from US American men. While such groupings may assist in understanding the similarities between US American women and the Chinese in general, it can lead to the misconception that all cultural characteristics of the two groups are similar or the same.

The second type of positive stereotyping is the **lumping fallacy**. This occurs when a person makes a false grouping in reference to two other groups (Scollon, Scollon & Jones 2012, p. 275). An example of this would be the statement that Westerners consider all Asians to be members of the same group, thus ignoring the contrasts between the groups and that such groupings include a diversity of different cultures and languages. In summary, negative stereotyping involves regarding members of a group as being polar opposites, whereas with positive stereotyping the members of different groups are viewed as being identical (Scollon, Scollon & Jones 2012, p. 275).

Stereotypes, whether positive or negative, limit our understanding of human behaviour and can lead to miscommunication in intercultural discourse because, as Scollon, Scollon and Jones (2012, p. 272) conclude, 'they limit our view of human activity to just one or two salient dimensions and consider those to be the whole picture'. People need to consider the differences and similarities that exist between people and cultures. In other words, no individual member of a group encompasses or displays all of the characteristics of his or her group. Individuals belong to a variety of different groups and thus their identity and characteristics can be asserted differently, depending on the situation. This is especially so for those who relate to more than one ethnic or cultural group.

Culture has been shown to be a complex phenomenon here. Furthermore, the ways in which individuals position the self and the other with regard to culture(s) have been shown to be potentially limiting. Yet, individuals from different cultures need to communicate with one another perhaps more than ever in the era of globalisation. The remainder of this chapter introduces the role that language plays in intercultural communication and lays the foundation for the rest of this linguistically focused book.

1.3 COMMUNICATION, LANGUAGE AND VARIATION

COMMUNICATION

Communication in its most basic sense may be defined as 'a sharing of elements of behaviour or modes of life' (Cherry 1996, p. 12). Animal communication is often linked to mere response to direct environmental stimulus. For instance, a bee may communicate to other bees the direction and distance to a food source. A male grasshopper communicates to others its desire to mate (as well as its satisfaction at having done so). Communication plays a critical role in the sharing and regulation of behaviour and modes of life for both human and non-human animals alike.

Human beings stand out among animals both in terms of the complexities of our social behaviours and the communicative means through which we manage these behaviours. As established above, human culture(s) and individuals' senses of self and other are complex and shifting. Human language has either evolved to manage these complex relationships or these complex relationships have evolved as a result of human language. In either case, complex social function is linked to an increase in size in the mammalian neo-cortex (i.e. the spongy, outer part of the brain). This growth has been exponentially more significant in humans than other mammals.

Human wants and needs and the information related to these wants and needs are also complex. These wants, needs and information are communicated and achieved through infinitely more sophisticated, patterned ways than those of our animal counterparts. A bee can communicate information about an immediate food source but can't tell you about a tasty food source from last year. A male grasshopper is limited to six communicative messages, all related to lovemaking and territory. Humans, on the other hand, have seemingly infinite ways of communicating information, including information about events displaced in time and space. More so, humans can communicate who told them where to find food or mates (or, on a technological plane, how to or who can fix their computers or cars) and how reliable this information may be.

Humans are, as Terrence W. Deacon (1997) points out, 'the symbolic species'. Deacon (1997, p. 423) writes that 'we humans have access to a novel higher-order representation system that . . . guides the formation of skills and habits'. He adds that 'we do not just live our lives in the physical world and our immediate social group, but also in a world of rules of conduct, beliefs about our histories, and hopes and fears about our imagined futures'.

This higher-order representation system is language, and this is the primary focus of this book. Throughout this book, we make reference to cross-cultural and intercultural communication. These terms are sometimes used interchangeably in the literature. However, we use **cross-cultural communication** to refer to research that compares communication practices of one language/cultural group with another. **Intercultural communication**, on the other hand, is focused on communication between speakers from different language/cultural backgrounds.

Most modern research on cross-cultural and intercultural communication takes into account that communication is affected by different aspects of the context, including cultural expectations, social relations and the purpose of the communication. The following sections introduce the fluid relationship between language and context, a theme that underlies the remainder of this book.

LANGUAGE

Language refers to the system of sounds, affixes, words and grammar, among other symbols, that human beings use for communication. Monolinguals, like English speakers in Anglo countries, are particularly apt to think of language in isolated, named and monolithic ways (Makoni & Pennycook 2007; Otsuji & Pennycook 2010). These speakers become obsessed with notions of proper English, French, Spanish and so on and prescribe rules for standard usage (e.g. Standard English).

However, some have argued against the view of language in terms of these inflexible named systems. In other words, instead of viewing language in terms of 'German', 'French' and so on we should think about language in more fluid ways. They advocate a focus on what a sound, word or way of speaking can 'do' in a particular context and whether its use is appropriate to that context from the perspective of the interlocutors. Linguistic labels, they argue, have become particularly problematic in the era of globalisation (Blommaert & Rampton 2011). **Globalisation** has meant increased contact between peoples and languages through migration and technology. This, in turn, has led to the increased likelihood that individuals use one or more languages beyond those found in the home. It is now more likely that spouses speak different languages to one another and/or to their children. Also, in globalised contexts, people may not attain or maintain full competency in a language as such. For example, recent adult migrants to Australia might acquire enough English to run errands and make basic requests but otherwise speak the language or languages of the country of origin at home and with friends and family (see Willoughby 2007). Conversely second-generation migrants to Australia might select elements of their parents' languages for identity goals in otherwise English conversations (see also Canagarajah 2013 for young Tamil migrants in the United States, the United Kingdom and Canada).

Blommaert (2010) describes language use like this in terms of a truncated repertoire. A **truncated repertoire**, especially that of migrants, consists of 'highly specific "bits" of language and literacy values combined in a repertoire that reflects the fragmented and highly diverse life-trajectories and environments of such people' (Blommaert 2010, p. 8). He notes that a truncated repertoire should not be all that surprising as a concept since 'No one knows *all* of a language . . . Native speakers are not perfect speakers' (Blommaert 2010, p. 103). However, we should note, as with culture above, that we do not wish to throw the baby out with the bathwater in our shift away from language labels and towards symbolic meaning and interpretation. There is a rich body of literature that discusses language use in terms of these labels and we ourselves use them in this book for ease of reference. In short, it would be silly to dispense of language labels altogether.

We adopt a largely semiotic approach to language and intercultural communication in this book. Semiotics requires that we introduce the concept of linguistic signs, if briefly. A **linguistic sign** consists of a physical form (pronunciation and meaning) and 'the discrimination it makes in the domain of language which sustains the coordination of behaviour' (Foley 1997, p. 25). For instance, the imperative English command *come!* consists of the physical combination of the sounds *c* (known in phonetic terms as a voiceless, velar stop [k]), *o* (an open-mid back unrounded vowel [ʌ]) and *m* (a bilabial nasal [m]). Combined, these sounds carry the general meaning 'movement towards or so as to reach the speaker' (Oxford English Dictionary 2013a). This combination of sounds functions in a discriminatory way to command a hearer to move from his or her current location and towards the speaker. Indeed, we will show throughout this book how risky such behavioural discriminations can be, especially as they take place across cultures.

Peirce (1991) proposes that signs may be classified into three categories: icons, indexes and symbols. An **icon** refers to a form in which there is a perceptible likeness between the form and meaning. For instance, the ways in which individuals describe eating show iconic similarities across cultures. A US English speaker says *nom nom*, a French speaker *miam miam* and a Thai speaker *ngam ngam*. In each of these cases, the form is repeated as if to mimic the open and closed mouth action of eating. Furthermore, each of the forms is pronounced with the air redirected through the nasal tract rather than the vocal tract. This also mimics, albeit more subtly, the physiological process of eating.

An **index** is a form that only derives its meaning from the context in which it is uttered. Personal pronouns (*I, you, she, he, it, they*) are perhaps the best example of indexes. For instance, the personal pronoun *you* is generally used to address or refer to one or more person or people, animal(s) or personified thing(s) (Oxford English Dictionary 2013b). However, the exact referent (or nature of the thing) only becomes clear in the immediate context. Indexes are also relevant to the discussion of social evaluations of language usage or pronunciation. For instance, though often cited as 'sloppy speech', there is nothing inherently incorrect about double negation (e.g. *he don't got no money*). In informal working-class contexts, among intimate interlocutors, this might be viewed as entirely appropriate (and even required). However, it is generally viewed as inappropriate in formal or education contexts, for instance.

The final linguistic sign is the **symbol**, which is entirely conventional in that it is not linked to context nor does it bear an iconic relationship to its referent. In other words, English speakers generally agree that a furry, four-legged mammal that barks (among other things) is called a *dog* regardless of the context. Persian-language (Farsi) speakers call the same animal a *sag*, Javanese speakers an *asu* and so on. There is nothing iconic about *dog*, *sag* and *asu*, yet we can discuss this animal across contexts with speakers of these respective languages.

This section has introduced and deconstructed the concept of language as it relates to intercultural communication. We have also hinted at the relevance of context to interpreting linguistic meaning. The full relevance of context becomes clearer below and throughout this book. However, it is important first to introduce language variation and point out that just as individuals harbour stereotypes and hold prejudices against others, they do the same for languages and their speakers.

LANGUAGE VARIATION

Those engaged with the study of language variation take as their starting point the proposition that there are at least two ways to say the same thing. For instance, bilingual or multilingual individuals might select among two or more languages to refer to the four-legged mammal referred to above (e.g. *dog* in English or *sag* in Farsi). Bilingual individuals often alternate between languages within a single conversation or context in what is known as **code-switching**.

Variation is also pervasive within a single language variety like English. For example, the English word *dog* may be pronounced differently depending on one's geographic location. A speaker from some areas of the US East Coast pronounces *dog* with the same vowel as in *for* [ɔ] whereas many other English speakers pronounce this with the vowel in *far* [a]. There are innumerable accent, lexical (e.g. *truck/lorry*) and spelling differences (*favor/favour*) between American, British and Australian Englishes (and other varieties of English again). Many people become angry or confused if a speaker selects a word from another dialect. For instance, Australians, British and New Zealanders bristle at what they perceive to be the Americanisation of English.

Language variation may also be linked to particular situations and over time these situations may foster their own varieties. For instance, in technical scientific discussions or texts, a *dog* might be referred to as *canis lupis familiaris*. Legal discussions (e.g. court, contracts) also take place in a specified way and through a special vocabulary. Most individuals are unfamiliar with legal ways of speaking and writing and need to hire a legal professional to navigate these ways. Furthermore, individuals from minority cultures (e.g. Indigenous Australians) are often doubly disadvantaged because legal ways of speaking are typically rooted in the dominant culture's traditions.

In any case, individuals vary their language from moment to moment in order to response to or to re-create the context at hand and this is known as **stylistic variation**. Stylistic variation includes shifts in usage for features associated with particular speakers (i.e. languages, dialects) or with particular situations (i.e. registers) (Schilling-Estes 2004). It also extends to variation in the way in which individuals accomplish speech acts, such as asking questions, making requests, thanking and so on.

Variation is socially meaningful and this influences how language is used for strategic goals. Languages, language varieties and language features are ideologically non-equivalent (Coupland 2001). For instance, English speakers often link French to culinary superiority and German to technical sophistication and these links are used by advertisers to sell products (Kuppens 2009). Individuals have been found to evaluate language variation along dimensions of **prestige** and **pleasantness**. For instance, Coupland and Bishop (2007) investigated the language attitudes of 5000 British individuals and found they rated the Queen's English as most prestigious. However, these individuals rated accents similar to their own among the most pleasant (second only to Standard English).

Stylistic variation is utilised for a number of strategic goals, as will be shown throughout this book. However, accommodation to the hearer is among the strongest factors influencing stylistic variation. Researchers have found that speakers converge towards the speech of a hearer to increase intimacy or diverge from the hearer to decrease intimacy (Giles & Powesland 1975). Discussed under the label **Communication Accommodation Theory**, this behaviour is motivated by a speaker's desire to appear more attractive and promote communicative efficiency with a hearer when that hearer has been evaluated positively (Coupland 2007).

The factors motivating stylistic variation are many. Among other things, stylistic variation has been linked to upward mobility (e.g. Labov 1972b), topic shift (e.g. Rickford & McNair-Knox 1994), irony (e.g. Clift 1999) and identity (e.g. Coupland 2007). A full discussion of these factors is beyond the scope of this work (for such a discussion see Coupland 2007; Eckert & Rickford 2001). What is critically relevant to this book is that even a monolingual speaker has more than one way to say the same thing and that language variation is socially meaningful. Yet, a speaker's intended meaning critically requires a hearer who understands that meaning or is willing to work cooperatively towards it.

Herein lies the potential flashpoint in intercultural communication. Speakers and hearers do not always share the same understanding of linguistic signs and variation even when they share the same language. This is particularly the case in this era of globalisation, which is characterised by increased contact between diverse peoples. We have established that cultural practices differ (as if you needed to be reminded!) and that individuals tend to evaluate their own group's practices at the expense of others'.

In spite of these potential stumbling blocks, a global world entails the need to communicate across cultures. Language is the means through which we engage with others in global endeavours driven by the economy, educational attainment and personal needs, among other things. This book provides a linguistic perspective on how intercultural communication may successfully be achieved. This emerges from a sophisticated but accessible discussion of linguistic theory as it relates to cross-cultural and intercultural practices. This knowledge will empower the reader to avoid intercultural transgressions wherever possible and to repair these transgressions when they take place. Communication by its very nature is a co-constructed, ritualistic event. Erving Goffman (1959) aptly discusses participation in this event in terms of a theatre performance. To these ends, the dear reader might consider this book her or his acting notes for communicating across cultures.

1.4 COMMUNICATION ACROSS CULTURES
STUDYING LANGUAGE, PRAGMATICS AND CONTEXT

This book approaches intercultural communication in terms of pragmatics and unfolding discourse. There are innumerable definitions for the study of pragmatics, each of which suggests a slightly different approach

(Archer & Grundy 2011). Crystal (2010, p. 124) explains **pragmatics** as follows:

> Pragmatics studies the factors that govern our choice of language in social interaction and the effects of our choice on others. In theory, we can say anything we like. In practice, we follow a large number of social rules (most of them unconsciously) that constrain the way we speak.

On the one hand, for instance, Crystal (2010) points out, there is no law that one shouldn't tell jokes at a funeral but it is not generally done. On the other hand, comedians violate these unspoken guidelines for a living. Comedian Sacha Baron Cohen often does this when his characters (e.g. Ali G, Borat) ask interview questions that are considered ignorant, ill informed or inappropriate by interviewees. In short, individuals usually have a sense of what is considered appropriate, polite and/or preferred behaviour in cultures with which they are familiar. Engaging with unfamiliar cultures means running the risk of not following the rules or not knowing them well enough to violate them successfully.

Context is an essential, if not *the* essential, concept in the study of pragmatics (see Archer & Grundy 2011). Context critically influences how individuals vary their language(s) and also how the meaning of others' variation is interpreted. **Context** may be viewed as a frame (see Goffman 1974) around a focal event that provides the hearer with the resources for interpreting that event (Duranti & Goodwin 1992). Not only does context influence language, but language is influenced by context as well. For instance, a dinner party guest might wish to ask another to pass some salt (i.e. the focal event). Any number of contextual factors might influence the guest's choice of language. More polite language might be required if the addressee is older, higher in status and/or not well known to the guest. Likewise, a formal rather than informal dinner would require suitably more formal language. Thus, the guest carefully selects language to actualise the real-world event of 'passing the salt' within the context. Yet, in doing so, the guest also reaffirms such contextual elements as 'formal dinner' and the guest's and addressee's relationship within this dinner.

The use of verbal and non-verbal resources to respond to and construct context is known as contextualisation. Contextualisation is accomplished through the use of indexical signs known as **contextualisation cues** (Gumperz 1996). Speakers exploit variation at a number of levels (e.g. sound, affixes, intonation or word selection) to act as contextualisation cues (Gumperz 1992; Li Wei 1998). Furthermore, contextualisation cues may also be gestural and kinesic (see Kendon 1990). For instance, adding *please* and/or *ma'am* or *sir* to the salt request above contextualises this event as polite. Not using *please* (or *ma'am* or *sir* if appropriate) might be interpreted as rude. Raising one's voice and pointing at the addressee for this event, even if using *please* and *sir*, marks a shift that will likely be interpreted as rude or even aggressive.

Social groups and individuals have preferred ways of speaking and in context-focused pragmatics these are observed on two levels: contextual felicity and contextual update (Roberts 2006). **Contextual felicity** refers to 'the aptness of an utterance' in 'expressing a proposition that one could take to be reasonable and relevant in light of the context' (Roberts 2006, p. 199). Contextual felicity derives from presupposed content, including the semantic meaning of an utterance, its relationship to prior discourse and beliefs about how it should be used. For instance, the utterance *can I have an ice cream?* is infelicitous when addressed to a policeman. An untruthful utterance is infelicitous because individuals (in Anglo culture at least) expect a cooperative conversationalist will tell the truth to the best of his or her ability (see Chapter 2). Contextual felicity also refers to the aptness of the utterance in successfully conveying interpretable indexical values, such as pronouns. For example, an utterance is infelicitous if a speaker says *he did it* and the hearer knows neither whom *he* or *it* are. Also, returning to the dinner example above, the failure to use the appropriate level of respect and intimacy with the addressee would render the utterance contextually infelicitous.

The second level, **contextual update**, is 'the part of the content of an utterance that determines how the context of the utterance will be updated' (Roberts 2006, p. 201). A contextual update consists of preferred content that either accepts/reaffirms the direction of the current context or alters/challenges it in some way. For instance, selecting the appropriate level of respect and intimacy with the addressee at the dinner would reaffirm all elements of the context in the example above. Pointing and demanding the salt, as noted above, would involve a change in the context. Conversation is ideally an orderly affair wherein each utterance marks a 'preferred' update of context through preferred content (see Chapter 5).

In sum, individuals have preferences about the way in which contexts should unfold and be updated. These preferences have been highlighted by researchers working from philosophical, cognitive and social action perspectives (Archer & Grundy 2011). The remainder of this book draws on these three perspectives to outline a number of cross-cultural preferences as well as what happens when seemingly different preferences interface in intercultural communication.

ORGANISATION OF THIS BOOK

This book explores the nuances of context and shows how the many aspects of context influence the interpretation of language. We take the position that a cross-cultural and intercultural understanding of context leads to mutual understanding in this global world. To be explicit, we argue that a sophisticated knowledge of the mechanisms of context is central to this understanding.

Pre-theoretically, the word context is used in conjunction with any number of settings, including legal contexts (e.g. Haffner 2012), medical contexts (e.g. O'Neil 2011) and education contexts (e.g. Turner & Hiraga 2012), among others. In this book, we too investigate context in relation to settings such as the courtroom, the clinic room and the classroom. However, we build towards these settings in the theoretical sense rather than taking them as a starting point. In other words, we first establish how preferred ways of speaking underlie context as a theoretical concept.

We categorise preferred ways of speaking in terms of established theoretical concepts, including speech acts, politeness and conversational preference organisation. We then show how these are brought to bear in intercultural legal, medical and business contexts, among others. This approach partially emerges from Blommaert and Rampton's (2011, p. 9) two-part proposition: 'a) the contexts for communication should be investigated rather than assumed'; and 'b) analysis of the internal organization of semiotic data is essential to understanding its significance and position in the world'.

This book is organised in three main parts. In Part I (Chapters 2–4), we introduce the most basic elements of context and contextual felicity. Chapter 2 outlines the notion of the direct and indirect message respectively as well as the concept of speech acts. These concepts are first introduced with regard to the work of Grice and Searle and then with regard to ethnographic approaches and speaker 'voicing'.

Chapter 3 outlines the complex and well-contested notions of politeness and face. We introduce Brown and Levinson's approach to face and politeness before presenting contemporary critiques and alternative frames for face and politeness, including rapport management (Spencer-Oatey 2008). We also introduce the notion of impoliteness, which has increased in relevance as a field in its own right rather than being a mere secondary aspect of politeness.

Chapter 4, drawing on the previous chapter, positions speech acts more explicitly with regard to face and politeness. This enables a discussion about the relationship between speech acts as focal events and face and politeness as contextual elements.

Part II (Chapters 5–8) moves outwards from the relationship between the speech act and face and politeness to discuss the structured nature of communication. More so, it presents human communicative structure as both ordered and flexible phenomena and thus context something that can be updated (i.e contextual update).

Chapter 5 introduces the study of conversation. Among other things, we show how conversation may be understood in relation to pair parts (e.g. question–answer) and preferred and dispreferred responses. We show how the latter are notoriously tricky to accomplish, especially across cultures.

In Chapter 6 we delve into notions of role, power and gender and show how these concepts may be either static or fluidly negotiated in the course of conversation. We pay particularly attention to how managerial roles can be difficult to manage across cultures.

We turn our attention to naming and address in Chapter 7. Address terms are among the most pragmatically salient indices of identity for speakers, hearers and analysts (see Errington 1985b; Kiesling 2004, 2009). We focus on address terms as the most crucial mediators of social relations. There are so many naming systems that Clyne and Platt (1990) suggest that people need to be alert, to enquire and not to be surprised about differences when they encounter people from different cultural groups.

Written discourse becomes the focus in Chapter 8. We show that cultures, such as Anglo-based cultures, favour presenting ideas in a linear progression, while in other cultures the presentation of ideas may be more 'digressive' or tend towards different rhythms, such as symmetry or parallelism. We explore the implications of this for the contemporary and global university. We also extend this discussion to computer-mediated communication, which spans the boundary of the written and spoken.

The third and final part of this book (Chapters 9–11) shows how the many facets of intercultural communication and context come to bear on institutional and professional settings. Chapter 9 first addresses the interpreting and translating context. Interpreters and translators play a critical role as linguistic mediators. Therefore, it is our position that examining this role is revealing for those of us for whom intercultural communication is a peripheral but essential part of our job (government officials, legal experts, educators).

Chapter 10 explores intercultural communication in professional and workplace settings more generally. International business (and intercultural medical) encounters often fail due to inadequate training (Ferraro 2002;

Rost-Roth 2007). Among other things, different cultural expectations may also shape the behaviour and interpretation of different parties engaged in intercultural business negotiation.

In closing, Chapter 11 posits nuanced ways through which successful intercultural communication may be achieved at the linguistic level. Research on spoken discourse in the Australian multicultural workplace by Monash University researchers (e.g. Clyne 1994; Bowe 1995; Neil 1996), involving participants from different cultures who are engaged in natural communication in a language that is not a first language to any of the speakers, has shown that individuals can develop ways to construct a 'common ground' and avoid many of the problems inherent to intercultural communication.

SUGGESTED FURTHER READING

There is a rich body of introductory texts for intercultural communication. They represent wide and varied approaches to the topic. Some of our favourite texts are listed here. They address Hofstede's, Hall's and similar 'macro' work on intercultural communication in greater depth. There are also a number of texts that provide a series of useful and foundational readings for language and intercultural communication. Spencer-Oatey's and Kiesling and Paulston's are particularly good. Lastly, Foley's introduction to anthropological linguistics provides a fascinating and in-depth discussion of language, meaning and culture.

Foley, W. 1997 *Anthropological Linguistics: An Introduction*. Malden, MA: Blackwell.

Kiesling, S. & Paulston, C. (eds) 2004 *Intercultural Discourse and Communication: The Essential Readings*. Boston, MA: Wiley Blackwell.

Martin, J. & Nakayama, T. 2004 *International Communication in Contexts*. 3rd edn. Boston: McGraw Hill.

Samovar, L., Porter, R., McDaniel, E. & Roy, C. 2013 *Communication Between Cultures*. 8th edn. Boston: Wadsworth Cengage.

Sorrells, K. 2013 *Intercultural Communication: Globalization and Social Justice*. Thousand Oaks: Sage.

Spencer-Oatey, H. (ed.) 2008 *Culturally Speaking: Culture, Communication and Politeness Theory*. 2nd edn. London: Continuum.

Part I
Contextual felicity across cultures

2 | Direct and indirect messages

2.1   INTRODUCTION

AT THE outset, mappings between one language and another can seem relatively straightforward. For instance, the English *thank you* corresponds rather directly to the French *merci*. However, cultural conventions and the communicative context can influence the interpretation of what are seemingly straightforward utterances. An English speaker often uses a simple *thank you* to accept an offer of food. Conversely, a French speaker uses *merci* to refuse an offer of food (Crystal 2010). In an Anglo context, failing an offer of food, a hungry individual in a kitchen might say *something smells good* to solicit such an offer. A Malagasy individual in search of a free meal would ask *iona no maska*: 'what's cooking?' (Myers-Scotton 2006). Cultures and contexts provide varying expectations as to how speakers use and interpret linguistic signs. They also guide the degree to which individuals use direct or indirect messages to accomplish goals.

It is at the level that might be called 'reading between the lines' that cultural differences may arise and these may contribute to misunderstandings in intercultural communication. For instance, Bailey (2001) has shown how interactions between Korean American shop owners and African American customers in Los Angeles may result in misunderstandings. Korean American shop owners most typically focus on the transaction at hand whereas African Americans view these interactions as an opportunity to reaffirm relationships through small talk. When the Korean Americans do not reciprocate, the African Americans perceive the shop owners to be unfriendly and even racist. African Americans often confront them on this point and this only serves to frighten the shop owners and aggravate the situation.

In this chapter we examine some of the ways in which we can identify and understand the complexities of form, function and meaning, especially as they pertain to direct and indirect messages. We first review and critique the seminal work of the philosophers/rationalists Austin, Searle and Grice. Then, in line with much contemporary thought, we shift away from philosophical/rationalist accounts of language use and towards a more ethnographic perspective.

2.2 GRICE, COOPERATIVE CONVERSATION AND IMPLICATURE

Grice (1975) presumed conversation to be mostly a cooperative affair. He used this presumption to set out principles for explaining why hearers make judgements as to the literal or non-literal truth of an utterance. Grice posited an overarching dictum for such judgements known as the Cooperative Principle. The **Cooperative Principle** states a speaker should 'Make [his or her] conversational contribution such as is required, at the stage at which it occurs, by the accepted purpose or direction of the talk exchange' (Grice 1989, p. 7). The speaker's adherence to or violation of this principle enables the hearer to 'deduce the implication' of an utterance, and thus its conversational implicature (Crystal 2010, p. 444). Horn (2006, p. 3) writes: '**Implicature** is a component of speaker meaning that constitutes an aspect of what is *meant* in a speaker's utterance without being part of what is *said*' (italics added).

Grice (1975) identified four expectations that adult English speakers seem to use in interpreting literal and implied meaning in a conversation. He called these expectations **conversational maxims**, and argued that these maxims guide the interpretation of conversations under the aegis of the Cooperative Principle (Horn 2006). Grice's maxims (1975, pp. 45–7) may be summarised as follows:

Quantity:	Make your contribution as informative as is required (for the current purpose of the exchange).
	Do not make your contribution more informative than is required.
Quality:	Do not say what you believe to be false.
	Do not say that for which you lack adequate evidence.
Relation/Relevance:	Be relevant.

Manner:	Avoid obscurity of expression.
	Avoid ambiguity.
	Be brief.
	Be orderly.

These maxims represent norms that hearers can expect speakers to have followed, if they are engaged in cooperative conversation. However, Allan (1991) makes the essential point that the maxims should be regarded as 'reference points for language interchange' and not as 'laws to be obeyed' (see also Leech 2007). In effect, we use these norms as a base, against which conversational exchanges can be compared. When a hearer encounters communication that does not meet these norms, the hearer then searches for **non-literal interpretations** (conversational implicatures).

The following hypothetical example illustrates how the maxims assist in determining the difference between the level of literal meaning and the level of implied meaning.

Trevor climbs a ladder to fix a broken tile on the roof. When he reaches the roof, he accidentally kicks the ladder and it falls to the ground, leaving him stranded.

Jason: Do you want me to put the ladder back so you can climb down?

Trevor: (On the roof) No! I just want to hang around up here all day!

In terms of Grice's maxims, there ought to have been no need for Jason's question. It was obvious from the context that Trevor would need Jason to replace the ladder. So in terms of Grice's maxim of **Quality**, Jason's question was asking the obvious. It was superfluous in the context and therefore it flouted the maxims of **Quantity** and **Relevance**. In return, Trevor replies using sarcasm. His reply was literally untruthful; hence, it also flouted the **Quality** maxim.

Jason would be able to interpret Trevor's reply as sarcasm using the maxims and the Cooperative Principle. When Trevor's reply was not a direct answer to Jason's question, the Cooperative Principle would require Trevor to find a suitable interpretation other than the literal meaning, and he could thus conclude that the reply was an instance of sarcasm.

Levinson (1985, p. 102) provides the following additional example:

A: Where's Bill?

B: There's a yellow VW outside Sue's house.

Levinson suggests that B's contribution, taken literally, fails to answer A's question, and thus seems to violate at least the maxims of **Quantity** and **Relevance**. B's utterance could then be interpreted as a non-cooperative response, ignoring A's concerns by changing the topic. Yet, Levinson suggests, it is clear that despite the *apparent* failure of cooperation, we try to interpret B's utterance as nevertheless cooperative at some deeper (non-superficial) level. We do this by assuming that it is in fact cooperative, and then by asking ourselves what possible connection there could be between the location of Bill and the yellow VW, and hence arrive at the suggestion (which B effectively conveys) that, if Bill has a yellow VW, he may be in Sue's house.

Grice (1975, p. 49) recognised that language users sometimes fail to observe the four maxims. A maxim might not be observed if, for example, a person deliberately tells a lie or cannot speak clearly for whatever reason (e.g. speaking while eating, a person with stage fright). Grice listed three methods by which a speaker could fail to observe a maxim:

- opting out of a maxim
- violating a maxim
- flouting a maxim.

Opting out of a maxim means choosing not to answer for one reason or the other. For instance, a speaker might choose not to answer what he or she perceives to be too personal a question. Alternatively, a criminal might refuse to answer a policeman in order to not implicate him or herself in a crime. These individuals might clearly indicate their respective intentions by saying, *that's none of your business* or *I don't have to tell you nothing, cop!*

Violating a maxim means quite broadly not obeying a maxim. A deceptive speaker who wishes to lie or an individual who does not adhere to the maxims intentionally or unintentionally is violating them. This contrasts with **flouting a maxim**, which entails a speaker blatantly failing to observe a maxim with the deliberate intention of causing an implicature. In such contexts, the speaker, however, does not intentionally mean to deceive or mislead the hearer, only to induce the hearer to search for an additional meaning to that of the expressed meaning. Trevor's sarcasm above is an example of a speaker flouting a maxim. Levinson's speaker above may be violating, flouting or even obeying the maxims.

Grice's work has been critiqued on a general theoretical level (Sperber & Wilson 1986; Brumark 2006; Horn 2006; Lee & Pinker 2010; Silverstein 2010; Pinker 2011; Kecskes 2013a; Sanders 2013) and for its Anglo-centric nature (e.g. Clyne 1987, 1994; Wierzbicka 1991, 1994a; Foley 1997). For instance, at the theoretical level, neo-Gricean philosophers and rationalists such as Horn (2006) have elevated Quality to be the most privileged of the four maxims. Cognitive researchers such as Sperber and Wilson and Pinker have also modified or rejected Grice's work. For instance, Sperber and Wilson (1986) find merit in Grice's work but elevate relevance (and thus **Relevance Theory**) rather than cooperation as the overarching conversational principle. The maximisation of relevance, they contend, is the primary concern of human cognition (Schourup 2011). Pinker and his colleagues (Lee & Pinker 2010; Pinker 2011) have critiqued Grice's and others' emphasis on the 'cooperative' nature of conversation. However, unlike other theorists, Pinker and others do not emphasise any one maxim or principle as being most pertinent to conversation. Rather, they argue that the agentive and strategic speaker engages in cooperation and conflict among other behaviours. (Lee and Pinker's **Strategic Speaker Theory** follows from this argument.)

Many researchers have critiqued the Anglo-centric nature of Grice's theory either directly or indirectly. For instance, many cultures have varying expectations about Quantity and the ways in which an appropriate level of Quantity is achieved. In Chinese and Vietnamese cultural contexts, the notion of cooperation entails saying only a small amount in order to avoid conflict, whereas in some cultures (e.g. Jewish, Israeli and African American) contrariness (and therefore saying a lot) and immodesty are considered to be cooperative (Clyne 1994, p. 12). Marriott (1997) found Japanese and Australian business people had differing expectations about how the norms of Quantity should be met. The Japanese found that the Australians did not give enough information during sales pitches. Conversely, the Australians were disappointed that the Japanese did not ask more questions. Such questions, the Australians believed, would have enabled them to provide more information.

The maxim of Quality is also viewed as having a European bias in terms of the meaning of 'truth'. Clyne (1994, p. 193) suggests that the European notion of 'truth' as an absolute value is not regarded as being of vital importance in such cultures as Vietnamese and Chinese, and argues that in such cultures 'in any competition with harmony, charity or respect, "truth" not only need not, but should not, be a criterion'. In South-East Asian communities, the core value of harmony directly contrasts with the Western European/Middle Eastern perception of 'truth'.

Manner is regarded as being the most 'culturally limiting' of all the maxims (Clyne 1994, p. 193). The concept of orderliness is highly valued in the Anglo-based cultures of England, the United States and Australia.

In cultures such as the Vietnamese, Japanese and Javanese ones, where implicitness or non-assertiveness is a core value, the maxim of 'Avoid obscurity of expression' may be regarded as being meaningless. Cam Nguyên (1991, p. 43) has identified what she terms the Vietnamese 'tolerance for ambiguity'. This tolerance for ambiguity is accompanied by a preference for a circular discourse structure, which involves merely suggesting examples of an implicit perception and continually returning to this perception to expand upon it.

Ide (1989) also postulates that the 'tolerance for ambiguity' relates to the tendency of indirectness at the pragmatic level of some Asian languages. For instance, as will be discussed further below, utterances in some Asian languages (e.g. Japanese, Chinese, Indonesian) permit the omission of the 'doer' (*I gave the book to you*), the direct object (*I gave **the book** to you*) and/or the indirect object (*I gave the book **to you***). Thus, single-word utterances such as 'gave' may be acceptable and require the hearer to discern the omitted referents within the context. More so, in Japanese, the act of 'giving' between humans is encoded on four levels, depending on the direction of giving, social status and social distance (Liddicoat 2009). These levels impact the language styles used by interlocutors to 'give' and to discuss giving (this is discussed further in Chapter 7).

Critique of Grice's maxims has led to a number of alternative theories. However, none of these alternative models have had the same impact as Grice's. Sperber and Wilson's Relevance Theory is sometimes employed as an alternative to the Gricean Anglo-centric approach (see Jary 1998; Žegarac 2007, 2008; Žegarac & Pennington 2008). Relevance as a general human cognitive concern is seen universally to transcend cross-cultural critiques of Grice's maxims. Clyne (1994) proposes revisions and additions to the four maxims in an investigation of intercultural workplace talk in Australia (see the review at the end of this chapter). And, as noted above, Pinker and his colleagues reject the frame of cooperation in favour of a more fluid, strategic and agentive understanding of the speaker and hearer relationship.

Notwithstanding the criticisms and revisions, Grice's approach, in its original and many adapted forms, has served as a basis for an enormous amount of research in the area of pragmatics (e.g. Horn 2006), code-switching (e.g. Myers-Scotton 1993) and intercultural communication (e.g. Clyne 1994). Grice's framework provides a necessary bridge in overcoming the gap between what is expressed, what is actually meant by the speaker (the intended meaning) and how the hearer perceives that meaning. Yet, the most sophisticated understanding of the difference between literal and implied meaning has emerged from Speech Act Theory and the work of the 'ordinary language' philosophers J. L. Austin and John Searle.

2.3   SPEECH ACT THEORY

Austin (1962, 1970) and Searle (1969, 1975) focused on the ways in which we use words to get things done. This led Searle to outline the conditions through which such speech acts (e.g. *requests, apologies, invitations*) could be accomplished. This in turn spawned many subsequent researchers to attempt to categorise the innumerable ways in which these acts are used to get things done. Sadock (2006) points out that pre-theoretically almost any utterance may be considered a speech act. For instance, producing sounds, combining words to form an utterance or insulting a guest are all 'acts done in the process of speaking' (Sadock 2006, p. 53). Yet, **Speech Act Theory** is primarily concerned with understanding the intentions and conventions linked to an utterance and what this utterance can do.

Speech Act Theory is particularly concerned with the gap between literal and implied meaning and the many ways in which goals can be accomplished by drawing on or even exploiting this gap. In order to account for the fact that the interpretation of non-literal meanings by the hearer may not necessarily coincide with the intentions of the speaker, Austin (1962) and Searle (1969) characterise utterances in the following way (explanations in parentheses provided by the present authors):

> **Locution:**   **the actual form of the utterance**
> (what is actually said)
> **Illocution:**   **the communicative force of the utterance**
> (what was intended by the speaker in making the utterance)
> **Perlocution:**   **the communicative effect of the utterance**
> (what the hearer interprets as the meaning intended by the utterance)

This characterisation of the tripartite nature of communication helps us to see how miscommunication might occur. Even when the speaker and the hearer come from the same culture, there is the possibility that the message received may not equate with the message intended. The likelihood of miscommunication increases greatly when the speaker and the hearer come from different cultures and may have different expected norms.

Illocutionary acts are the central aspect of Speech Act Theory and there have been many attempts to classify these acts into types. At the outset, as Sadock (2006) points out, we can see there is a **conventional** aspect to speech acts. We generally agree as per the introduction that uttering *thank you* accomplishes the act of 'thanking' in English and *merci* the same act in French. However, sometimes the act of thanking might be accomplished more subtly and this is critically linked to our ability to interpret a speaker's **intention**. For instance, an individual might thank someone for a box of chocolates by saying *I love chocolates* (Sadock 2006). This utterance is not a conventionalised form of 'thanking' but may be interpreted as this act in the context.

Austin (1962) was among the first to try to understand and categorise communicative intent, form and interpretation of utterances. He established a distinction between **statements** (or **constatives** in his words), which are utterances that may be assigned a truth value, and **performatives**, which he claims have no truth values. Drawing on Austin, Searle (1979) further subdivided performatives into five subcategories. The following is adapted from Searle (1979, pp. 12–29).

Types of speech acts[1]

Assertives: An act that commits the speaker (S) to the truth of the proposition (P) (e.g. *affirm, conclude, deny, report, believe*).

Directives: Attempts by the speaker (S) to get the hearer (H) to do something (e.g. *command, request, insist, ask, challenge*).

Commissives: Acts that commit the speaker (S) to a future act (A) (e.g. *promise, offer, guarantee, give one's word, declare intention*).

Expressives: Acts in which the speaker (S) makes known his or her attitude about a proposition to the hearer (H) (e.g. *thank, forgive, blame, complain, apologise*).

Declarations: Acts that bring about correspondence between the propositional content and the reality (e.g. *baptise, name, appoint, declare war*).

It must be noted that Searle's assertives may be judged as having truth value because these comment on a state of affairs in the world (Liu 2011).

---

[1] Searle (1979) uses the term *illocutionary act*, where he earlier used the term *speech act*. The latter term is used here because it has subsequently received wider use.

Table 2.1 Felicity conditions for 'requests' and 'thanks'

	Request	Thank (for)
Propositional content	Future act (A) of hearer (H).	Past act (A) done by hearer (H).
Preparatory	1. H is able to do A. Speaker (S) believes H is able to do A. 2. It is not obvious to both S and H that H will do A in the normal course of events of his own accord.	A benefits speaker (S) and S believes A benefits S.
Sincerity	S wants H to do A.	S feels grateful or appreciative for A.
Essential	Counts as an attempt to get H to do A.	Counts as an expression of gratitude or appreciation.

(Searle 1969, pp. 66–7)

The remaining four speech acts are not considered to have a truth value in line with Austin's view of performatives. In both cases, the actions performed by Searle's speech acts are viewed in terms of whether they are felicitous or infelicitous (see Allan 1986, 1994).

Specific **felicity conditions** must be met for a speech act to be considered successful and thus felicitous. The felicitous accomplishment of a speech act relates, among other things, to the speaker's sincerity, the preparatory conditions underlying and leading up to the utterance and whether the utterance counts as the speech act in question. The felicity conditions for the speech acts *request* (a type of directive) and *thank (for)* (a type of expressive) are outlined in Table 2.1 (see the Appendix for the table in its entirety).

Requests differ only slightly from other directives such as *orders* and *commands*. For instance, *commands* and *directives* merely have the additional preparatory condition that the speaker (S) must be in a position of authority over the hearer (H) (Searle 1969). Not unlike Grice's maxims, when the felicity conditions for speech acts aren't met, hearers may look for alternative explanations (Crystal 2010). For instance, a hearer might interpret a speaker's (S) act of *thanking* as sarcasm if there was no past act (A) done by that hearer (H). This is reflected in the statement *thanks for nothing*.

Searle (1969, ch. 3) points out that the forms of indirect speech acts are routinely built upon the felicity conditions. For instance, continuing our discussion of the speech act *request*, there are a variety of ways to *request* someone at the dinner table to *pass the salt*:

1. Pass the salt (please).
2. Can you pass the salt?
3. Can you reach the salt?
4. Would you mind passing the salt?
5. I would appreciate it if you would pass the salt.
6. Would you pass the salt?

Utterance (1) is a direct request, which takes the form of an **imperative**. The illocutionary force of this direct request (as well as any of these six requests) may be 'downgraded' with the possible addition of *please* (also known as a downtoner, minimiser or hedge) (Spencer-Oatey 2008). This contrasts with strategies that 'upgrade' the illocutionary force of an utterance (also known as an intensifier, a maximiser or booster). An example would be the use of *now* instead of *please* in utterance (1).

Utterances (2), (3) and (4) above are **interrogatives** (questions) based on the preparatory condition. Utterances (2) and (3) take the form of a question about the hearer's ability to do the act. Utterance (4) relates to the hearer's attitude towards the proposed act. These three utterances illustrate that indirect messages often have a primary and secondary illocutionary force (Searle 1975). In other words, a primary illocutionary force (in this case, request) is often strategically used alongside another illocutionary act (ability or attitude) in indirect messages (see also Flowerdew 2013). This is obvious to English-speaking children who may counter the indirect request *can you pass me the salt?* with a reply such as *I can but I won't*.

Utterance (5) is a **statement** (in contrast to an imperative or an interrogative) and relates to the sincerity condition. This statement invokes the speaker's desire for the hearer to perform the act. Once again it illustrates the multilayered nature of indirect messages as a request is used alongside desire. Lastly, utterance (6) above is an interrogative that relates to the essential condition. This is because it counts as an attempt to get the hearer to do the act and this attempt is a secondary illocutionary force alongside the primary force of a request.

The important role of the culturally oriented assumptions of mutually shared background and cooperative conversation explains where interpretations might be misconstrued in certain contexts, including intercultural contexts. This is particularly the case because direct directives are used

Table 2.2 Request form types

Form type ('routine' texts)	Occurrences	Form type ('relational' texts)	Occurrences
please + imperative	3	please + neg. imperative	1
would you please	3	please + imperative	1
please could you	3	you will need to	1
could you	1	they should ensure that	1
can you please	1	I suggest you enclose	1
I would be grateful if you would	1	I suggest we discuss	1
I would be obliged if you would	1	I would like to see	3
it is intended to add	1	will you please	2
		could you please	1
		can you please	1
		can we please	1
		I would be grateful if	1
		I would be grateful if you could	4
		I would appreciate your	1
		I would very much appreciate your	1
		I believe it would be worthwhile	1
		I would be grateful if you would	2
		perhaps you may like to	1
		perhaps we could	1
		perhaps we can	1

(Bargiela-Chiappini & Harris 1996, p. 644)

relatively infrequently in the languages of the world. Indirect forms, such as utterances (2)–(6) above, are far more common. Furthermore, in contexts where direct forms are used, they tend to be employed among similarly aged siblings, friends and other equals.

Bargiela-Chiappini and Harris (1996), who analysed 32 authentic texts written by and to the managing director of an international joint venture, found that the forms of requests tended to vary according to whether the request was of a 'routine' type or whether it was more complex (which they labelled 'relational'). Table 2.2 illustrates the more restricted set of request forms that they found were used in 'routine' contexts, compared with the broader, more elaborate set of request forms used by the managing director.

The many ways in which requests and other speech acts may be accomplished across cultural contexts will be discussed at length in Chapter 4. We pay particular attention to what has been called the 'most carefully conceived, comprehensive study in cross-cultural pragmatics': the 'Cross-Cultural Speech Act Realization Project' by Shoshana Blum-Kulka and colleagues (Archer & Grundy 2011, p. 341).

Like Grice's maxims, Speech Act Theory has been critiqued at the general theoretical level (Levinson 1983; Holtgraves 2005; Sadock 2006; Silverstein 2010) and for its Anglo-centric nature (Foley 1997; Ogiermann 2009; Shariati & Chamani 2010; Liu 2011). For instance, at a theoretical level, Holtgraves (2005) explored attitudes towards speech acts and found that most individuals categorised speech acts according to emotional impact (and thus perlocution). This led Holtgraves to question the cognitive relevance of Austin and Searle's illocution-based categorisations of speech acts. Other researchers (e.g. Levinson 1983) have also questioned the theoretical focus on illocution at the expense of other speech act dynamics. Not unlike Holtgraves (2005), these researchers find the focus on speaker intention and illocution somewhat limiting.

Speech Act Theory has also been critiqued for its perceived 'Western' focus. For instance, Duranti (1988) argues that in Samoan culture speech acts do not belong to the speaker or hearer but rather are achieved collectively by the wider group. Thus, Foley (1997, p. 280), reviewing Duranti, points out: 'Samoans practice interpretation as a way of publicly controlling social relationships rather than as a way of figuring out what a given person meant to say' (see Rosaldo 1982 for a similar albeit more cooperative process among the Illongot of the Philippines). Cultures vary in the manner and frequency at which speech acts are used and perceived. For instance, Chinese speakers generally use more declaratives than English speakers (Liu 2011). There may be more opportunities to declare in Chinese cultural contexts through 'more meetings, more banquets, and more officials who are authorized [to declare] by the masses and by themselves' (Liu 2011, p. 1815). Also, Chinese speakers generally view apologies as positive, emotional and hearer-focused affairs in contrast to English speakers' more neutral and speaker-focused view of this speech act. Consequently, Liu (2011) extends Holtgraves' critique of Speech Act Theory into the cross-cultural realm by noting that the perlocution of apologies is more relevant than illocution for Chinese speakers.

Yet, the most powerful and frequent critique of Speech Act Theory, both cross-culturally and more generally, is its focus on the form rather than function of speech acts (e.g. Duranti 2001; Walker, Drew & Local 2011) and its under-reliance on context (e.g. Roberts 2006; Silverstein 2010). Duranti (2001) notes there are critical social acts other than speech acts that cannot be labelled in convenient ways. Ignoring these unnamed acts while elevating named acts undersells the complexities of how language is used to get things done. Silverstein (2010) takes an even more critical view of Speech Act Theory, dismissing it as 'folk linguistics' that institutionalises and fixes language to specific time and place.

Silverstein's critique highlights the growing relevance of context in the late modern study of intercultural communication and linguistics more generally. As Spencer-Oatey (2008, p. 31) writes, 'context can have a very major influence on people's use of directness-indirectness and this can interact with cultural differences'. For instance, she points out that the British might be considered indirect by Germans and Poles but direct by the Chinese and Japanese. Furthermore, as established in Chapter 1, context is a fluid phenomenon and speakers use language to respond to as well as to redefine it. Thus, as Roberts (2006, p. 201) points out: 'Besides felicity, the other way that an utterance interacts with its context during interpretation is by inducing an update of that context.'

Speech Act Theory has been and remains a fruitful field of inquiry for intercultural communication. Speech Act Theory and the Cooperative Principle underlie many of the discussions throughout this book. However, in recent years, there has been a greater emphasis on context and the value of ethnography for uncovering the nuances of context. Consequently, the next section introduces ethnography as a complementary way of understanding conversation, speech acts and sociolinguistic practices more generally.

2.4 ETHNOGRAPHY, VOICING AND INDIRECTNESS

Ethnography is essential for researchers concerned with goal-oriented individuals operating in fluid intercultural contexts. From the Greek *ethnos* ('people') and *graphein* ('writing'), the modern sense of ethnography finds its roots with anthropologists such as Geertz (1960), who spent extended periods of time with the Javanese to understand their ways of living. Ethnography came to the forefront of communicative studies with Gumperz and Hymes' (1972) edited volume *The Ethnography of Communication*. This volume's papers sought to observe and explain how cultural norms and ways of speaking were both interpreted and reinterpreted by individual speakers. Findings emerge from in-depth observations, interviews and/or recordings of naturally occurring conversations.

Saville-Troike (2003, p. 3) summarises **ethnography** as follows:

> 'Doing ethnography' in another culture involves first and foremost fieldwork, including observing, asking questions, participating in group activities, and testing the validity of one's perceptions against the intuitions of natives. Research design must allow an openness to categories and modes of thought and behaviour which may not have been anticipated by the investigator. The ethnographer of communication cannot even presuppose what a community other than his own may consider to be a 'language', or who or what may 'speak' it . . .

To illustrate this final point, at the extreme, we might consider the Ojibwa people who consider 'thunder' to be a language variety (Saville-Troike 2003). We might also consider the Navajo people who believe that dogs can understand the Navajo language (Saville-Troike 2003).

Ethnographers' openness to categories and thought and behaviour leads to a more nuanced understanding of utterances and implicature in local contexts. For instance, Morgan (2010) examined evaluations of prominent African Americans such as Barrack Obama by white Americans. These comments on their surface could be interpreted as the speech act of 'complimenting' in that they count as presenting a positive evaluation of these African Americans. However, Morgan (2010) shows how utterances such as 'he's articulate' and 'he speaks well' may be understood as negative compliments and indirectly racist. In other words, it shouldn't need to be said that Barack Obama is well spoken in light of his Harvard background.

Ethnographers have adopted a series of approaches to understanding language use in context (we outline the popular but dated S.P.E.A.K.I.N.G. model in Chapter 5). Duranti (2001) posits two main means through which one may explore the links between culture and ways of speaking. First, researchers may start with linguistic forms, utterances or conversational routines and examine how these interact with existing socio-cultural practices. For instance, a researcher might choose to examine 'greetings' in a situation where individuals are merely passing by one another and do not want to talk. Pinto (2011b) examined the forms used among Spaniards and US Americans respectively. He found that Spaniards often used *adios* ('bye') and *hasta luego* ('see you later') for these situations where the US Americans would use *hi, hello* or *how are you?* Pinto (2011b, p. 371) linked these differences to English speakers' social concern with maintaining harmonious relations while not impinging on another's personal space. He contrasts this with the Spaniards who prefer to be more direct while at the same time maintaining solidarity.

Second, and alternatively, ethnographers might use as a starting point socio-cultural constructs (e.g. gender, power or race) or social processes (e.g. conflict, advertising or performance) (Duranti 2001). For example, researchers interested in the processes of globalisation have often used hip hop as a frame for understanding how language forms are borrowed across time and place (e.g. Pennycook 2003; Alim 2006; O'Hanlon 2006; Alim, Ibrahim & Pennycook 2009). Alim (2006), for instance, has shown how African Americans used Arabic *Qur'anic* text and non-standard English to position themselves simultaneously within the global *umma* ('Islamic community') and the global hip hop community. Pennycook (2003) shows how the Japanese hip hop group Rip Slyme uses English to connect with the wider hip hop community. However, Pennycook also shows that this English is influenced by Japanese phonology and syntax and thus positions Rip Slyme within the global hip hop phenomenon albeit in a Japanese way.

In any case, contemporary research, especially ethnography, has involved a revival of the works of philosopher/literary theorist Mikhail Bakhtin (1981, 1986) and sociologist Erving Goffman (1959, 1967, 1974). Consequently, rather than being viewed as entirely 'new' per se, the late modern ethnographic and pragmatic endeavour should be seen in term of innovative uses of traditional philosophies and approaches. These 'newer' approaches are introduced here with regard to indirect messages and expounded upon throughout this book, but especially in Chapter 6 and Chapter 7.

VOICING AND INDIRECTNESS

Bakhtin (1986, p. 89) writes: 'Our speech . . . is filled with others' words, varying degrees of otherness and varying degrees of our-own-ness, [which] carry with them their own evaluative tone, which we assimilate, rework and re-accentuate.' In short, language features are imbued with semiotic potential due to their social history. Individuals activate this potential by **voicing** the features in a context. For instance, returning to our hip hop examples above, some non-standard English features (e.g. *aks* instead of *ask*) carry semiotic potential by virtue of links to hip hop and African Americans more generally. Many speakers, African American or otherwise, activate this potential through voicing in a range of contexts. For example, white middle-class males might use *aks* to invoke the coolness or masculinity linked to African Americans and their language styles (see Cutler 1999).

White middle-class males, among others, do not use this feature because they 'want to be African American' as many folk linguists assert. Rather, individuals find these language styles to be useful to accomplish contextually relevant identity (e.g. projecting a tough persona) and discourse goals (e.g. intimidating someone). This point was originally made by Elinor Ochs (1992), who asserted that linguistic features normally viewed with direct links to gender were, in fact, indirectly related. Ochs argued that linguistic features such as tag questions (e.g. *isn't it? don't they?*) weren't inherently feminine as many had suggested. Rather, these forms were used for cooperative and inclusive conversational stances, which in turn combined with other stances to construct the social category femininity.

Voicing (see also styling in Coupland 2007) may be used to accomplish any number of identity and discourse goals. The remainder of this chapter investigates how voicing is used for indirectness across cultures. We illustrate this function by focusing on the relationship between voicing, role and genre. The discussion of role here lays the foundation for the discussion in Chapter 6 of how social roles are both static and fluid and negotiable across contexts and cultures. Genre is intertwined with role and it is a concept to which we return throughout this book.

ROLES AND INDIRECTNESS

Bakhtin's notion of voicing is echoed in Goffman's work (Clift 1999). Goffman (1967) views language in terms of interactional ritual and posits that this is how analysts should approach communication, especially as it serves as a mediator between social actors (Silverstein 2010). Goffman (1959) uses the theatre as a metaphor to describe how we use language to act out roles through voicing. This metaphor, his concept of dramaturgy, raised the notion of roles (the notion of the self) and rules (micro-social norms) (Adler, Adler & Fontana 1987). With regard to roles, Adler, Adler and Fontana (1987, p. 220) write: 'Goffman's actors intentionally and manipulatively role-play for the purpose of managing others' impressions of them.' These actors do so by aligning with or creatively redefining micro-societal rules.

Goffman (1974) argues that an individual may 'frame' an utterance a particular way in order to distance him or herself from the proposition contained in the utterance. This overlaps with Bakhtin's observation that writers often use quotation marks to distance themselves from a word or phrase (Clift 1999). Goffman (1974) proposed three role divisions through which individuals may frame an utterance in this way. The **author** is the original composer of the utterance, the **animator** is the person who speaks the utterance and the **principal** is the person committed to the proposition contained in the utterance. Clift (1999, p. 5) outlines this concept with reference to the following text from a BBC radio report:

> The UN Secretary-General Boutros Boutros-Ghali has in an interview with the New York Times said that criticism of him in the British Press was – and I'm here quoting him – 'maybe because I'm a wog.'

Here, the author of the words is the UN Secretary-General and the animator of the words is the radio announcer. The radio announcer is at pains here to clarify he is neither the author nor the principal.

Many researchers have shown how individuals may exploit the fluid nature of role to distance the self from a proposition, and thus be indirect. For instance, code-switching is a well-established means through which individuals may use the voice of the 'other' to soften the impact of an utterance by obfuscating its intention or truthfulness (Heller 1988; McConvell 1988; Woolard 1988). For instance, Manns (ms.) shows how young Javanese speakers select English to present negative assessments of the attributes and behaviours of present and non-present others. English speakers are construed as more direct and bluntly honest than the Javanese themselves, who are guided by ideologies of politeness and harmonious relations (Geertz 1960; Wolfowitz 1991; Keeler 2001). Therefore, by invoking the voice of English speakers, young Javanese can subtly attribute their viewpoints to this voice.

Many, if not most, languages provide strategies other than code-switching for shifting responsibility to another principal. For example, Shoaps (2009) notes that Mayan Sakapultek speakers have an affix at their disposal which they can use to shift responsibility for an utterance onto an unknown rather than known principal. Thus, adding the prefix *xa'* to an utterance signals what Shoaps labels 'moral irony', a socio-culturally shared evaluation linked in the immediate context to an implicit but unknown principal. Many languages use grammatical strategies to omit the responsible parties altogether. For instance, English speakers may do this through the use of passive voice. The utterance *mistakes were made* has often been used by American politicians to 'apologise' without explicitly referencing the person responsible for the transgression (see Broder 2007). This has been referred to in the popular media as 'bureaucratic passive tense' (Lieberman 2013). Also, as noted above, many Asian languages permit the omission of subjects, objects and direct objects. This enables a speaker of, for instance, Indonesian to make an indirect request to borrow an item by saying *boleh dipinjam?* ('can [it] be borrowed?') where an English speaker might say *can I borrow that from you?*

GENRES AND INDIRECTNESS

Bakhtin (1986) has laid the groundwork for studies of modern genre as social practice. From Bakhtin's perspective, **genres** 'consist of historically transmitted, relatively stable frameworks for orienting the production of discourse' (Foley 1997, p. 359). Bakhtin asserts that social categories are constructed when they become attached to genres and voices (Bauman & Briggs 2003). Many institutionalised genres – such as political speeches, lectures, interviews and stand-up comedy routines – are clearly defined and have established frameworks (Coupland 2007). People easily recognise and frequently label genres such as these and understand their norms. Other genres are less clear and are difficult to categorise. For instance, some might categorise sub-types of conversations, such as small talk, gossip, verbal play, flirting and storytelling, as genres though these are more diffuse and at times difficult to recognise or label (Coupland, J. 2000; Coupland, N. 2007).

Genres are simultaneously firm and flexible. On the one hand, speakers and writers need to subscribe to the social rules set out by genres for structuring talk (Coupland 2007). On the other, as Foley (1997, p. 361) points out: 'Genres do vary to the extent that they involve dialogic expansion and richness.' For example, the phrase *once upon a time* generally suggests the opening of a fairy tale in Anglo cultural contexts. However, a speaker or writer might also use *once upon a time* in an atypical context – for instance, to give a folksy or traditional feel to an academic paper (Foley 1997). Returning to our discussion of voicing above, *once upon a time* has been imbued with semiotic potential as a result of its historical links to the genre of fairy tales. However, it may be used to creatively manipulate the genre of an academic paper.

Genres interact with roles to provide individuals in many cultures with strategies of indirectness. For example, Hill and Irvine (1993) explain that the family of a man in the Wolof tribe of Senegal may use the pre-marriage ritual of *xaxaar* to convey insults about bride-to-be's family. The man's family will hire a *griot* – a professional verbal artist – to chant poetic insults about the bride's family in the *xaxaar*. Hill and Irvine (1993, p. 12) point out: 'The employers of the *griots* evade responsibility because the words of the insults are not theirs. The *griots* avoid responsibility because they perform only for hire.' Audience members often repeat the insults in the wider community and are absolved of responsibility because they merely report what they have heard.

African American cultural practices include a number of genres that provide ritualistic opportunities for indirectly criticising others and praising oneself (Labov 1972a; Mitchell-Kernan 2001). These include *playing the dozens, capping* and *signifying*, all of which reputedly emerged as a non-violent way of resolving tensions during the slave era. Signifying takes as its starting point that dictionary entries for words are never sufficient for expressing or interpreting meaning (Mitchell-Kernan 2001). Consequently, signifying entails using utterances with multiple potential meanings and leaving it to a hearer to work out the intended meaning. For instance, in the following exchange, a wife sees her husband, who doesn't typically wear a suit to work, heading out the door in the suit:

Wife:	Where are you going?
Husband:	I'm going to work.
Wife:	You're wearing a suit, tie, and white shirt? You didn't tell me you got a promotion.

(Mitchell-Kernan 2001, p. 155)

The wife in this instance has no reason to believe that her husband has received a promotion, so she is *signifying* that he is lying.

2.5   SUMMARY

Language is critically used to get things done but there is often a gap between a speaker's words and his or her intended meaning. It is at the level of reading between the lines that misunderstandings often emerge in intercultural communication. Discerning speaker meaning can be a difficult task even in instances where speakers share cultural conventions. For example, the point of *signifying* is to put the onus of interpretation on the hearer. Felicitous communication is particularly difficult when cultural conventions are not shared. As we outlined in Chapter 1, contextual felicity results from presupposed, conventional content, including an utterance's meaning, its relationship to prior discourse and beliefs about its appropriate use. This chapter has shown that differences in cultural preferences emerge with regard to what constitutes cooperative conversation and appropriate strategies of indirectness. In the next chapter, we frame these preferences in terms of 'schemas', 'politeness' and 'face'.

2.6   REVIEW

1. **Key terms**

   Speech acts, locution, illocution, perlocution, Cooperative Principle, maxims of conversation (Quality, Quantity, Relation/Relevance, Manner), conversational implicature, inference, ethnography, voicing, genre.

2. **Key ideas**

   Having read this chapter you should:
   a. understand the difference between direct and indirect speech acts
   b. appreciate how people of different cultures may draw different inferences from the same utterance
   c. be aware of the significance of such cultural differences for intercultural interaction.

3. **Focus questions**

   a. Flouting a maxim

   Consider the following extract from section 2.2:

   > **flouting a maxim** [entails] a speaker blatantly failing to observe a maxim with the deliberate intention of causing an implicature. In such contexts, the speaker, however, does not intentionally mean to deceive or mislead the hearer, only to induce the hearer to search for an additional meaning to that of the expressed meaning.

   Provide an example of flouting a maxim. Indicate the social interaction, cultural norms and environmental factors that influence the interpretation of its conversational implicature.

   b. Speech acts (use the table in Appendix 1 for this)

   Using Searle's (1979) subdivision of performatives, provide an example for each of the five types of speech acts. Indicate their propositional content as well as the preparatory, sincerity and essential conditions for each type of speech act.

   c. Indirect speech acts

   (i) Provide an example of an indirect speech act and describe its primary illocutionary and its secondary illocutionary force using Searle's (1975) definition. Explain the influence of the cultural assumptions of mutually shared background on the interpretation of this indirect speech act.

   (ii) How could this indirect speech act be misunderstood in an intercultural context? Give an example of the linguistic and cultural context in which it could be misconstrued.

4. Research analysis: Grice's maxims

a. Grice's original maxims Grice (1975, pp. 45–7) were revised by Clyne (1994). See section 2.2 for Grice's original formulations and consider Clyne's revisions below:

Manner:	Avoid obscurity of expression.
	Avoid ambiguity.
	Be brief.
	Be orderly.
Manner:	*Supermaxim* – 'Be perspicacious'.
	Sub-maxims (summarised from Clyne 1994, pp. 194–5):

1. 'Do not make it any more difficult to understand than may be dictated by questions of face and authority.'
2. 'Make clear your communicative intent unless this is against the interests of politeness or of maintaining a dignity-driven cultural core value, such as harmony, charity or respect.'
3. 'Make your contribution the appropriate length required by the nature and purpose of the exchange and the discourse parameters of your culture.'
4. 'Structure your discourse according to the requirements of your culture.'
5. 'In your contribution, take into account anything you know or can predict about the interlocutor's communication expectations.'
   (i) Why are Clyne's (1994) revisions of the maxim of Manner regarded as being more appropriate for interpreting utterances in an intercultural context?
   (ii) Why is Clyne's fifth maxim of Manner important to the interpretation of an utterance in intercultural contexts? Provide an intercultural communication example that might illustrate this.
   (iii) Is the concept of 'orderliness' highly valued in your culture? Describe the appropriateness of Grice's 'be orderly' in your daily communication patterns.
   (iv) Based on your answer to the previous question, do you think Clyne's revisions relating to 'be orderly' overcome the limits of Grice's maxim? Give reasons for your answer.

b. Now further consider the extract taken from the above discussion on the maxim of Manner:

> Cam Nguyên (1991, p. 43) has identified what she terms the Vietnamese 'tolerance for ambiguity'. This 'tolerance for ambiguity' is

accompanied by a preference for a circular discourse structure, which involves merely suggesting examples of an implicit perception and continually returning to this perception to expand upon it. Ide (1989) also postulates that the 'tolerance for ambiguity' relates to the tendency of 'indirectness' at the pragmatic level of some East (and South-East) Asian languages.

(i) Would you describe your own culture as having a 'tolerance for ambiguity'? Give reasons.

(ii) How does having a 'tolerance for ambiguity' or a lack of 'tolerance of ambiguity' affect the discourse structures in your culture?

(iii) Describe some possible negative perceptions and consequences that may arise in an intercultural communication context where there are two people, one from a culture that values ambiguity, another from one that values a higher level of certainty. Provide at least two strategies of how such negative perceptions and consequences may be overcome and successful intercultural communication can occur.

5. **Research exercise**

   a. There are a variety of ways to ask someone at the dinner table to *pass the salt*:

   Pass the salt (please).
   Can you pass the salt?
   Can you reach the salt?
   Would you mind passing the salt?
   I would appreciate it if you would pass the salt.
   Would you pass the salt?

   Using the above example as a guideline, conduct a survey of at least five people to determine their interpretation of different request forms and their literal and non-literal meanings. You can use the above request forms of English, or design your own request forms using a language that you know well.

   b. Contemporary ethnographers have often shown an interest in service encounters such as those described by Bailey (2001) in this chapter's introduction. For instance, Gaudio (2003) conducted a sophisticated ethnography of Starbucks coffee shop in order to understand the role of this shop in contemporary society. Among other things, he showed how ways of speaking had been commodified. Conduct an ethnography of speaking at a restaurant. What do you find with regard to speech acts, indirectness, voicing, genre, etc.? How might these ways of speaking pose a problem to those not familiar with their conventions?

SUGGESTED FURTHER READING

We suggest revisiting the seminal works (e.g. Austin, Goffman, Grice, Searle) for a firm foundation in Speech Act Theory, Grice's maxims, role and direct/indirect messages. The following works complement or expound upon this chapter's introduction of these topics. Horn and Ward's *The Handbook of Pragmatics* is a particularly handy reference book for pragmatic theory. Duranti's *Linguistic Anthropology* reader is a goldmine for ethnographically informed approaches to language. Silverstein provides a particularly vociferous critique of Speech Act Theory before emphasising the need for a semiotic approach for understanding direct and indirect speech acts. Clyne's (1994) work exemplifies how theories with perceived Anglo-centric foci have been revised to better account for intercultural communication.

Duranti A (ed.) 2001 *Linguistic Anthropology: A Reader*. Malden, MA: Blackwell.

Horn, L. 2006 'Implicature'. In Horn, L. & Ward, G. (eds) *The Handbook of Pragmatics*. Malden, MA: Blackwell, pp. 53–73.

Levinson, S. C. 1983 *Pragmatics*. Cambridge: Cambridge University Press.

Mitchell-Kernan, C. 2001 'Signifying and marking: Two Afro-American speech acts'. In Duranti, A (ed.) *Linguistic Anthropology: A Reader*. Malden, MA: Blackwell, pp. 151–64.

Morgan, M. 2010 'The presentation of indirectness and power in everyday life'. *Journal of Pragmatics*, vol. 42, pp. 283–91.

Sadock, J. 2006 'Speech acts'. In Horn, L. & Ward, G. (eds) *The Handbook of Pragmatics*. Malden, MA: Blackwell, pp. 53–72.

Saville-Troike 2003 *The Ethnography of Communication*. Oxford: Basil Blackwell.

Silverstein, S. 2010 '"Direct" and "indirect" communicative acts in semiotic perspective'. *Journal of Pragmatics*, vol. 42, pp. 337–53.

3 | Schemas, face and politeness

3.1   INTRODUCTION

A̲ₗₗ social groups have preferred ways of speaking. For instance, contemporary English greetings include *hi, what's up?, how's it going?, how are you?, hello, how do you do?* and *g'day* (for many Australian English speakers, at least!). Furthermore, social groups tend to have preferred ways of speaking for particular contexts. For example, *how do you do?* would be highly valued at a formal occasion but it would not be a good way to greet your friend in the morning. You would need something cooler, more humorous – even perhaps a loud groan!

Most languages have differing styles of communication according to:

- levels of familiarity (e.g. family, friends, acquaintances, strangers)
- levels of formality (e.g. extremely formal to informal)
- types of situations (e.g. professional, business, sport, private, public)
- relative age
- gender.

Getting these levels correct is often called socially appropriate behaviour or **politeness**.

Not surprisingly, politeness formulas vary across cultures. For instance, Chinese and Indonesian speakers often greet one another by asking *where are you going?* or *have you eaten?* Individuals from Anglo-European cultures can find these questions invasive, not recognising them as mere formulaic greetings akin to *how are you?* In other words, a Chinese or Indonesian stranger may not care where you are going any more than an English stranger cares about your general state of being. Moreover, a lengthy explanation of the day's eating and travel plans would be as inappropriate in China or Indonesia as a discussion of your physical or mental ailments would be in Australia, the United States or the United Kingdom.

Avoiding conflict and confrontation is an integral element of appropriate language usage, finding its way into the language of almost all social groups – and it is this that is generally recognised as politeness. In this chapter we examine what makes an utterance appropriate in one social context but not in another. This basis will contribute to an understanding of parallel complexity in intercultural communication. We begin with a cognitive perspective on contextual felicity through a brief discussion of cultural schemas. We then outline what has been labelled the 'first wave' of politeness research (see Culpeper 2011b), with a particular focus on Brown and Levinson's work on face and face-threatening acts. A subsequent critique of Brown and Levinson's theory leads to an introduction of the 'second wave' of politeness research. Perhaps the most interesting aspect of the second wave is its pursuit of impoliteness as a concept.[1] In other words, our knowledge of politeness conventions enables us not only to avoid conflict or confrontation but to incite it where strategically relevant.

3.2   CULTURAL SCHEMAS

From the cognitive perspective, appropriate or preferred behaviour may be understood in terms of cultural schemas. **Schemas** refer in a general sense 'to units of human knowledge that result from the cognitive processes of deriving patterns either from our perception or from our construal of the world' (Sharifian 2006, p. 11). By extension, units of cultural knowledge of this type are **cultural schemas**. Cultural schemas guide the ways in which individuals accomplish speech acts (e.g. Sharifian 2004, 2006; Intachakra 2012), conceptualise their relationships with others (e.g. Sharifian 2004, 2006; Intachakra 2012; Wyatt & Promkandorn 2012), communicate love (e.g. Caldwell-Harris, Kronrod & Yang 2013) and interact more generally (e.g. Grainger, Mills & Sibanda 2010).[2]

---

[1] Some researchers (e.g. Grainger 2011; Shum & Lee 2013) discuss politeness studies in terms of three waves. However, we take the position that the two-wave model is more apt. Lakoff's, Leech's and Brown and Levinson's work, as well as critiques of these works, sit neatly within a first wave of research. However, since the turn of the century a dizzying array of models has emerged. These, to our mind, sit neatly within a second wave of studies, which are often 'radically different in some respects' but also provide 'many specific improvements to the classic politeness models' Culpeper (2011b, p. 414).

[2] Many studies implicitly draw on the notion of cultural schema without explicitly making reference to the concept. For instance, Grainger, Mills and Sibanda (2010) discuss the practices of a Zimbabwean

Sharifian (2004, pp. 123–5) illustrates the way in which a cultural schema known as *sharmandegi* (sometimes translated as 'being ashamed') is evident in the Persian language (Farsi) in a number of speech acts (translated literally here):

Expressing gratitude:
    'You really make me ashamed.'
Offering goods and services:
    'Please help yourself, I'm ashamed, it's not worthy of you.'
Requesting goods and services:
    'I'm ashamed, can I beg some minutes of your time.'
Apologising:
    'I'm really ashamed that the noise from the kids didn't let you sleep.'

Sharifian (2004, p. 125) suggests that in all cases, the *sharmandegi* schema 'seems to encourage Iranians to consider the possibility that in the company of others they may be doing or have done something wrong or something not in accordance with the other party's dignity'. He further comments that the idea of a common schema underlying the various uses of the expression *sharmandegi* is also supported by the observation that all those speech acts may be responded to by the same formulaic expression, such as *doshmanetoon sharmandeh basheh*, literally meaning 'your enemy be ashamed'.

Sharifian relates the *sharmandegi* schema to a higher-level 'overarching' cultural schema that defines a core value of culture related to social relations he calls *adab va ehteram*, roughly glossed as 'courtesy and respect' in English (2004, p. 125). He suggests that this 'higher-level schema encourages Iranians to constantly place the presence of others at the centre of their conceptualizations and monitor their own ways of thinking and talking to make them harmonious with the esteem that they hold for others' (2004, p. 125).

Sharifian argues that such 'cultural schemas' are conceptual structures that develop at the cultural level of cognition, rather than the psychological level. These schemas are knowledge templates that are represented in a distributed fashion across the minds in a cultural group. Cultural schemas are abstracted from social interactions between the members of a cultural group, who 'negotiate' and 'renegotiate' these schemas across generations. Such schemas can motivate thought and behaviour that are

choir director in Britain in terms of the Southern African cultural concepts of *hlonipha* ('pay respect') and *ubuntu* ('the belief individuals are all connected through shared humanity').

considered appropriate to a particular cultural group. Sharifian suggests that 'Unfamiliarity with such schemas may lead to discomfort or misunderstanding during the process of intercultural communication' (2004, p. 127).

3.3 FIRST WAVE OF POLITENESS RESEARCH: THE MODELS

The first wave of politeness research includes the 'pioneers' who set out the first models of politeness in the 1970s and 1980s (Culpeper 2011b). It also includes those researchers who examined, supported and/or critiqued these models, mostly in the 1980s and 1990s. Here we briefly introduce conversational maxim-based models, which emerged from Grice's work discussed in Chapter 2. We then discuss Brown and Levinson's influential 'face management' model in great depth. Brown and Levinson sought to move away from a maxim-based approach, instead seeking to describe why and how speakers make language choices. In spite of critiques, Brown and Levinson's work remains influential and many researchers continue to draw on it to describe such diverse contexts as language classrooms (e.g. Al-Gahtani & Roever 2013), healthcare (e.g. Backhaus 2009; Brown & Crawford 2009) and the media (e.g. Bayraktaroğlu & Sifianou 2012; Migdadi, Badarneh & Momani 2012).

MAXIM-BASED MODELS

The seminal works on politeness emerged from Grice's Cooperative Principle and its four maxims. Lakoff (1973) was among the first researchers to adopt Grice's constructs to elaborate upon politeness (Fraser 1990). It can be inferred from Lakoff's work that politeness is the avoidance of offence (Fraser 1990, p. 223). In a later work, Lakoff claims that politeness is 'a device used in order to reduce friction in personal interaction' (Lakoff 1979, p. 64). Lakoff (1973) proposes the following two rules of Pragmatic Competence:

1. Be clear (essentially Grice's maxims).
2. Be polite.

In addition, Lakoff posits the sub-maxims:

Rule 1: Don't impose.
Rule 2: Give options.
Rule 3: Make your hearer feel good.

Leech (1983) has also used Grice's Cooperative Principle and maxims as the basis for his approach. He has, however, elaborated his model to include what he calls the Politeness Principle. Where the Cooperative Principle explains how speakers convey messages, the Politeness Principle seeks to explain why (Culpeper 2011b). Like Grice's model, the Politeness Principle operates along a series of maxims:

Tact maxim:	Minimise hearer costs: maximise hearer benefit.
	(Do not put others in a position where they have to break the Tact maxim.)
Generosity maxim:	Minimise your own benefit; maximise your hearer's benefit.
Approbation maxim:	Minimise hearer dispraise; maximise hearer praise.
Modesty maxim:	Minimise self-praise; maximise self-dispraise.
Agreement maxim:	Minimise disagreement between yourself and others; maximise agreement between yourself and others.
Sympathy maxim:	Minimise antipathy between yourself and others; maximise sympathy between yourself and others.

Leech and Lakoff use the term maxim in a very different manner to Grice. Grice's maxims focus more on expectations about language and how information is conveyed in everyday conversations whereas Leech's and Lakoff's maxims are more concerned with interpersonal relationships. Furthermore, Leech (1983) indicates from the outset his maxims would not be equally relevant across cultures. For instance, one might expect the Tact maxim to be more relevant to some British cultures and the Modesty maxim more pertinent to some Japanese cultures (Culpeper 2011b).

BROWN AND LEVINSON'S POLITENESS MODEL

The best known and most widely researched model of politeness is Brown and Levinson's (1978) (revised slightly and discussed at length in 1987). This model consists of three basic notions: face, face-threatening acts (FTAs) and politeness strategies. Brown and Levinson's account of politeness was based on the analysis of three unrelated languages and cultures, namely English, Tamil (a Dravidian language) and Tzeltal (a language of the Mayan family of Central America) and was claimed to have universal applicability.

Face is the first notion of Brown and Levinson's model. The origin of face, as it is used by modern researchers, can be linked to mid-nineteenth-century books and documents written in pidgin English in China (St Andre 2013). China-focused anthropologists sought to develop the term in the mid-twentieth century. Goffman (1955, 1967) subsequently divorced 'face' from its Chinese roots and developed it as a universal concept of interaction (St Andre 2013). **Face,** as used by Brown and Levinson, is derived from both the English folk perception of 'being embarrassed or humiliated, or "losing face"' (Brown & Levinson 1987, p. 61) and the work of Goffman (1955, 1967). In Brown and Levinson's terms, the concept of 'face' refers to the desire that all people have to maintain and defend their own self-image.

The second basic notion of Brown and Levinson's model is the concept of **face-threatening acts** (FTAs). Face is something that can be lost, maintained or enhanced, and any threat to face must be continually monitored during an interaction. It is believed to be in everyone's best interest that face be maintained. Brown and Levinson (1987, p. 24) suggest that some acts are intrinsically **threatening to face** and require softening. Therefore, language users develop politeness strategies to reduce the face loss that may result from an interaction that is face-threatening.

Brown and Levinson (1987, p. 61) make a distinction between positive and negative face, which they define in a way that many find counterintuitive, but which is still widely used in the literature. Brown and Levinson's definitions are as follows:

Positive face: the positive consistent self-image or 'personality' (crucially including the desire that this self-image be appreciated and approved of) claimed by interactants.

Negative face: the basic claim to territories, personal preserves, rights to non-distraction – that is, to freedom of action and freedom from imposition.

Regardless of the problems with this terminology, the key observation is that politeness has two important aspects: preserving a person's positive self-image and avoiding imposing on a person's freedom.

The above aspects of face can give rise to the following four types of FTAs, identified by Brown and Levinson (1987, pp. 65–6):

- acts threatening to the hearer's negative face (freedom of action): e.g. ordering, advising, threatening, warning
- acts threatening to the hearer's positive face (self-image): e.g. complaining, criticising, disagreeing, raising taboo topics
- acts threatening to the speaker's negative face (freedom of action): e.g. accepting an offer, accepting thanks
- acts threatening to the speaker's positive face (self-image): e.g. apologising, accepting a compliment, confessing.

Brown and Levinson (1987, p. 74) suggest that the assessment of the seriousness of an FTA involves three dimensions in many and perhaps all cultures:

> **D** the *social distance* between the speaker and the hearer (i.e. the degree of familiarity and solidarity they share, or might be thought to share)
>
> **P** the *relative power* of the speaker with respect to the hearer (i.e. the degree to which the speaker can impose on the hearer)
>
> **R** the *absolute ranking* of the imposition in a particular culture (in terms of (1) the expenditure of goods and/or services by the hearer, (2) the right of the speaker to perform the act and (3) the degree to which the hearer welcomes the imposition).

Brown and Levinson (1987, p. 80) illustrate the interaction of these variables by citing the subsequent examples. In the case of requests for 'free goods' or small services (low imposition R) between members of the public (P not relevant), then either of the following might be used by the speaker on account of the relative social distance between the speaker and the hearer:

1. Excuse me, would you by any chance have the time?
2. Got the time, mate?

It is Brown and Levinson's intuition (1987, p. 80) that (1) would be used where the speaker and the hearer were distant (speakers from different parts, for instance), and (2) where the speaker and the hearer were close (either known to each other, or perceptibly 'similar' in social terms).

In regards to the P variable (relative power), D and R being more or less constant and having small values (e.g. if the speaker and the hearer know each other and the imposition is for free goods), then either of the following might be used depending on the relative power between the speaker and the hearer:

3. Excuse me sir, would it be alright if I smoke?
4. Mind if I smoke?

Brown and Levinson (1987, p. 80) suggest that (3) might be said by an employee to his or her boss, while (4) might be said by the boss to the employee in the same situation. (Now that smoking is less widely acceptable, the contexts in which such utterances would be appropriate are more restricted, yet we believe the comparison still holds.)

In regards to the R variable (degree of imposition), Brown and Levinson (1987, p. 81) provide the following illustration: supposing P is small and D is great (e.g. the speaker and hearer are strangers), and P and D are held constant, then either of the following might be used depending on the degree of imposition (R):

5. Look, I'm terribly sorry to bother you but would there be any chance of your lending me just enough money to get a railway ticket to get home? I must have dropped my purse and I just don't know what to do.
6. Hey, got change for a quarter?

Brown and Levinson suggest that both might be uttered at a railway station by a frustrated traveller to a stranger, but that their intuitions are that in saying (5) the speaker considers the FTA to be much more serious than the FTA in (6). 'Our conclusion is that in the ranking of impositions in Anglo-American culture, asking for a substantial amount of money without recompense is much more of an imposition than a request to search one's pocket for change' (Brown & Levinson 1987, p. 81).

The third and final notion of the Brown and Levinson model relates to the choice of **Redress Strategies**, which are employed when the weight of the imposition is perceived as being face-threatening. Brown and Levinson acknowledge that the degree to which a given act rates as face-threatening and also the social importance of distance and power are culturally determined, and may differ according to the situation within a particular cultural environment (1987, pp. 76–9). However, they do assert that P, D and R 'seem to do a remarkably adequate job in predicting politeness assessments' (1987, p. 17).

Brown and Levinson's schematic representation of possible politeness strategies is summarised in Figure 3.1. The top options (e.g. do the FTA) are considered appropriate if the imposition is relatively small, whereas the bottom options (e.g. don't do the act) are appropriate if the risk to face is high.

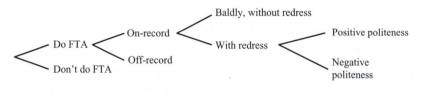

Low face risk to the participant

High face risk to the participant

Explanation of terms

On-record – when only one intention can be identified by the participants
    e.g. 'I promise that I will pick you up at 4 o'clock.'

If the participants decide that 'I' (the speaker) has unambiguously declared the intention of committing the above future act, then it is regarded as 'on-record'.

Off-record – the avoidance of direct impositions
    e.g. 'I'm out of cash. I forgot to go to the bank today.'

Baldly, without redress – involves undertaking an act in the most direct, unambiguous and clear manner
    e.g. 'Clean your room' ('Do X!').

People will only do an FTA in such a manner if the speaker does not fear retribution from the hearer.

    Redressive action – 'gives face' to the hearer, meaning that the speaker tries to overcome any possible damage from the FTA by modifying their behaviour i.e. positive or negative politeness strategies.

    Positive politeness – strategies addressed to the hearer's self-image (positive face), e.g. by treating him or her as a member of an in-group, a friend, a person whose wants and personality traits are known and liked. (Thus involving expressions of solidarity, informality and familiarity.) e.g. exaggerate interest in H, sympathise with H and avoid disagreement.

    Negative politeness – is oriented towards the hearer's negative face and involves expressions of restraint, self-effacement and formality e.g. being conventionally indirect, giving deference, using hedges, apologising for imposing.

Figure 3.1 Possible politeness strategies
(summary of Brown & Levinson 1987, pp. 69–70)

Brown and Levinson's model thus tries to account for choices that speakers make in avoiding threats to a hearer's self-image (positive face) or freedom from imposition (negative face). The model assumes that in choosing how to phrase speech acts that may threaten the hearer's positive or negative face, a speaker takes into account these factors: relative power between the speaker and hearer (P), relative social distance between the speaker and hearer (S), and the relative degree of the imposition involved (R).

The concepts inherent to the Brown and Levinson model have formed the basis of much subsequent research in a range of different contexts and across cultures. In the following sections we review some of the subsequent work on politeness, almost all of which can be seen to have been informed in some way by the work of Brown and Levinson.

3.4 FIRST WAVE OF POLITENESS RESEARCH: THE CRITIQUES

The model proposed by Brown and Levinson (1978, 1987) has been the subject of much comment and criticism. Some of the most vociferous critiques of the model have addressed its focus on FTAs at the expense of other contextual factors, its decontextualisation and oversimplification of language use, its conceptualisation of face and its linking of indirectness to politeness.

One of the key problems of Brown and Levinson's politeness model is that it is concerned principally with politeness strategies in the context of FTAs (see Paramasivam 2011; Intachakra 2012). Yet, interaction does not exist entirely of FTAs. This is something that Brown and Levinson themselves concede (Culpeper 2011b).The building of positive relationships through mutual caring and assistance over time is surely important, and is usually accompanied by the expression of mutual appreciation and praise. Spencer-Oatey (2008) has proposed a model that specifically tends to the fostering of rapport, as will be discussed in section 3.5 below.

The second problem with Brown and Levinson's model relates to their decontextualisation and simplification of a discursively constructed process (Mills 2003; Backhaus 2009; Ogiermann 2009). For example, Wolfowitz (1991) argues that for Javanese in Suriname a house guest's positive face is attended to through emphasised violations of that guest's negative face. A guest may not feel valued if food or drink is not performatively being pushed in his or her direction. Along similar lines, in many cultures, banter and ritual insults such as *signifying* (discussed in Chapter 2) contribute to an individual's positive face through the seeming violation of his or her positive face (see Haugh & Boufield 2012; Mugford 2013; Yu 2013)

Politeness and its associated strategies have also encountered resistance from Japanese linguists. Ide (1989) argues that Brown and Levinson's distinction between positive and negative politeness strategies does not account for the Japanese notion of *wakimae* (which Ide translates as 'discernment'). She believes that Japanese social interactions do not allow for interactional choice, because social norms are predetermined by a person's place in society. According to Ide (1989), Brown and Levinson's approach does not accommodate such predetermined forms of interaction because it is not a matter of establishing the level of imposition, rather of the superior–inferior relationship in society. In this context, Goffman's original interpretation of 'face' in terms of its volitional features and social-indexing perspectives is perhaps more appropriate for such cultures.

While Ide (1989) describes 'politeness' in relation to 'discernment', other approaches to politeness have employed the term 'deference' (e.g. Adegbija 1989; Blum-Kulka 1989). Meier (1995a, p. 348) points out that such a term is quite often used interchangeably with politeness and that this is not surprising given that 'Brown and Levinson derived their model from Goffman (1967), whose two forms of deference are transformed by Brown and Levinson into their two types of politeness strategies'.

This hints at another weakness in Brown and Levinson's model that is relevant in Western cultures, too. This model oversimplifies positive politeness strategies by only describing them in terms of expressions of solidarity, informality and familiarity. This pays little heed to issues of respect and deference. For instance, there are many social contexts in the English-speaking world in which affirmation of the positive self-image of an addressee who is senior in age, experience or status, or socially distant from the speaker, is overtly expressed, sometimes with formality, and deference. In other cultures, particularly Asian cultures, the expression of deference and respect is almost mandatory with addressees who are senior in age, experience or status. In certain restricted contexts, for example, among employees who have worked together for a significant period, private exchanges might be less formal, but in public, conventional deference to seniors would be mandatory.

To account for the under-representation of deference in the Brown and Levinson model, researchers have drawn attention to the fact that the model is based on the individual, rather than the social group. This, many argue, may be linked to the way in which Brown and Levinson conceptualise face (Matsumoto 1988, 1989; Mao 1994; de Kadt 1998; compare Ide 1989; Grainger, Mills & Sibanda 2010). Mao (1994) suggests that Brown and Levinson's concept of 'face' as an image that intrinsically belongs to the individual, to the 'self', contrasts with Goffman's original interpretation of 'face' as a 'public property' that is seen as given or 'loaned' to individuals depending on the situation. De Kadt (1998) argues that this difference in the interpretation of 'face' is of great significance when discussing this concept in terms of universality, especially for non-Western cultures. De Kadt suggests that Goffman's original concept has the advantage of better accommodating both volitional and social indexing aspects of politeness.

For instance, Goffman (1967, p. 44) regarded 'face' as an element present in every society and indicated that societies everywhere, if they are to be societies, must mobilise their members as self-regulating participants in social encounters. Goffman suggested that 'each person, subculture and society seems to have its own characteristic repertoire of face-saving practices, yet these are all drawn from a single logically coherent framework of possible practices' (1967, p. 13). Such a perspective seems to be in opposition to Brown and Levinson's concept of face in that, according to Goffman, 'face' is used in terms of 'persons' and 'societies', not just 'individuals'.

De Kadt (1998, p. 188) found that Zulu speakers use both verbal and non-verbal means of communication to address the issue of 'face'. Greeting rituals are viewed as being compulsory and are generally performed by the subordinate person in the interaction. These greetings are followed by enquiries into the status of the other's health and wellbeing, not by the subordinate, but this time by the person of higher status. Generally, in such interactions, terms of address are used that specify the participants' roles in the coming conversation. For example, de Kadt (1998, p. 188) reports that:

> an adult male could be referred to by his wife as *baba ka Sipho*, 'father of Sipho', by pupils at the school where he teaches as *thisha*, 'teacher', by his colleagues as *mngame wami*, 'my friend', (and) by men of the same age as *infowethu*, 'my brother'.

This example shows that for the Zulu speaker, the status of the participants determines the choice of terms and phrases. In such a society the concept of *face* is one of mutuality and is paid attention to by both participants throughout the interaction. De Kadt argues that Goffman's broader definition of 'face', in contrast to Brown and Levinson's, is thus more appropriate in understanding the social indexing and volitional aspects of Zulu politeness. 'Such a perspective diverges from the more limiting focus on FTAs, which is present in the Brown and Levinson model' (de Kadt 1998, p. 189).

Brown and Levinson's focus on 'individual face' has also attracted much criticism from Japanese linguists. Matsumoto (1988, 1989) argues that this notion of *face* with its focus on individual territorial rights is difficult to apply to the Japanese language context. Matsumoto (1988) and Ide (1989) argue that individual rights are not so important in the Japanese culture because cultural norms focus more on the positional relation to others than with individual territory.

A final criticism of Brown and Levinson's model to be addressed here has been the connection between politeness and indirectness. Brown and Levinson suggest that there is a direct link between indirectness and politeness – the more obscure the intention of an utterance, the more polite it is; the more direct or clear the intention, the less polite it is. As Shum and Lee (2013, p. 53), drawing on Watts (2003), point out: 'equating indirectness to politeness seems to be an overgeneralization and simplification, particularly when it comes to the explanation of overly polite or impolite behavior or communication that is different from social expectation.' House and Kasper (1981), Tannen (1981), Wierzbicka (1985, 1991, 2003), Blum-Kulka and House (1989), and Bialystok (1993) have all examined the connection between politeness and the level of indirectness and found that the relationship between these two processes differs from culture to culture. For example, in Japanese discourse there is a closer link between politeness and indirectness than in American or Arabic cultures (Takahashi & Beebe 1993). Katriel (1986) found that in the Israeli Sabra culture there is a direct connection between politeness and directness. Wierzbicka (1985) suggests that Polish society is sometimes perceived as being generally 'impolite' or 'rude' due to the usage of performatives and imperatives for advice-giving and directives. Such types of utterances may be viewed as being 'too direct' in cultures that value indirectness as the norm.

Another problem with research that compares levels of directness and indirectness is that conclusions can only be relative to the cultures that are being contrasted. For example, if German speakers from House and Kasper's (1981) study, who are regarded as being direct, are compared with Greek speakers from Pavlidou's (1991), the Germans might be judged as being indirect in contrast to a higher level of directness of the Greek speakers. The same has been said about Australians who appear to be indirect when contrasted with Hebrew and German speakers (Blum-Kulka & House 1989).

In sum, as the above studies show, it is problematic to identify cultures solely in terms of a negative and positive orientation, especially when discussing indirectness and directness. Meier (1995b, p. 386) believes that describing cultures in relation to such orientations is misleading and 'risks perpetuating national stereotypes and "linguacentricity"'.[3] Furthermore, decontextualising politeness and reducing it to the mitigation of FTAs oversimplifies human communication and relationships more generally. In spite of these critiques, Brown and Levinson's model continues to influence the study of politeness, as noted in the previous section. Moreover, some researchers have sought to defend its general applicability (e.g. Backhaus 2009) and to dissect the East–West cross-cultural critiques proposed by scholars such as Ide, Mao and Matsumoto (e.g. Chen, He & Hu 2013). However, the past few decades have fostered an array of improvements to first-wave models as well as a number of new models and these are said to fall under the aegis of the second wave (Culpeper 2011b).

3.5   SECOND WAVE OF POLITENESS RESEARCH

Three of the more prominent concerns in the second wave of politeness research have been the discursive construction of politeness (e.g. Eelen 2001; Watts 2003; Mills 2003), the relational work of politeness (e.g. Locher 2006; Spencer-Oatey 2008) and impoliteness as a topic worthy of study in its own right (e.g. Bousfield 2008; Bousfield & Locher 2008). These theoretical foci emerge from some of the more vociferous criticisms of Brown and Levinson's theory.

Many researchers have emphasised the situated and discursively constructed nature of politeness. In other words, these researchers believed the imposition of inflexible, predictive models on human practice could potentially be counterproductive (Culpeper 2011b). This led Eelen (2001) and Watts (2003) and colleagues (e.g. Watts, Ide & Ehlich 1992) to draw a distinction between first-order politeness and second-order politeness. **First-order politeness** encompasses the many ways in which polite behaviour is viewed and enacted by non-specialist individuals operating in communities (e.g. 'commonsense notions of politeness') (Watts 2003, p. 9). **Second-order politeness**, on the other hand, refers to the theorisation of politeness by researchers such as those operating in the first wave of politeness inquiry. This involves theoretical observations about the social expectations (e.g. expected use of mitigators such as *please* and *sir* in speech acts) and power balance (e.g. relationships between roles such as manager

---

[3] The term 'linguacentricity' refers to the limitations of perspective that may result from using a single language as a model for understanding all others.

and employee) prevailing between the participants in a given interaction. Watts (1989) and Watts, Ide and Ehlich (1992) also term this second-order politeness as *politic* in order to contrast this with first-order *polite* behaviour (see also Watts (2003) and Meier (1995a, 1995b) for a further discussion of politic and polite behaviours).

Watts (2003) shows a primary concern for first-order politeness, noting the need to move beyond homogenous understandings of the notion of culture (see also Mills 2003; Pan 2011). Yet, he is not opposed to the explanatory power of second-order politeness and supports the relational approach (see Locher & Watts 2005), a second path of inquiry in the second wave of politeness research. The relational approach is concerned with the work individuals put into negotiating relationships with others (Locher & Watts 2005). Locher (2006, p. 262) summarises how the two orders may inform one another via a relational approach: 'a discursive approach to politeness stresses that we first of all have to establish the kind of relational work the interactants in question employ to arrive at an understanding of the then-current norms of interaction.' In short, not unlike the ethnographic approach, the relational approach does not presuppose how individuals perceive and enact politeness. It first observes practice and then links this practice to theory.

Many researchers (e.g. Spencer-Oatey 2005, 2008; Paramasivam 2011; Intachakra 2012) discuss the relational nature of language and politeness in terms of rapport. Spencer-Oatey (2005, 2008) arguably provides the most detailed framework for this approach with her notion of 'rapport management' (Culpeper et al. 2010). Rapport management conceptualises language and politeness along three dimensions: face, social rights and obligations and interactional goals (Spencer-Oatey 2008). With these three dimensions as a basis, rapport management may be used to uncover cross-cultural variations with regard to a number of factors. For instance, it raises the issue of how individuals assess contexts and whether they prefer directness or indirectness. Rapport management also shines a light on the necessity and frequency of specific speech acts relative to a particular culture as well as the linguistic resources (e.g. discourse markers, pronominal distinctions as in the French *tu/vous*) an individual has at his or her disposal to accomplish these acts. Lastly, it enables the analyst to understand how these assessments, resources and acts relate to fundamental cultural values, such as the schemas mentioned in section 3.2 above.

The third and final approach to be discussed with regard to the second wave of politeness inquiry is that of impoliteness. As with rapport management, the study of impoliteness also emerges from the discursive and relational focus on language and politeness (see Bousfield & Locher 2008).

Impoliteness and its many manifestations (e.g. banter, rudeness) have long been neglected in favour of a focus on politeness. Culpeper (2011b, p. 427) points out: 'one of the great lacuna in Brown and Levinson (1987) is that they do not treat banter at all'. Leech (1983) notably does posit a Banter Principle and this is often referenced in papers that deal with the role of banter or mock impoliteness in reinforcing relationships (e.g. Haugh & Bousfield 2012; Mugford 2013).

Impoliteness is certainly a worthy focus in its own right due to its strategic use for banter, struggles of power, and entertainment, among other things. In fact, impoliteness is licensed in many contexts, such as military recruit training (Culpeper 2008) and political debates (Harris 2001) and on certain television programs, such as *The Weakest Link* (Culpeper 2005; Bayraktaroğlu & Sifianou 2012). With regard to the latter, host Anne Robinson draws on a sophisticated and balanced series of politeness and impoliteness strategies to position guests on the *The Weakest Link* (Bayraktaroğlu & Sifianou 2012). For instance, in the following exchange, Robinson (AR) asks a series of seemingly innocent and even flirtatious questions that tend to a contestant's (Jason) positive face.

1	AR:	What do you do, Jason?
2	Jason:	I am a freelance videographer, Anne.
3	AR:	What, you make movies?
4	Jason:	Yes.
5	AR:	Where?
6	Jason:	At home basically. Anywhere that wants videos,
7		I do corporate videos, wedding videos [any _
8	AR:	/ [and would you
9		make a movie with me in it?
10	Jason:	Yeah, definitely.

(Bayraktaroğlu & Sifianou 2012, p. 152)

Robinson subsequently establishes, through more seemingly innocent and polite questioning, that Jason is unmarried and lives with his mother. She uses this information to set Jason up for the following impolite exchange:

19	AR:	/ So let me get this straight. You make private films in
20		the attic of your house where your mother lives.
21	Jason:	Yeah.
22	AR:	Is she still alive?
23	Jason:	(*laughs*) Are you comparing me to Norman Bates?
24	AR:	(*smiling*) I couldn't possibly comment . . .

(Bayraktaroğlu & Sifianou 2012, p. 152)

The coexistence of politeness and impoliteness in exchanges such as these, Bayraktaroğlu and Sifianou (2012, p. 156) conclude, 'stems from and reflects the fact that context is fluid and dynamic rather than static' (see also Culpeper 2011a).

3.6 METHODOLOGIES: NATURAL SEMANTIC METALANGUAGE

Wierzbicka (1972, 1985, 1991, 2003) has developed an approach to the study of cross-cultural semantics and cross-cultural pragmatics. She bases this approach on the explication of the meaning of words and illocutionary acts by the use of just over two dozen lexical primitives, which she suggests are semantic universals. Wierzbicka's methodology draws on the ideas of seventeenth-century thinkers such as Descartes, Leibnitz and Locke. These thinkers were interested in how simple words could be used to define others. Wierzbicka has posited the use of semantic primitives to compare differences of definition between similar words and concepts in different languages. Wierzbicka (1994b) introduced the term 'cultural scripts' to refer to her technique for articulating cultural norms, values and practices using natural semantic metalanguage.

The following example of differences in approach to 'self assertion' in Japanese and English (Wierzbicka 2003, pp. 72 ff.) contrasts the Western model (cultural script) based on the 'complex of individuality, autonomy, equality, rationality, aggression, and self-assertion' with the traditional Japanese 'complex of collectivism, interdependence, superordination-subordination, empathy, sentimentality, introspection and self-denial' as characterised by Lebra (1976, p. 257).

Wierzbicka suggests that the main difference between the two cultural perspectives with regard to self-assertion can be represented simply as:

Japanese: Don't say: 'I want this', 'I don't want this'.
Anglo–American: Do say: 'I want this', 'I don't want this'.

Wierzbicka continues: Japanese culture discourages people from expressing clearly their wishes, their preferences and their desires (what they would or wouldn't like or want), whereas Anglo-Saxon culture encourages them to do so.

Japanese: Don't say: 'I would/wouldn't like (want) this'.
Anglo-American: Do say: 'I would/wouldn't like (want) this'.

Furthermore, Japanese culture, in contrast to Anglo-American culture, discourages clear and unequivocal expression of personal opinions:

> Japanese: Don't say: 'I think this/I don't think this'.
> Anglo-American: Do say: 'I think this/I don't think this'.

Wierzbicka reports the observations of Smith (1983, pp. 44–5): 'the Japanese are at pains to avoid contention and confrontation . . . much of the definition of a "good person" involves restraint in the expression of personal desires and opinions'. This restraint manifests one of the greatest Japanese cultural values, called *enryo*, a word usually translated as 'restraint' or 'reserve'. 'One way to express *enryo* is to avoid giving opinions and to sidestep choices when they are offered. As a matter of fact, choices are less often offered in Japan than in the United States' (Smith 1983, pp. 83–4).

Rather than trying to translate the Japanese term *enryo* into English cultural concepts such as reserve, restraint, modesty or self-effacement, Wierzbicka (1991, pp. 76 ff.) considers the observations of Smith (1983), quoted above, and similar observations by Doi (1973, p. 12), Mitzutani and Mitzutani (1987) and Lebra (1976). She characterises the meaning of the Japanese word *enryo* in terms of concepts such as *want, think, say, good* or *bad*, in the following way:

> *enryo*
> X thinks:
> I can't say to this person: I want this, I don't want this
>   I think this. I don't think this
> someone can feel something bad because of this
> X doesn't say it because of this
> X doesn't do some things because of this.

Wierzbicka (2003, p. 76) observes that in English, on the contrary, one is expected to say clearly and unequivocally what one wants, what one would like or what one thinks. She suggests that 'uninhibited self-assertion' is allowed and encouraged in mainstream, Anglo-American culture:

> as long as it doesn't come into conflict with another cherished value of the culture, that is, personal autonomy. This means that while one is allowed to say in principle 'I want X', one is not allowed to say freely:

I want you to do X

since in this case, the speaker's right to 'self-assertion' would come into conflict with the addressee's right to personal autonomy.

Wierzbicka suggests that this is why English has a number of interrogative-directive devices (sometimes called 'whimperatives') such as:

Would you do X?
Will you do X?
Could you do X?
Can you do X?
Why don't you do X?

She suggests that this collection of utterances may be characterised with some reference to the autonomy of the addressee; for example:

I want you to do X.
I don't know if you will do X.
I want you to say if you will do it.

Returning to Japanese, Wierzbicka cites Matsumoto's (1988) observation that even though the use of interrogative structures is more limited in Japanese than it is in English, in Japanese 'the important thing is to show deference and acknowledge one's dependence on other people rather than to avoid the imposition'.

Wierzbicka concludes that, in many situations, it is easier (in Japanese) to say 'I want you to do X' than 'I want to do X' – as long as one acknowledges one's dependence on the addressee:

I want you to do X.
I know that you don't have to do it.
I say: it will be good for you if you do it.
I think: you will do it because of this.

Wierzbicka (2003, p. 78) summarises the comparison as follows:

In English, if one wants the addressee to do something, it is important to acknowledge the addressee's autonomy by inviting them to say whether or not they will comply with the request. Hence the proliferation and the frequency of 'whimperatives' in English. In Japanese, interrogative directive devices or 'whimperatives' exist, too, but their scope is much narrower than in English (see Matsumoto 1988; Kageyama & Tomori 1976).

Instead, there is in Japanese a proliferation of devices acknowledging dependence on other people, and deference to other people. Hence, the basic way of making requests in Japanese involves not 'whimperatives' (that is, quasi interrogative structures) but dependence acknowledging devices (usually combined with expressions of respect) . . .

Wierzbicka observes that, by contrast, in many other languages, for example, Polish, Russian, Hebrew, Italian and Hungarian, the bare infinitive is used much more freely, and the use of interrogative structures in directives is much more limited.

Wierzbicka (1972, 1980, 1991, 2003) and other scholars such as Goddard (1989, 2005, 2012), Wierzbicka and Goddard (2004), and Harkins (1990) have examined a variety of micro and macro concepts (cultural scripts) in a great number of languages incorporating an explication in terms of natural semantic metalanguage. Regardless of whether one is entirely happy with Wierzbicka's method of explication, this body of research on cross-cultural pragmatics is significant in terms of the comprehensive inventory of concepts that have been compared and discussed.

3.7   SUMMARY

As this chapter has shown, there has been considerable research interest on the phenomenon of 'politeness' spanning the last four decades. Brown and Levinson's model has provided an important foundation for analysing linguistic politeness and has drawn research attention to the relative importance of different aspects of politeness in different societies. Meier suggests that the study of politeness requires that we 'persist in placing language within its broader social context' (1995a, p. 353). The second wave of politeness research has sought to do just that by positing alternative frameworks that speak to some of the noted weaknesses of Brown and Levinson's approach. The use of natural semantic metalanguage to analyse cultural scripts (e.g. Wierzbicka 2003; Wierzbicka & Goddard 2004) provides further insight on aspects of politeness, and offers a further perspective from which to study cross-cultural communication.

3.8   REVIEW

1. **Key terms**
   Face (positive and negative), politeness (positive and negative), institutional power (P), social distance (D), relative imposition (R), speech–event, formality, sincerity, cultural script, natural semantic

metalanguage, cultural schema first-order politeness, second-order politeness.

2. **Key ideas**

Having read this chapter you should:

a. be able to differentiate between positive and negative face and positive and negative politeness

b. appreciate why different levels of politeness may be appropriate or expected in different situations

c. appreciate the different ways in which people express politeness

d. appreciate the significance of cultural differences in expressions of politeness and the reasons for such (e.g. different preferences for positive and negative face; differences in the ascription of P, D and R).

3. **Focus questions**

a. Face-threatening acts (FTAs)

Based on your own experience and language background, provide an example of an FTA and analyse it in terms of Brown and Levinson's (1987) factors of D, P and R that can be used to assess the seriousness of an FTA (section 3.3).

b. Different perspectives on politeness

We have introduced a number of perspectives on politeness. Which one do you believe is the best approach in understanding and analysing politeness across cultures? Give reasons for your choice.

c. Brown and Levinson

The approach of Brown and Levinson (1978, 1987) has been widely criticised by researchers.

  (i) Provide three of the key problems with their approach that have been identified by their critics.

  (ii) Based on your own experience and language background, do you believe that such criticisms are well founded? Give reasons for your answer.

4. **Research analysis**

Consider the following extract from Wierzbicka (1991, 2003) who refers to the observations of Smith (1983, pp. 83–4) in regard to the Japanese:

> the Japanese are at pains to avoid contention and confrontation . . . much of the definition of a 'good person' involves restraint in the expression of personal desires and opinions. This restraint manifests one of the greatest Japanese cultural values, called *enryo*, a word usually

translated as 'restraint' or 'reserve'. One way to express *enryo* is to avoid giving opinions and to sidestep choices when they are offered. As a matter of fact, choices are less often offered in Japan than in the United States...

(Smith 1983, pp. 44–5)

a. Would you describe your own culture and the associated linguistic communication practices as being similar to that of the Japanese? How are your own linguistic practices similar to or different from that described in the above quote?

b. In your own culture, is the avoidance of giving opinions and showing a high level of restraint in the expression of personal desires highly valued and seen as being 'polite'? Give at least two examples to illustrate your argument.

c. How would the politeness strategies of a Japanese speaker and a North American English speaker in an intercultural communication setting differ from each other? How would the concept of face and the strategies used to redress any FTAs differ among these two interlocutors?

Wierzbicka (2003, p. 78) further describes the politeness strategies used in English and Japanese. Consider the following extract:

In English, if one wants the addressee to do something, it is important to acknowledge the addressee's autonomy by inviting them to say whether or not they will comply with the request. Hence the proliferation and the frequency of 'whimperatives' in English. In Japanese, interrogative directive devices or 'whimperatives' exist, too, but their scope is much narrower than in English (see Matsumoto 1988; Kageyama & Tomori 1976).

Instead, there is in Japanese a proliferation of devices acknowledging dependence on other people, and deference to other people. Hence, the basic way of making requests in Japanese involves not 'whimperatives' (that is, quasi interrogative structures) but dependence acknowledging devices (usually combined with expressions of respect)...

d. Based on the above quote, are 'whimperatives' commonly used in your first language? Give two examples to illustrate your answer.

e. Using the above two extracts as a guideline for your answer, why are 'whimperatives' less likely to be used as a politeness strategy in Japanese than in English?

5. **Research exercise**

Conduct a brief survey of around six people from at least two different language backgrounds and ask them to define what the terms
'polite' and 'impolite' mean to them. Are the people's definitions consistent with Brown and Levinson's description of politeness strategies
(i.e. positive and negative politeness strategies)? Provide examples to
substantiate your findings.

SUGGESTED FURTHER READING

As with Chapter 2, we recommend revisiting the classics (e.g. texts by
Brown and Levinson) for a firm grounding in foundational concepts.
Culpeper provides a terrific overview of the first and second waves of the
study of politeness. Discussions of impoliteness are enlightening and can
be fun; Bousfield and Locher's edited volume provides the best overview
of current impoliteness research. 'Face' makes a great focus for discussions
of intercultural difference and a number of readings address this. Lastly,
many researchers focus on extremes to illustrate cultural difference (e.g.
the supposed East–West divide) but it can be enlightening to examine the
differences between seemingly similar cultures, as Haugh and Bousfield do.

Bousfield, D. & Locher, M. 2008 (eds) *Impoliteness in Language: Studies on its Interplay
with Power in Theory and Practice*. Berlin: Mouton de Gruyter.

Culpeper, J. 2011 'Politeness and impoliteness'. In Aijmer K. & Anderson G. (eds) *Pragmatics of Society*. Berlin: Mouton de Gruyter, pp. 391–436.

Haugh, M. & Bousfield, D. 2012 'Mock impoliteness, jocular mockery and jocular abuse
in Australian and British English'. *Journal of Pragmatics*, vol. 44, pp. 1099–114.

Mao, Lu Ming, R. 1994 'Beyond politeness theory: "Face" revisited and renewed'. *Journal
of Pragmatics*, vol. 21, pp. 451–86.

Sifianou, M. 2012 'Disagreements, face and politeness'. *Journal of Pragmatics*, vol. 44,
pp. 1554–65.

St Andre, J. 2013 'How the Chinese lost "face"'. *Journal of Pragmatics*, vol. 55, pp. 68–85.

4 | Speech acts and politeness

4.1   INTRODUCTION

STAFF AT a British airport once complained that newly hired Indian and Pakistani cafeteria workers were uncooperative and surly. This was in spite of few words being exchanged between the staff and new workers. Gumperz (2004 [1982]) studied communication between the groups and found the miscommunication could be linked to the intonation and manner of speaking of the cafeteria workers in the British context. For instance, the cafeteria workers would offer gravy (*gravy?*) to the ground staff using a falling intonation rather than the rising intonation typical of Anglo-English questions. Consequently, this utterance was interpreted by staff as a statement (*this is gravy*) or imperative (*have gravy!*) rather than the cafeteria worker's intended interrogative meaning (*gravy?*).

Preferred ways of speaking and the ways in which politeness and speech acts are accomplished are subtly different across cultures. An English speaker who wishes another to close a window will often say *can you close the window?* whereas a German speaker would be more likely to say *you should close the window.* We outline why this is the case through a synthesised discussion of the concepts of speech acts and politeness, introduced in the previous chapters. This discussion emerges from the influential Cross-Cultural Speech Act Realization Patterns (CCSARP) project (Blum-Kulka, House & Kasper 1989).[1] The work of the CCSARP project is also extended through discussions of the studies that have been conducted in the wake of

---

[1] The languages studied as part of the CCSARP project were Hebrew (Blum-Kulka and Olshtain), Danish (Faerch and Kasper), British English (Thomas), North American English (Wolfson and Rintell), German (House-Edmonson and Vollmer), Canadian French (Weizman), Argentinian Spanish (Blum-Kulka and House) and Australian English (Ventola). Publications from this study include

this project as well as more ethnographic and conversational approaches. As noted in Chapter 2, these latter approaches have sought to provide a more nuanced understanding of direct and indirect messages, speech acts and politeness.

These lines of research are frequently pursued respectively under the labels of interlanguage pragmatics (e.g. Kasper & Blum-Kulka 1993; Trosborg 1994; Ogierman 2009; Al-Gahtani & Roever 2013) and intercultural pragmatics (e.g. Marriott 1990; Béal 1992; Spencer-Oatey & Xing 2003; Kecskes 2013b; the journal *Intercultural Pragmatics*). **Interlanguage pragmatics** as a field seeks to understand the extent to which users of a second or subsequent language transfer pragmatic features of their first language, or fail to comprehend features of the newer language(s). **Intercultural pragmatics**, as the name suggests, is concerned with the cross-cultural pragmatic differences and how these pragmatic differences play out in intercultural communication.

We organise the current discussion of speech acts and politeness in terms of some of the most studied and problematic speech acts. We focus on how variation in linguistic forms contributes to an utterance being interpreted as more or less direct. We begin with requests, which are the most frequently studied speech act, the most central to Brown and Levinson's model and the core focus of the CCSARP study (Brown & Crawford 2009; Chen, He & Hu 2011). We next discuss complaints, which have increasingly been studied within professional settings and service encounters (e.g. Márquez-Reiter 2005, 2013; Holmes, Marra & Schnurr 2008). The focus then turns to apologies, which, as with requests, formed a critical concern of the CCSARP project. Lastly, this chapter closes with a critical but balanced discussion of the Discourse Completion Test. This approach to studying language has yielded rich data on speech acts and cross-cultural communication. However, it has been losing favour in recent years and, consequently, we reflect on the pros and cons of using this approach.

4.2 REQUESTS

Requests have been studied more frequently and in more languages than any other speech act (Chen, He & Hu 2011). Blum-Kulka (1987) examines

House & Kasper (1981), Blum-Kulka & Olshtain (1984), Blum-Kulka (1987), Cohen & Olshtain (1981) and the volume edited by Blum-Kulka, House and Kasper (1989).

Table 4.1 Examples of nine request categories

Descriptive category	Examples
1. Mood derivable (imperative)	Clean up the kitchen. Move your car.
2. Performative	I'm asking you to move your car.
3. Hedged performative	I would like to ask you to move your car.
4. Obligation statement	You'll have to move your car.
5. Want statement	I would like you to clean the kitchen. I want you to move your car.
6. Suggestory formulas	How about cleaning up? Why don't you come and clean up the mess you made last night?
7. Query preparatory	Could you clean up the mess in the kitchen? Would you mind moving your car?
8. Strong hints (A)	You've left the kitchen in a right mess.
9. Mild hints (B)	We don't want any crowding (as a request to move the car).

(Blum-Kulka 1987, p. 133)

indirectness and politeness in requests used by participants who were asked to rank a set of varied requests in Hebrew and in English in terms of directness and politeness. The research finds that while some types of requests were ranked similarly for indirectness and politeness within a given language or across languages, this was not the case for all request types.

The request types consisted of a set of nine mutually exclusive strategy types postulated to represent a cross-culturally valid set, which are described and exemplified in English in Table 4.1.

The research methodology involved students who were native speakers of Hebrew or English being asked to rank a series of randomly presented requests relating to five different situations in terms of either directness or politeness. Tables 4.2 and 4.3 show the findings for the directness ratings, and the politeness ratings respectively. The scores for the category means are included in Tables 4.2 and 4.3 as a way of seeing how distinct the separation is between different strategies.

Blum-Kulka (1987, p. 136) finds that the most direct strategy (**mood derivable – imperative**) is considered the most direct and the least polite in both Hebrew and English. Within and across languages there is some variation in the other categories. In neither language is the strategy that

Table 4.2 **Directness scales in Hebrew and English: requests**

HEBREW		ENGLISH		
Strategy type	Mean	Strategy type	Mean	
Mood derivable (imperative)	1.5	Mood derivable (imperative)	1.6	**Direct**
Want statements	1.6	Obligation statements	1.9	
Obligation statements	1.8	Performatives	2.5	
Performatives	2.17	Want statements	2.5	
Suggestory	2.5	Hedged performative	2.6	
Hedged performatives	2.8	Query preparatory	2.7	
Query preparatory	3.01	Suggestory	2.8	
Hints (A)	5.6	Hints (A)	5.12	
Hints (B)	7.1	Hints (B)	6.40	**Indirect**

(Blum-Kulka 1987, p. 133)

Table 4.3 **Politeness scales in Hebrew and English: requests**

HEBREW		ENGLISH		
Strategy type	Mean	Strategy type	Mean	
Mood derivable (imperative)	2.3	Mood derivable (imperative)	2.09	**Least polite**
Want statements	3.2	Obligation statements	2.84	
Obligation statements	3.36	Want statements	3.54	
Suggestory	4.18	Performatives	4.0	
Hints (A)	4.38	Suggestory	4.25	
Hints (B)	4.47	Hedged performative	5.09	
Performatives	6.06	Hints (A)	5.23	
Hedged performative	6.34	Hints (B)	5.33	**Most**
Query preparatory	7.08	Query preparatory	7.10	**polite**

(Blum-Kulka 1987, p. 133)

is judged as the most indirect judged as the most polite. In both languages **hints** are rated as the most indirect and **query preparatory**, which is achieved by means of conventional indirectness, (*could/would you...?*) as the most polite. There is some systematic variation between languages as to the relative politeness of **hints** compared to other forms of hedging or suggestion, with English speakers regarding **hints** more towards the **politeness** end of the continuum than do the Hebrew speakers. English speakers, on the one hand, regarded **want statements** as more polite than **obligation statements**, while the reverse was true for Hebrew speakers.

Blum-Kulka (1987, p. 135) notes that request forms drawn from natural speech samples were 'stripped' of both internal and external modifications, such as hedges or politeness markers (*please*) and reason justifications. We suggest that this creates a somewhat non-representative sample because *would/could you please...* is probably more frequent in English usage than *would/could you...* Despite this slight drawback, this methodology has resulted in some interesting cross-cultural comparisons.

House and Kasper (1981) report on research involving German and British subjects using a similar methodology to that reported in Blum-Kulka (1987), but with a focus on requests with a **low degree of imposition** between equals. House and Kasper found that the most preferred request type for English speakers was the **query preparatory** type, for example, *can you close the window?*, while the most preferred type for German speakers was the **locution derivable** (i.e. **obligation statement**) type, for example, *you should close the window* (*du solltest das Fenster zumachen*). Thus, they concluded that, on the whole, German students selected more direct requests than did their English counterparts.

House and Kasper (1981) also include a section examining the use of hedges of various kinds, which they called **modality markers**. Such an inclusion acknowledges the fact that although *come here, please come here* and *come here will you* are all **mood derivables (imperatives)**, the addition of *please* and *will you* (and their German counterparts *komm doch bitte mal her, ja*) also affect the directness of the utterance. House and Kasper (1981, pp. 166–70) further identify two types of modality markers, which they call downgraders and upgraders. **Downgraders**, which include *please* and *will you*, play down the impact that the speaker's utterance is likely to have on the hearer, whereas **upgraders**, such as *absolutely*, *really* and *certainly*, increase the force or the impact an utterance is likely to have on the addressee.

The CCSARP study has yielded fascinating data on the variation of linguistic forms and an utterance's perceived directness or indirectness. Like Brown and Levinson's work on politeness, the CCSARP project remains a key reference point for the study of speech act realisation and interpretation. Yet, a number of recent studies have sought to provide a more nuanced understanding of links between micro-cultural practices and wider macro-cultural norms. Many of these studies have adopted the analytical categories that emerged from the CCSARP study (e.g. Al-Gahtani & Roever 2012). However, in line with those proposing a relational- and rapport-based approach (see Chapter 3), many contemporary researchers aim for a more discursively based understanding of speech acts and politeness.

From this research, for example, we find that although indirectness is most often linked to politeness, many researchers argue that indirectness in some cultures can be perceived as impoliteness. In short, indirectness increases the interpretive effort of the hearer and can even lead an individual to perceive a speaker as untruthful or manipulative (Ogierman 2009). To these ends, Ogierman (2009), reviewing Zemskaja, notes that indirectness can be viewed as a waste of the hearer's time. Therefore, some cultures (e.g. German, Polish, Russian) show a preference for direct rather than conventionally indirect utterances (Ogierman 2009). That said, Wierzbicka (e.g. 1991) has argued that the illocutionary force of direct Polish utterances is often downgraded though the use of diminutives. Ogierman (2009) concedes that diminutives and other downgraders play a role but not to the degree that Wierzbecka and others have proposed.

Many preferences with regard to requests can be linked to wider cultural values. For example, British and Australian university students respectively use different strategies to make email requests to lecturers (Merrison et al. 2012). Merrison et al. (2012) investigate these email requests by drawing on CCSARP categories but extending these categories to a discourse analytical approach. They find that British students most often orient their requests to institutional hierarchy (e.g. the use of academic titles such as 'Dr') and present the request in terms of a potential imposition. Consequently, British students often make requests alongside apologies. Australian students, on the other hand, present their requests in a more egalitarian manner. Rather than showing concern for imposition, students are more genial and tend to index closeness, well-wishing and common ground. The Australian and British strategies, Merrison et al. (2012) argue, can be linked to the wider cultural concerns of these societies (egalitarianism and status-consciousness respectively).

The cultural norms guiding requests can be quite complex and this even leads to intra-cultural miscommunication. For instance, Intachakra (2012) describes how a Thai politeness schema known as '$k^hwa:mkre:\eta t\varepsilon aj$' influences speech acts. Literally meaning 'fear of hearts', this schema is more generally construed as meaning 'consideration or concerns for others' feelings' (Intachakra 2012, p. 619). This schema often leads a Thai individual to have a thought but leave that thought not explicitly expressed. Thus, as is often the case with high-context cultures (see Chapter 1), an interlocutor must read between the lines and may or may not be successful in doing so. For example, the employee in the following case (based on Intachakra 2012, p. 626) is gathering her things to go home when her boss approaches and this exchange takes place:

> Boss: It's already 4 o'clock. You may go home now.
> Employee: That's OK. I don't have any specific plan this evening.

The employee decides to work for an additional half hour and completes the next day's workload. The boss, in a later interview, indicated that this was merely a passing comment and he had not expected the employee to stay on.

Many researchers have posited the need to understand speech acts as they emerge across multiple turns. This assertion will be revisited a few times in this chapter and extensively from Chapter 5 onwards. For instance, Al-Gahtani and Roever (2012) examined requests in role-playing exercises among Saudi Arabian learners of English. One scenario entailed one participant, due to a heavy homework load, needing to ask another to go to buy bread from the supermarket. The second participant was reticent to go because he or she was watching television. Al-Gahtani and Roever found that beginning learners would rarely preface the request with any preliminaries and if they did these would be brief, as in this example below:

> 1 P: Excuse me::
> 2 I: Yes
> 3 P: I (.) want bread
> 4 I: Ok
>   (Al-Gahtani & Roever 2012, p. 50)

Even a request across two turns such as this demonstrates the sequential nature of a request and highlights some of the weaknesses of the single utterance-focused CCSARP study. This becomes even clearer with advanced learners, whose increased language abilities entail a greater ability to mitigate this act across multiple turns:

```
 1   P:   hi ((name))
 2   I:   hi ((name))
 3   P:   hhh >actually< I wanna ask you something?
 4   I:   Su::re.
 5   P:   hhh today I have too many (.) assignments to do =
 6        I: = Yeah
 7   P:   so I have no:: more time (.1) to do my shopp[ing
 8   I:   [hh
 9   P:   for today (.) a::nd I'm running out (.) the bread so could
          you (.3) buy
10        some bread for me?
11   I:   su::re (.) yeah
```
(Al-Gahtani & Roever 2012, pp. 51–2)

Both examples illustrate the sequential nature of requests and how a CCSARP approach, while valuable, is also reductionist with regard to how human communication truly unfolds. Indeed, second-language learners seem to grasp the complexities of acts like the one above and tend to mitigate this act when they have adequate language to do so.

4.3   COMPLAINTS

Complaints typically occur when the addressee has done an action (P) that the speaker interprets as bad for him or herself. House and Kasper (1981) suggest that a complaint may include the following components:

- the action is referred to explicitly
- the speaker's negative evaluation of the action is expressed explicitly
- the addressee's agentive involvement is implicitly or explicitly expressed, and/or
- the negative evaluation of both the addressee's action and of the addressee him or herself are implicitly or explicitly stated.

House and Kasper (1981, pp.159–62) characterise eight levels of directness by using a single situational context in which the addressee (Y), who is well known to the speaker (X) and often borrows X's things, has stained X's new blouse. Progressing from the least direct to the most direct, House and Kasper exemplify the range of levels of directness as follows:

1. By performing the utterance in the presence of Y, X implies that he knows that the P has happened and he implies that Y did P.

Odd, my blouse was perfectly clean last night.
Seltsam, gestern war meine Bluse doch noch ganz sauber.

2. By explicitly asserting that P was done, X implies that Y did P.
   There's a stain on my blouse.
   Das ist ein Fleck auf meiner Bluse.

3. By explicitly asserting that P is bad for him, X implies that Y did P.
   Terrible, this stain won't come off.
   Schrecklich, dieser Fleck wird wohl nie wieder rausgehn.

4. By explicitly asking Y about conditions for the execution of P, or stating that Y was in some way connected with the conditions for the doing of P, X implies that Y did P.
   Did you wear my blouse by any chance?
   Hast du etwa meine Bluse angehabt?

5. X explicitly asserts that Y did P.
   You've stained my blouse.
   Du hast den Fleck draufgemacht.

6. By explicitly stating that the action P for which Y is agentively responsible is bad, or explicitly stating a preference for an alternative action not chosen by Y, X implies that Y is bad/or X asserts explicitly that Y did P and that P is bad for X, thus also implying that Y is bad.
   You shouldn't have taken my blouse without asking my permission/You have ruined my blouse.
   Du hättest die Bluse nicht ohne meine Erlaubnis nehmen sollen/Du hast meine ganze Bluse ruiniert.

7. X asserts explicitly that Y's doing of P is bad.
   I think it's mean that you just take my things.
   Ich finde es gemein von dir, dass du einfach mein Sachen nimmst.

8. X asserts explicitly that Y is bad.
   You are really mean.
   Du bist wirklich unverschämt.

House and Kasper (1981, pp. 159–60) point out that 'on all the lower levels the addressee Y must perform an inference process on the basis of the situational context, especially the relationship holding between the interlocutors X and Y and the social norms recognized by both X and Y'. They suggest that 'through this inference process Y is enabled to work out for himself both an adequate propositional content and the intended illocutionary force of X's utterance'.

Table 4.4 is taken directly from House and Kasper (1981), which outlines their findings relating to 80 complaints in English and 107 complaints in German.[2]

House and Kasper (1981, p. 161) found that in the English data, levels 7 and 8, the most direct levels, did not occur at all in a total of 80 complaints, whereas in the German data, level 8 occurred once (0.9 per cent) and level 7, eight times (7.5 per cent) out of a total of 107 complaints.

Level 6 was by far the most frequently used complaint level in the German data (36 instances out of a total of 107, i.e. 33.6 per cent). In English, level 6 was also the most frequently used, but by only a small margin (18 instances out of a total of 80, i.e. 22.5 per cent) compared with 17 instances for level 4. House and Kasper comment that whereas level 6 is the 'standard complaint form' for German that level was most frequently used in English in contexts of familiarity and equality.[3]

Beyond linguistic form, as with requests above, complaints are nuanced, sequential and linked to wider socio-cultural concerns. For instance, complaints may be formulated in a way that strategically blurs their interpretability as complaints and the role of the speaker as a 'complainer' (Edwards 2005). Sacks (1992) notes that speakers do not like to be seen as complaining. Therefore, he writes: 'if you don't want your complaining to be the topic, you might have to avoid making things which are formulatable as complaints' (Sacks 1992, p. 638). Some researchers (e.g. Holt 2010; Clift 2012) demonstrate how laughter plays a role in blurring the status of an act as a complaint. Clift (2012), reviewing Drew and Walker (2009), shows how some speakers do this through a combination of laughter and reported speech. For example, in the following utterance, a speaker reports on her problems with the phone company British Telcom: 'I said to them, (laughter) "This is British Telecom for you" (laughter)' (Clift 2012, p. 1310). Laughter and reported speech here enables the speaker to distance herself from the utterance and blur her role as complainer (see also Edwards 2005).

Furthermore, complaints often unfold across multiple turns (Drew 1998; Edwards 2005; Márquez-Reiter 2005, 2013; Drew & Walker 2009) or, in the case of written complaints, multiple sentences (Henry & Ho 2010). Henry and Ho (2010) show how complaint letters to Brunei newspapers are structured across multiple sentences. These letters almost always

---

[2] The data on which this table is based included examples of a range of social distance and authority relationships.

[3] We have replaced House and Kasper's phrase 'minus social distance and minus authority constellations' with 'contexts of familiarity and equality'.

Table 4.4 Directness levels in German and English: complaints

Directness level	1	2	3	4	5	6	7	8	9
GERMAN									
Number of instances	7	8	18	10	19	36	8	1	107
Relative frequency	0.065	0.075	0.168	0.093	0.178	0.336	0.075	0.009	1
ENGLISH									
Number of instances	11	5	14	17	15	18	–	–	80
Relative frequency	0.138	0.063	0.175	0.213	0.188	0.225	–	–	1

(House & Kasper 1981, Table 1)

set out the background for the complaint in addition to the explicit complaint itself. Furthermore, these complaint letters sometimes include reference to prior letters, buffers to avoid offence and/or statements about the consequence of the offending act.

The ways in which complaints are set out are often guided by wider socio-cultural conventions. For instance, Holmes, Marra and Schnurr (2008) note that complaints in Māori workplaces in New Zealand are often implicit and group-oriented. Complaints in Pākehā (European New Zealander) workplaces, on the other hand, can be explicit, confrontational and individual-focused. In Uruguay, Márquez-Reiter (2005) finds, callers to a caregiver service provider often frame their complaints in less formal and intimate language (e.g. the use of familiar pronouns, terms of endearment) in the hopes of establishing solidarity with the call taker to have their complaint resolved. When it becomes clear the issue will not be resolved, the caller often engages in a *desahoga*, which is 'a form of self-disclosure through which callers volunteer rather intimate or private details about themselves and/or their next of kin' (Márquez-Reiter 2005, p. 509). The caller in the following text engages in a *desahoga* and then acknowledges having done so:

5	Caller:	And no (.) look when the girl tried to sit her on the toilet (.) my mom almost fell down to the bottom = this meant that my poor mom spent hours without urinating (.) it is terrible to see Mom like that (.) I cannot cope anymore . . . lines 6–12: *desahoga* continues . . .
12	Call taker:	Yes Mrs but the request for change doesn't appear [in]
13	Caller:	Yes (.) I've already understood (.) but I'm telling you that it's not possible that things [work like this]
14	Call taker:	[The thing is]
15	Caller:	I thank you anyway for having listened to me (.) because you listen to what you didn't have to hear (Márquez-Reiter 2005, pp. 506–7)

Márquez-Reiter argues that *desahogas* like these form part of a wider Uruguayan socio-cultural reality. This reality includes cultural schemas that permit the sharing of personal information with strangers and a developing Uruguayan socioeconomic infrastructure, which does not protect consumer rights (Márquez-Reiter 2005).

4.4   APOLOGIES

Apologies are speech acts that come under the broad category of **expressives**, along with thanking, forgiving, blaming, complaining and apologising. Searle (1969) characterises **apologies** as speech acts in which the speaker makes known his or her attitude about a proposition to the hearer. Searle does not provide detailed conditions for apologies; however, Clyne (1994) examines apologies in some detail, and illustrates how these may vary across cultures. Clyne (1994, p. 77) notes that the definition of an apology in the *Concise Oxford Dictionary* refers to three components of an apology:

- regretful acknowledgement of failure or fault
- assurance of no offence intended
- explanation or vindication.

Cohen and Olshtain (1981, pp. 113–34) (also Olshtain & Cohen 1983; Blum-Kulka, House & Kasper 1989, p. 289) actually identify six major components of apologies, as follows:

1. Illocutionary force indicating devices (IFIDs)
   An expression of regret, e.g. *I'm sorry.*
   An offer of apology, e.g. *I apologise.*
   A request for forgiveness, e.g. *Excuse me/Forgive me/Pardon me.*
2. Explanation of account
   Any external mitigating circumstances, 'objective' reasons for the violation, e.g. *The traffic was terrible.*
3. Taking on responsibility
   a. Explicit self-blame, e.g. *It is my fault/my mistake.*
   b. Lack of intent, e.g. *I didn't mean it.*
   c. Expression of self-deficiency, e.g. *I was confused/I didn't see you/I forgot.*
   d. Expression of embarrassment, e.g. *I feel awful about it.*
   e. Self-dispraise, e.g. *I'm such a dimwit!*
   f. Justify hearer, e.g. *You're right to be angry.*
   g. Refusal to acknowledge guilt
      Denial of responsibility, e.g. *It wasn't my fault.*
      Blame the hearer, e.g. *It's your own fault.*
      Pretend to be offended, e.g. *I'm the one to be offended.*
4. Concern for the hearer, e.g. *I hope I didn't upset you/Are you all right?*
5. Offer of repair, e.g. *I'll pay for the damage.*
6. Promise of forbearance, e.g. *It won't happen again.*

Table 4.5   Apology formulas: English, Hungarian and Polish

English (14 subjects)

Sorry	Excuse	Forgive	Apologize
89	14	1	1

Hungarian (20 subjects)

Sjanálom	Elnézést	Bocsánat	Ne haragudjon
(Sorry)	(Excuse)	(Forgive)	(Don't be angry)
26	34	37	58

Polish (76 subjects)

Przepraszam	Przykro mi	Wybacz	Nie gniewaj sie
(I apologize)	(Sorry)	(Forgive)	(Don't be angry)
291	47	27	6

(Suszczyńska 1999, p. 1057, Table 1)

Suszczyńska (1999) used a discourse completion test based on the above categories of apologies to compare the types of apologies provided by 110 subjects – 14 American, 20 Hungarian and 76 Polish native-speaking students. The test comprised eight situations with varying degrees of offence. Table 4.5 provides a summary of the different types of apologies reported by Suszczyńska (1999) for the three groups. Here, Suszczyńska focuses on four subtypes of Blum-Kulka, Olshtain and Cohen's type (1) apologies (IFIDs).

Suszczyńska (1999, p. 1058) points out that the three IFID sets cannot be perfectly mapped onto one another because, for example, Hungarian lacks a true performative verb; English does not seem to use the expression 'don't be angry' as an apologetic formula; and Polish, unlike English or Hungarian, has no equivalent of 'excuse me' for smaller offences but simply uses *Przepraszam* (*I apologise*) in all such situations. Yet, more generally, there are obvious similarities to be observed. In all three languages, there are IFID formulas expressing regret, asking forgiveness, or pleading to withhold anger, which reflect common human experience. Suszczyńska makes the point that what is important from the perspective of cross-cultural comparison is the question of which of these expressions have been routinised in a particular language group.

In English, the overwhelming expression is one of regret (*I'm sorry*), with a few cases of *excuse me* and sporadic cases of *forgive me* or *I apologise*, the latter being used more in written apologies. However, Suszczyńska shows that this is not the case for the Hungarian and Polish data. In the Hungarian data all four strategies are well represented and routinised. There is a preference for *Ne haragudjon* ('Don't be angry'), then comes *Bocsánat* ('Forgive me'), followed by *Elnézést* ('Excuse me') and *Sjanálom* ('Sorry'), which is used least of all. In Polish, the performative verb *Przepraszam* is used most often (literally translated as 'I apologise'). There are fewer cases of *Przykro mi* ('I am sorry') and *Wybacz mi* ('Forgive me'), and just a handful of *Nie gniewaj się* ('Don't be angry').

Apology strategies may also be linked to wider socio-cultural factors as with requests and complaints above. For example, in a role-play study of apology strategies used by Chilean Spanish and Australian English speakers with their 'bosses' (workplace superiors), Cordella (1990) found that Chilean and Australian cultural values were reflected in the act of apologising. Chilean apologies, she found, tended to be more hearer-oriented compared to the more speaker-oriented Australian apologies. In other words, Australian speakers showed a preference for apologies wherein a speaker expressed regret for the transgression. Conversely, the Chileans preferred apologies that involved the hearer in terms of asking to be excused or forgiven. Cordella (1990) links these preferences to a greater concern for the group in Chile compared to Australia's more individualistic society.

The circumstances for which one apologises as well as to whom one apologises vary across cultures. Sugimoto (1998) investigated norms of apologies depicted in American and Japanese literature on manners and etiquette and found the range of people to whom apologies are considered appropriate differed greatly. In general, American etiquette texts focused on apologies for individual behaviour in public contexts (including the acts of the individual's small children and pets). In contrast, the Japanese manuals dealt mainly with apologies in situations involving people who know each other (e.g. friends, neighbours, colleagues) rather than strangers. Sugimoto (1998, p. 258) observes that in general, the Japanese indicate sincerity and respect by conforming to cultural norms involving formulaic expressions appropriate to different social relationships, while US Americans strive for spontaneous and original messages of apology because it is felt that originality is indicative of sincerity.

Apologies have become a frequent feature of for-profit communication (Cameron 2000; Park, Lee & Song 2005). For instance, Cameron (2000) notes that apologies have become part of the opening sequence of many call centres (e.g. *I am sorry to keep you waiting*). Yet, their use in for-profit communication varies across cultures. For example, apologies often appear in Korean spam (unsolicited email) messages where they wouldn't in English spam. Park, Lee and Song (2005) link this to Koreans' belief that apologies are acceptable and even expected in advertising discourse. Koreans were more apt to view an advertisement as honest if it used an apology. That said, the use of apologies in spam and advertising more generally has not yet been linked to greater sales. Park, Lee and Song (2005) merely link the use of apologies in spam to wider socio-cultural concerns for such acts in Korea more generally (see Hatfield & Hahn 2011).

As with the speech acts discussed above, apologies are sequentially constructed acts. For instance, Clyne (1994) provides the following example of an apology and the eventual acceptance of the apology from his multicultural workplace data. In this apology, Krysztina, a Polish operator, is 'apologising' to Jennifer (her workplace supervisor of Malaysian–Chinese background) in a self-initiated stretch of discourse. Clyne (1994, p. 78) observes that ostensibly Krysztina wants to be 'freed from her guilt' for she fears the consequences of an error she committed at work. Clyne suggests that in actual fact, she is 'fishing' for an assurance that nothing will happen to her, or rather, that Jennifer will support her if necessary. Clyne represents the apology by the below schemas. Clyne makes the point that Krysztina continues to elaborate her apology until her superior explicitly 'accepts' the apology.

a. admission of guilt
   It was . . . probably it was my fault.
b. doubts about her guilt
   I don't know whose fault but I take my . . . I blame myself for it.
c. explanation of 'what went wrong'
d. anxiety about the reactions of another worker
e. appeal for compassion
f. an assurance that the delay in reporting the matter to Jennifer is not the result of antipathy (or prejudice?)
g. seeking a reassurance.

4.5 METHODOLOGIES: DISCOURSE COMPLETION TESTS

Many of the studies above use the Discourse Completion Test to explore variation in the enactment of speech acts across cultures. This approach formed the basis for the CCSARP study and it remains a frequently used means for exploring speech acts. A **Discourse Completion Test (DCT)** most typically presents participants with one or more hypothetical situations and asks how they would respond in these situations. For example, the following is one of 10 scenarios Nureddeen (2008) used to study apologies in Sudanese Arabic (translated from the original colloquial Arabic):

While travelling, Jamal placed a heavy bag on the bus shelf. The bus stopped suddenly and the bag fell on a passenger.

The passenger: Oh God! What was that?

Jamal: _____

Nureddeen (2008, p. 300)

The DCT is presented to the study participant in the form of a written questionnaire, a spoken interview, a role play or a listening exercise. For instance, with regard to the latter, Adrefiza and Jones (2013) investigated apology responses (i.e. how individuals reacted to apologies) by asking participants to listen to pre-recorded apologies. Respondents were then asked to give their responses to the pre-recorded apologies.

DCTs have come under scrutiny in recent years in part because of the increased focus on ethnographic and discourse analytical approaches. As noted in Chapters 2 and 3, adherents to those approaches prefer not to approach human communication with preconceived ideas of social categories or even, at times, theories. These researchers emphasise the need to collect and analyse naturally occurring data. DCTs, these researchers argue, decontextualise language. DCTs require research participants to provide hypothetical answers to hypothetical situations in hypothetical roles that they themselves may not have filled. For instance, I may have never been a bus passenger whose bag has fallen on a person and I may not be very good at acting like I am. Furthermore, DCTs do not capture the dynamic and unfolding nature of naturally occurring human behaviour. They attempt to reduce speech acts to one or two utterances whereas we have established above these acts often unfold across multiple turns. In sum, many researchers avoid DCTs and others employ them with some critical distance. We recommend a balanced view of DCTs and it is worth outlining their usefulness here.

DCTs are useful for collecting large amounts of standardised data for comparison with other data sets. DCTs may be used to collect data quickly and efficiently. Furthermore, the CCSARP study and the follow-up studies in its wake provide an established body of work with which to compare newly collected data. In short, the CCSARP study has been useful in establishing the linguistic strategies used for directness and indirectness across eight languages. This project has spawned a large number of follow-on studies on other speech acts and languages. It is more difficult and time-consuming to isolate and analyse speech acts in naturally occurring data (Ogierman 2009). Furthermore, speech acts collected in naturally occurring data are often collected in varied contexts and this reduces the standardised nature of the speech act. This, in turn, reduces its comparability to some degree with the same speech act in other naturally occurring contexts in other languages (Ogierman 2009). In sum, to discount DCTs entirely would be to discount the invaluable work of the CCSARP project, which has been discussed at length in this chapter.

Many researchers have attempted to modify and/or augment the DCT in response to critics (e.g. Bardovi-Harlig & Hartford 1993; Beebe & Cummings 1996). For instance, whereas DCTs were traditionally delivered as written exercises, recent projects have sought to provide audio examples of the hypothetical situations (e.g. Adrefiza & Jones 2013). However, arguably the two most reasonable proposals in dealing with the weaknesses of the DCTs come in the form of alternative, complementary data and a proposed shift in the way in which analysts view the kind of data gleaned through the DCT. Ogierman (2009) is among those who use and extol the positive aspects of the DCT. However, she is also quick to note that the DCT yields a particular kind of data that should be complemented with other kinds of data, such as natural speech. Bella (2012) also uses a DCT but she notes that rather than yielding naturalistic data the DCT sheds light on participants' metapragmatic knowledge. In other words, the DCT is more useful for uncovering individuals' surface knowledge about how language should be used rather than how they would necessarily use it in a natural context.

4.6   SUMMARY

In this chapter we have examined research on requests, complaints and apologies to exemplify the types of cultural variation that can occur in relation to speech acts, and taken account of some of the social contexts that contributes to this variation. While there seems to be a 'universal' set of features that tend to be found in requests, complaints and apologies, a particular subset may be preferred by members of particular cultures. We have also outlined the pros and cons of the oft-used but frequently maligned DCT. We noted its established value for collecting a particular kind of very comparable data quickly. Yet, we also note that the DCT's findings should be complemented with other kinds of data.

At the extreme, some researchers have advocated abandonment of a traditional speech act approach to human communication altogether (e.g. Kasper 2006; Silverstein 2010). We do not take this view as evidenced by our lengthy discussion of speech acts in this and the preceding chapters. Speech acts are a core element of human communication and their study can reveal much about appropriate and inappropriate behaviour in a context. Yet, human communication is ultimately a co-constructed phenomenon. Therefore, analysts and individuals not only need to attend to the relationship between speech acts and contextual felicity. They also need to attend to the way in which context is updated in unfolding conversation. This latter phenomenon offers both risks and opportunities. On the one hand, the processes of updating a context entail more potential flashpoints for miscommunication. On the other, in unfolding conversation, there are more opportunities to repair miscommunication. This marks a turning point in this book and we now turn to the fluid nature of human communication through an increased focus on contextual update.

4.7   REVIEW

1. **Key terms**
   Speech acts (direct and indirect), request, directive, apology, complaint, hint, conventionally indirect request, discourse completion test.
2. **Key ideas**
   Having read this chapter you should:
   a. understand the structure of speech acts, particularly requests, directives, apologies and complaints
   b. understand the differences between direct and indirect directives and requests
   c. appreciate why speakers from different cultures and backgrounds may have different expectations in relation to particular speech acts
   d. appreciate the significance of these different expectations for intercultural communication.
3. **Focus questions**
   a. Requests
      (i) Which of the Blum-Kulka request categories presented in Table 4.1 are you least likely to use in English?
      (ii) Does this differ if you are using another language?
   b. Complaints
      (i) Which of the House and Kasper (1981) complaint forms would you be most likely to use if you suspected that a roommate/family member had borrowed a piece of your clothing and got it dirty?
      (ii) What components does this complaint include?

c. Apologies

(i) How would you apologise to a classmate for having forgotten to return a book you had borrowed?

(ii) How would you classify your apology in terms of Cohen and Olshtain's characterisation of apologies?

4. **Research analysis**

Consider the following extracts from the screenplay of the *Titanic* (Cameron 1996, pp. 94–5).

In these two extracts the screenwriter represents interactions between a steward on the upper decks with his passengers and stewards in steerage with their passengers.

Extract 1: Upper deck

There is a loud knock on the door and an urgent voice. The door opens and their steward puts his head in.

Steward Barnes: Sir, I've been told to ask you to please put on your lifebelt, and come up to the boat deck.

Cal: Get out. We're busy.

The steward persists, coming in to get the lifebelts down from the top of a dresser.

Steward Barnes: I'm sorry about the inconvenience, Mr Hockley, but it's Captain's orders.

Please dress warmly, it's quite cold tonight.

(He hands a lifebelt to Rose.)

Not to worry Miss, I'm sure it's just a precaution.

Extract 2: Steerage

BLACKNESS. Then BANG! The door is thrown open and the light snapped on by a steward. The Cartmell family rouse from a sound sleep.

Steward #2: Everybody up. Let's go. Put your lifebelts on.

IN THE CORRIDOR outside, another steward is going from door to door along the hall pounding and yelling.

Steward #3: Lifebelts on. Lifebelts on. Everybody up, come on. Lifebelts on.

People come out of the doors behind the steward, perplexed. In the foreground a SYRIAN WOMAN asks her husband what was said. He shrugs.

    a. Compare the ways in which the three stewards ask their respective passengers to put on their life jackets and go upstairs, using the categories of requests defined by Blum-Kulka (1987) (see Table 4.1).

    b. Considering TV dramas with which you are familiar, select and describe one character/context in which formal/polite language (similar to that used by Steward Barnes to the upper deck passengers) is used and give some approximate examples.

    c. Select and describe one character/context in which extremely informal language (such as that used in Extract 2) is used. Give some approximate examples.

    d. Note the reference to the Syrian woman in the last stage note. This represents a typical case of non-communication often experienced by international travellers. How is it possible to avoid potentially dangerous situations such as this? What obligations does a tourist operator have to issue warnings that can be understood?

5. Research exercise

Construct three DCTs to elicit forms of apology – varying P, D and R (see also Brown & Levinson 1987, ch. 3).

SUGGESTED FURTHER READING

We recommend the CCSARP literature as a starting point for understanding variations in speech act patterns (e.g. work by Blum-Kulka, House and Kasper). For more recent work, the journal *Intercultural Pragmatics* is a great start. In contrast to the CCSARP project, a number of studies address how speech acts unfold across multiple turns (e.g. Márquez-Reiter, Drew & Walker, Al-Gahtani & Roever). Clift exemplifies the complexities of speech acts and laughter's place in speech acts. It also highlights the relevance of role (and blurred roles) in conversation (see Chapters 2 and 6). Lastly, DCTs have long been critiqued and many of the earlier attempts to revise this approach are the most revealing (e.g. Bardovi-Harlig & Hartford).

Al-Gahtani, S. & Roever, C. 2013 'Proficiency and sequential organization of L2 requests'. *Applied Linguistics*, vol. 33, no. 11, pp. 42–65.

Bardovi-Harlig, K. & Hartford, B. 1993 'Refining the DCTs: Comparing open questionnaires and dialogue and completion tests'. In Bouton, L. & Kachru, Y. (eds) *Pragmatics and Language Learning, Monograph 4*. Urbana-Champaign, IL: University of Illinois, Division of English as an International Language, pp. 237–645.

Blum-Kulka, S. 1989 *Cross-Cultural Pragmatics: Requests and Apologies*. Norwood, New Jersey: Ablex.

Clift, R. 2012 'Identifying action: Laughter in non-humorous reported speech'. *Journal of Pragmatics*, vol. 44, pp. 1303–12.

Drew, P. & Walker, T. 2009 'Going too far: Complaining, escalating and disaffiliation'. *Journal of Pragmatics*, vol. 41, pp. 2400–14.

Márquez-Reiter, R., 2005 'Complaint calls to a caregiver service company: The case of desahogo'. *Intercultural Pragmatics*, vol. 2, no. 4, pp. 481–514.

2013 'The dynamics of complaining in a Latin American for-profit commercial setting'. *Journal of Pragmatics*, vol. 57, pp. 231–47.

Part II
Structure and contextual update across cultures

5 | Conversation across cultures

5.1   INTRODUCTION

MISCOMMUNICATIONS EMERGE in conversations between Korean shopkeepers and African American customers in Los Angeles, as we observed at the start of Chapter 2. We linked this miscommunication to the two groups speaking at cross-purposes: financial transactions and social exchanges respectively (Bailey 2001). Yet, even when these groups speak with the same purpose, miscommunication can result from differing conversational styles. In the following social exchange, an African American customer ('cust') describes a recent trip to Chicago to a Korean shop owner ('own'), who has been in the United States for 20 years and has a degree from the University of California, Los Angeles:

```
1   Own:    Is Chicago cold?
2   Cust:   Uh:::h! ((lateral headshakes)) ((1.4-second pause)) man I
            got off the plane and walked out the airport and I said 'oh
            shit.'
3           heh heh heh
4   Own:    I thought it's gonna be a nice spring over there
5   Cust:   Well not now this is about a month – I been there – I was
            there
6           but you know (.) damn ((lateral headshakes))
7           ((1.4-second pause)) Too co:l'
8           I mean this was really cold.
                                    (adapted from Bailey 2001, p. 131)
```

The African American customer's style is emotional, performed and involved. This includes the use of falsetto voice, engaged body language (e.g. lateral headshakes) and profanity. The Korean shopkeeper's style is less involved. He is looking at the floor and unsmiling as the customer recounts his trip.

The shopkeeper's lack of engagement in lines 6–8 is particularly problematic from an African American perspective. African American conversational styles emphasise a call and response ritual in which 'one actor's words receive an immediate, often overlapping, response and confirmation from others' (Bailey 2001, p. 133). This can be seen in African American ritual genres, including speeches, sermons and hip hop (e.g. Preacher: *Can I get amen?* Congregation: *Amen!*). Yet, the call and response ritual extends to everyday conversation. This arguably accounts for the African American's 1.4-second pauses as well as his repeated observations about how cold the weather was. He is anticipating an engaged and emotional response whereas the shopkeeper's responses are unengaged and fact-focused (e.g. *I thought it's gonna be a nice spring over there*) (Bailey 2001).

This chapter explores some of the complexities of cross-cultural and intercultural conversation. As we have pointed out a few times now, conversation and context are co-constructed activities. Individuals have preferences about how contexts should unfold. These preferences are nuanced and extend to each subsequent utterance and how that utterance updates the context. In other words, when a speaker produces an utterance there is generally a preferred and dispreferred response to that utterance. For instance, in the extract above, a preferred response on the part of the shopkeeper would have been more intensity and involvement (see Tannen 2007). A preferred response on the part of the African American, from the perspective of the shopkeeper, might have been a less performative and more fact-based account of Chicago and the weather.

We examine conversational preference in this chapter by focusing on its smallest and most nuanced units. We begin by exploring the management of turn-taking in conversation, drawing on the field of research known as Conversation Analysis (e.g. Sacks, Schegloff & Jefferson 1974; Sidnell 2010). We then provide some examples of how turn-taking can be managed by speakers from different cultures, among other things through minimal responses and laughter. This, in turn, leads to a discussion of how these many aspects of conversational preference can coalesce into culture-specific conversational styles (e.g. the Korean American and African American styles above). In closing, we take a closer look at ethnography as a methodological approach. This lays the foundations for a more ethnographically informed discussion of language use and conversation in subsequent chapters.

5.2   TURN-TAKING IN CONVERSATION

Crystal (2010, p. 120) notes: 'Conversation [is] a highly structured activity, in which people tacitly operate with a basic set of conventions.' We introduced some of these conventions in the previous chapters. Yet, perhaps nowhere is the structured nature of conversation clearer than in turn-taking. Sacks, Schegloff and Jefferson (1974), in their seminal work on **turn-taking** in conversation, observed the following three key features in its organisation:

- one party talks at a time
- transitions are finely coordinated for speaker change
- utterances are constructed in such a way as to show coordination of turn transfer and speakership.

Sacks, Schegloff and Jefferson identified **adjacency pairs** as a key feature of conversation. They pointed out that most conversation is composed of pairs of utterances, with the prototypical example being a **question–answer** sequence. There is a sense in which the question as a first part of the adjacency pair 'requires' the answer as the second part. This is illustrated by Clark (1996, pp. 196–7) who, drawing on Schegloff and Sacks (1973), outlines five essential properties of adjacency pairs:

- Adjacency pairs consist of two ordered utterances – the *first pair part* and the *second pair part.*
- The two parts are uttered by different speakers.
- The two parts come in types that specify which part is to come first and which second.
- The form and content of the second part depends on the type of the first part.
- Given a first pair part, the second pair part is *conditionally relevant* – that is, relevant and expectable – as the next utterance.

Clark (1996, pp. 196–7) illustrates these properties through an extensive discussion of a single text, drawn from the London-Lund corpus of British English (Svartvik & Quirk 1980). The text is a brief telephone conversation from the corpus:

Jane:	(Telephones Miss Pink's office.)
Kate:	Miss Pink's office, hello.
Jane:	Hello, is Miss Pink in?
Kate:	Well, she's in, but she's engaged at the moment, who is it?
Jane:	Oh, it's Professor Worth's secretary, from Pan-American College.

Kate: Mmm...
Jane: Could you give her a message [for me?]
Kate: [Certainly.]
Jane: Umm... Professor Worth said that, if Miss Pink runs into
          difficulties on Monday afternoon... with the standing sub-
          committee... over the item of Miss Panoff...
Kate: Miss Panoff?
Jane: Yes.
Jane: That Professor Worth would be with Mr Miles all
          afternoon – so she only had to go round and collect him if
          she needs him...
Kate: Ah... thank you very much indeed, right.
Jane: Right.
Kate: Panoff, right [you are].
Jane: [Right.]
Kate: I'll tell her.
Jane: Thank you.
Kate: Bye bye.
Jane: Bye.

(adapted from Clark 1996, pp. 196–7)

Jane and Kate's conversation illustrates a number of adjacency pairs in English (and indeed some relevant to many other languages and cultures). This is seen by re-examining the text with these adjacency pairs noted:

Adjacency pair		Example
1. Summons	Jane:	(rings)
2. Response	Kate:	Miss Pink's office
1. Greeting	Kate:	Hello
2. Greeting	Jane:	Hello
1. Question	Kate:	Who is it?
2. Answer	Jane:	Oh, it's Professor Worth's secretary
1. Assertion	Jane:	Oh, it's Professor Worth's secretary
2. Assent	Kate:	Mmm...
1. Request	Jane:	Could you give her a message [for me?]
2. Promise	Kate:	[Certainly.]
1. Promise	Kate:	I'll tell her
2. Acknowledgement	Jane:	Thank you
1. Thanks	Kate:	Thank you very much indeed
2. Acknowledgement	Kate:	Right
1. Goodbye	Kate:	Bye bye
2. Goodbye	Jane:	Bye

In each case, the second pair part (2) is regarded as **conditionally relevant** upon the first pair part (1). For example, in the question–answer sequence, Jane's question is the first pair part, and Kate's answer the second.

1. Question   Kate: Who is it?
2. Answer   Jane: Oh, it's Professor Worth's secretary

Given Jane's question, Kate's answer is conditionally relevant as the next utterance. Clark (1996, p. 200) suggests that an adjacency pair may be seen as a type of action–response pair, or the proposal and uptake of a joint project. On one level, the entire conversation is one type of joint project. However, he argues that the minimal joint project is the adjacency pair – a proposal plus its uptake.

Individuals' expectations about how conversations will unfold and how smoothly these conversations do unfold are discussed in terms of preference organisation. In sum, first pair parts tend to have preferred second pair parts. This is set out in the following hypothetical exchange:

Boy: Would you like to go out this Friday?
Girl: Um . . . well, I'm afraid I already have plans.

The girl's refusal in this instance is a dispreferred second pair part. The preferred second pair part to an invitation is most typically acceptance (in Anglo-based cultures). Focusing on another example, the preferred second pair part to an assessment (e.g. *that test was difficult*) is agreement (*it was!*). A dispreferred second pair part would be disagreement (*nah, it was easy!*). Preferred second pair parts tend to latch neatly onto the first pair part and result in conversational cohesion (Pomerantz 1984; Li Wei 1998). Dispreffered second pair parts, on the other hand, can be risky and often disturb the flow of conversation. When speakers recognise an upcoming, potential dispreferred response, they tend to preface this dispreferred second pair part with pauses (e.g. *um . . .*) and hedges (*well*), as seen in the example above (see Pomerantz 1984).

Many cultures have differing expectations with regard to preference organisation and second pair parts. Not surprisingly, this can lead to mis-communication. For instance, some cultures might present invitations where the preferred second pair part is a refusal. The Iranian cultural schema of *taarof* influences individuals to make polite but disingenuous invitations of food, accommodation and even personal possessions. However, *taarof* conventions also mean acceptance of these invitations and offers is entirely inappropriate. On the other hand, US Americans often make casual, vague and disingenuous invitations to an interlocutor in order to foster positive feelings (and thus positive face) (Pinto 2011a; compare Goddard 2012). In situ, the preferred second pair part is casual acceptance of such invitations. However, foreigners living in the United States sometimes get angry or disappointed when the proposed event never materialises (Pinto 2011a).

The coordination of turn-taking is a nuanced and potentially problematic affair. Sacks, Schegloff and Jefferson (1974) cite the transition-relevance place (TRP) as a key point at which turn-taking is mediated:

> any syntactically defined turn-constructional unit of speech is followed by a transition-relevance place (TRP). At these TRPs, turn allocation takes place, and a transition to a new speaker may occur. At every TRP, a set of rules for turn allocation is applied by the participants: the current speaker may select the next; the next speaker may self select; or, if neither of these possibilities is taken, the current speaker may continue his or her turn.

In certain circumstances, a speaker may want to have a longer turn than usual – for example, if the speaker wants to tell a story. To do this, the speaker usually foreshadows his or her intention with what Sacks (1992) calls a **story preface**. Such a story preface could be 'Something awful happened to me today' and would be perceived as an intention to undertake the activity of telling a story. It might therefore be responded to in the next turn by an acceptance such as 'what?' In such contexts, the primary speaker has the right to talk until the completion of his or her speech, and the recipient can respond with continuers, but the recipient will not generally take over the floor.

There are considerable differences in the way in which turns are managed or allocated across and within cultures. Focusing on intra-culture variation, the oft-cited and idealised Anglo rule for conversation is 'no gap, no overlap'. However, a simple comparison of gender even within Anglo culture shows the truth is much more complex. Burridge and Florey (2002, p.169), reviewing Pamela Fishman, note that women do much of the 'conversational shitwork' in Anglo culture. Women encourage turn-taking through questions, politeness markers and supportive discourse markers (e.g. tag questions) (Holmes 1995). Men, on the other hand, tend to interrupt, overlap and compete for the floor (Holmes 1995). Woods (1988) investigated work settings and found that high-status individuals (i.e. supervisors), whether men or women, were more successful in interrupting conversations than low-status individuals (Foley 1997). However, she also found that low-status men were normally also successful in interrupting women of higher status. We return to gender in the next chapter.

We can contrast turn transitions across cultures by examining one factor which indexes turn transition: silence. There are different cultural expectations with regard to silence and the role it plays in a society. For some cultures, as Atawneh and Sridhar (1993, p. 294), drawing on Tannen, point out: 'silence is the extreme manifestation of politeness'. The Western Apache Indians and the !Kung tribesmen of southwest Africa believe that if one does not talk then potential offence is kept to a minimum (Wardhaugh 2010). There are also differing views of the silence in the shopkeeper example at the start of this chapter. For instance, in a general sense, there tend to be few silences in casual African American conversations. Therefore, the African American likely interpreted the 1.4-second silence in this text as uncomfortable and expected a turn transition. The Korean, on the other hand, likely viewed his silence as polite in the sense that it kept misunderstandings to a minimum (Bailey 2001). Aboriginal Australians often preface an answer with a silence. This creates problems in Anglo-Australian courtrooms where lawyers claim Aboriginal people are difficult witnesses (Eades 2007).

5.3   BACK-CHANNELLING

Conversation participants not holding the floor typically provide acknowledgement that they are continuing to follow what the speaker is saying through **back-channelling**. In English, this is typically done by utterances such as *mmm* and *uh-huh*. Mexicans show similar uses of *uh-huh* (Kjaerbeck 1998). The Javanese often use *ya* or *iya* ('yes') or *huh eh*, the latter being an acknowledgement device that sounds like the English negation marker *uh-huh* to the uninformed. It has been suggested that Japanese speakers may use the word *hai* ('yes') as a **back-channel** device, not necessarily indicating agreement but rather indicating 'I am listening' (see Cutrone 2005). Kjaerbeck (1998) notes use of *ja ja* ('yes') in Danish more as a positive back-channel device than as a clear marker of agreement.

Not using back-channelling can be problematic because a speaker might not think that a hearer is engaged. For instance, Phillips (2004 [1983]) shows how US American teachers sometimes view Native American students as unengaged due to a lack of back-channelling (see also King 2011 for Japanese universities). That said, using back-channelling devices can be equally problematic. There is clearly the potential for misunderstanding when one considers the overlap between the meaning of a form or utterance (e.g. 'yes') and its function as a back-channel device (see Eades 2007; Berk-Seligson 2009 for a discussion of the problems this creates in the intercultural courtroom). Repetition is used for back-channelling and this may lead to miscommunication. Repetition in Javanese culture means more than mere agreement or acknowledgement of information (Keeler 2001). It has the same effect as an English speaker saying *you bet* (Keeler 2001). Such repetition by Javanese speakers interacting with individuals from Anglo cultures might be perceived as mimicry if done too frequently. Indian English speakers might use a breathy *very nice* as a back-channelling device and this may be interpreted by individuals from Anglo cultures as having sexual overtones (Gumperz 1982).

Back-channel responses sometimes contribute to misunderstanding in interactions between US university students and international teaching assistants ('tutors' in the Australian university context) (Chiang 2011). For instance, the international teaching assistant in the following exchange, Ms Feng, provides a series of minimal responses (*mmm, yeah*) that are meant to continue the conversation. Ms Feng doesn't seem to understand Adam's question and whether Adam is asking a question at all at points. However, the minimal responses might be interpreted as back-channel devices on the part of the student and this leads to some confusion.

5	Adam:	In the (0.1) chapter six you =
6	Ms Feng:	= mmm
7		(1.2)
8	Adam:	You're talking about the price ceilings =
9	Ms Feng:	= Yeah
10		(1.7)
11	Adam:	I don't get that.
12	Ms. Feng:	mmm
13		(2.1)
14	Adam:	It has to be above it?
15		(1.0)
16	Ms Feng:	mmm
17	Adam:	The equilibrium price?
18	Ms Feng:	mmm
19	Adam:	What happens when it's above it?
20		(1.0)
21	Ms Feng:	Yeah, if (0.3) price ceiling is (0.2) above the equilibrium price, (0.2)

(adapted from Chiang 2011, p. 3322)

Line 11 (*I don't get that*) could reasonably be assumed to be an indirect request (Chiang 2011). However, Ms Feng acknowledges this utterance with an *mmm*, and this is followed by a 2.1-second silence. Adam realises that in spite of the *mmm* his question has not been understood, so he reformulates this question three more times before Ms Feng understands the query.

5.4   GREETINGS AND LEAVE-TAKING

Some of the most ritualistic aspects of conversation can be found in the way individuals open and close conversation through greetings and leave-taking (Crystal 2010). Writing the most influential paper on Conversation Analysis, Schegloff and Sacks (1973) dealt with openings and closings in telephone conversations. Telephone conversations (and more recently video relay services) have continued to yield valuable data on the way in which individuals engage in the ritualistic behaviour of greetings and leave-taking (e.g. Goddard 1977; Clark & French 1981; Hellerman & Cole 2008; Brown & Crawford 2009; Sun 2012; Warnicke & Plajert 2012). This research is discussed here alongside a more self-reflective discussion of these practices in daily life.

At the start of Chapter 3, we briefly considered English greetings such as *hi, what's up?, how's it going?, how are you?* and *hello, how do you do?* Each of these expressions is only the first part of the greeting, and is conventionally followed by at least a second part (response). More frequently, the first part is followed by a series of exchanges. Thus, the response to *how do you do?* might be *very well, thank you* and the response to *hi* might be *hello*, or vice versa, but to simply leave it at that would be unusual except if you are passing someone, perhaps on the stairs.

The convention in English is to follow the greeting exchange with at least one further exchange, which may take a number of forms, including:

- a question about health: *How are you? How are you doing?*
- a comment on the weather: *Terribly hot, isn't it?*
- a comment on the length of time between contact: *Haven't seen you for ages*
- a question about activities: *What have you been up to?*

The almost obligatory nature of at least a second exchange is obvious on talkback radio where we have noticed that many callers feel the need to enquire about the radio host's health and the host feels obliged to reply, even though he or she may have given the same reply several times in the last hour. In such contexts, a question about health seems to be the default, and this is probably the case in most of the English-speaking world. A further example of the conventional nature of the health enquiry is that at the beginning of a medical consultation, if the doctor asks *how are you?*, an English-speaking patient invariably feels the need to reply *fine, thanks*. It is sometimes then necessary to add a qualification such as *actually, I haven't been feeling quite so well* and the health issue that is the reason for the visit can at that point be raised.

The topic of health and wellbeing is not restricted to Anglo-Celtic cultures. In Chapter 3 we referred to de Kadt's (1998) findings that for Zulu speakers, greeting rituals are viewed as being compulsory and are generally initiated by the subordinate person in the interaction and then followed by enquiries into the status of one's health and wellbeing by the person of higher status. A Kenyan colleague[1] once reported that greeting rituals in her culture were so elaborate that if you happen to see a friend or relative approaching and you are in a hurry, it is better to avoid the person by crossing the road than to cut short the greeting ritual, which would of necessity include enquiries into the health and wellbeing of all family members in turn.

Farewells can be even more lengthy and complex, though perhaps this is changing to some extent due to the pressures of the modern world. In general, a short farewell, particularly after a special occasion, can seem strange unless some reason for an abrupt departure has been foreshadowed or a compelling reason develops. A short and abrupt farewell seems to devalue the interaction in some way. Ferguson (1976) suggests that the form of a farewell is influenced by factors such as degree of intimacy between the two participants, relative status, and length of contact or expected time apart.

Clark and French (1981), in a paper describing their research on telephone goodbyes offered to operators in routine enquiries to a university switchboard, identified three components of the closing sequence: (1) *topic termination*, (2) *leave-taking* and (3) *contact termination* (i.e. hanging up). The **topic termination** component typically involves the parties agreeing that they have nothing more to add, and is generally followed by an exchange of confirmations such as *okay*. In certain cases, the topic termination is not a simple matter, as one or the other of the participants may think of additional issues to raise. (Users of public telephones may recall waiting patiently as a previous user seems to be involved in a topic termination, only to find that one of the parties comes up with another

---

[1] Personal communication, Dr Angelina Nduku Kioko.

item of unfinished business, and this may happen several times over. It is almost impossible from the body language of a telephone user to tell when the topic termination phase begins.)

The **leave-taking** phase has been referred to as the *reaffirmation of acquaintance* and typically includes a goodbye exchange. Clark and French (1981, p. 4), following Goffman (1971), observe that:

> people from different cultures have different ways of breaking contact with each other. In small close-knit societies in which continuing relations among individuals are taken for granted, people may not need an elaborate form of leave-taking. In urban America, however, people generally need to reassure each other that the break in social contact is only temporary – that they are still acquainted and will resume contact at some time in the future.

Clark and French, drawing on Albert and Kessler (1976, 1978) and Knapp et al. (1973), report that in **leave-taking**, people may:

1. summarise the content of the contact they have just had
2. justify ending their contact at this time
3. express pleasure about each other
4. indicate continuity in their relationship by planning, specifically or vaguely, for future contact
5. wish each other well.

Albert and Kessler (1978) found, in fact, that statements of these five kinds occurred precisely in the above order. In most languages, the common terminal expressions incorporate one or the other of the last two functions, at least historically. *See you, auf Wiedersehen, au revoir* and *hasta la vista* are all derived from expressions of well-wishing. Thus, at least part of the reaffirmation process is generally expressed in the **terminal exchange** itself (Clark & French 1981).

Given that routine enquiries do not typically involve any type of acquaintance, for example, past acquaintance, or acquaintance arising from the interaction, Clark and French (1981, p. 5) predicted that such conversations would not end in a *goodbye* sequence but instead would conclude with a *thank you – you're welcome* sequence. In fact, they did find that the majority of simple requests ended as they predicted. When they examined conversations that contained more than minimal exchanges of one telephone number, they found that the likelihood of a goodbye exchange taking place increased with the complexity of the information requested and expressions of gratitude for the assistance. Significantly, a goodbye exchange was also initiated by female callers in conversations in which an 'operator mistake' occurred. Such mistakes included misspelled names and misquoted numbers, and would usually be followed by the correction and a short apology by the operator, such as *I'm sorry* or *My fault*. Clark and French make the insightful suggestion that complex requests on the part of caller and operator mistakes have in common a degree of **personalisation** of the encounter, and argue that the personalisation results in a feeling that callers have become acquainted enough with the operator to warrant a **closing section** and a *goodbye* exchange.

Telephone **opening sequences** have been studied by researchers beginning with Schegloff (1968) in the United States and extending to other contexts such as France (Goddard 1977) and Greece (Sifianou 1989) among others. Schegloff saw telephone openings as part of a broader category of summons–answer sequences – the telephone ring being the summons and the person picking up the telephone providing the answer, typically with *hello*. Schegloff commented on the fact that the typical sequence of exchanges for telephone openings (in the United States) does not provide for the identification of the caller, and that the caller's identity is usually deduced speculatively by the answerer (1968, p. 351).

Goddard's (1977, p. 211) account of the expected sequence of a French telephone opening may be summarised as follows:

Caller:	Dials number.
Answerer:	*Allo?*
Caller:	Checks number.
Answerer:	*Oui* ('yes').
Caller:	Identifies himself and either:

    1. answerer: recognises and interrupts caller

    2. caller: excuses him or herself and asks for addressee.

Goddard (1977, p. 212) comments that this sequence is explicitly taught and children are instructed that when they ring to speak to a friend they should:

1. check number
2. excuse yourself
3. name yourself
4. ask for your friend.

Goddard reports that with the exception of calls between intimate friends, where both the caller and the answerer would recognise each other's voice, the most common telephone beginning is the question *Is this X?*

He noted that on one occasion, when he was renting a house, a caller, hearing a foreign voice when expecting to hear her friend (the owner of the house), initiated the exchange with *Who are you?*, which he regarded quite negatively.

Sifianou (1989) further reports that telephone callers in England use somewhat of a mixture of the strategies identified by Goddard for French, depending on the context. For example, verification of the telephone number would only take place if there was something unexpected about the answerer. Sifianou (1989, p. 534) reports that Greeks, however, never answer their telephone by reciting their telephone number or giving their name. She offers the explanation that:

> Giving too much unnecessary information flouts Grice's maxim of quantity and can be interpreted as being insulting or even rude; identifying oneself on the phone in Greece seems to be interpreted in a similar way and, consequently, it is omitted. Callers presume that the answerer will recognize them from clues.

Sifianou suggests (1989, p. 529) that telephone callers in England are more likely to use negative politeness strategies as characterised by Brown and Levinson (1978), using indirectness, whereas Greek callers prefer to use positive politeness strategies such as in-group markers and more direct constructions.

Both Goddard (1977, p. 218) for the United States and Sifianou (1989, p. 539) for Greece report that the use of the telephone is an expected and almost obligatory means of maintaining social contact among family and friends who rarely see each other. Sifianou further observes that in Greece, 'such calls are customary even among friends and relatives who see each other quite frequently' and notes that 'a rough Greek equivalent to the English farewell formula *see you* is *θa tilefon θume* ('we'll ring each other'). Sifianou sees the enthusiastic use of the telephone as a logical extension of the Greek predisposition to closeness as well as their eagerness to share views and opinions and have frequent contact. She observes that in England the primary function of telephone conversations seems to be transactional, whereas in Greece the primary function seems to be interactional (Sifianou 1989, p. 527).

5.5   LAUGHTER IN CONVERSATION

Laughter and verbal humour play an important rapport and discursive role in conversation. Brown and Levinson (1978) regard joking as a strategy used to minimise the threat to one's positive face. Forman (2011) notes that verbal humour and laughter serve three psychological functions: to index superiority/aggression, to release inhibitions and as a response to incongruity. To these ends, research shows laughter functions in conversation both as a response and as a self-initiated comment on affairs (e.g. Gumperz 1982; Gavioli 1995; Clift 2012; Haugh & Bousfield 2012). Responsive laughter is laughter initiated by the hearer, which can fulfil the following functions:

- to acknowledge humour, wit
- to signal friendly support (solidarity)
- to minimise disagreement
- to show politeness (respect)
- to ridicule, to laugh at (conflict).

Self-initiated laughter (laughter by the speaker) on the other hand, can serve:

- to invite others to join in the conversation (managing social relationships)
- to encourage and support others
- to frame or modify an utterance
- to indicate:
  - irony
  - humour
  - modesty
  - uncertainty
  - anxiety.

Gavioli (1995) draws on conversational analysis to show how the use of laughter mitigates a hearer's frustration or disappointment when unexpected negative news is communicated. Gavioli examined the use of turn-initial versus turn-final laughter for initiating remedy in English and Italian bookshop service encounters to illustrate how laughter can be used differently in quite similar situations in different cultures. The contexts involved instances where the assistant had to supply a dispreferred response, such as a book required by the customer was not available, or the customer was not in the correct department.

Gavioli (1995, p. 374) found that in the English encounters 75 per cent of the instances of laughter occurred at or near the beginning of the turn and were accompanied or preceded by hesitations such as *well* or *um*, as exemplified in the example below. Thus, it served to introduce the explanation about to be offered by the assistant.

Assistant:	Well, (laughter) yeah, there isn't anything in here at all! There's the *Basic writings on phenomenology*, but there is no – no S – I'm getting mixed up with Hegel I'm afraid.
Customer:	Ah: yeah (that's it).
Assistant:	We haven't even got anything listed as no longer stocked, or out of print or anything.
Customer:	Aha. It might actually be more than a year ago then I suppose.
Assistant:	Yeah. I think you can forget that one altogether quite frankly, and I don't think it'd be worth looking even in *SLOV.*
Customer:	Oh: could you tell me where it is anyway, just so I can have a look through it?

In contrast, in the Italian encounters 90 per cent of the laughter occurred at the very end of a turn, as illustrated here:

Assistant:	No. I haven't got it then. Nothing doing (laughing).
Customer:	Because it was in the newspaper that –
Assistant:	that it had been published...
Customer:	That it is on sale on the...
Assistant:	Yes, erm, but we don't stock all the newest books so actually it is unlikely that we (laughing) stock it. If you want to try either at Muratori or perhaps at the Rinascita also.

Gavioli (1995, p. 378) concludes that:

> there are different preferred ways in which this mechanism works in the two languages. Whereas laughter in English usually prefaces some forthcoming excuse or account within the same turn, in Italian it marks the point where turn transition takes place, and it is left to the customer to elicit the remedy. So, the meaning of laughter in English could be considered something like 'excuse me, I am not doing very well but let me explain'. In Italian it signals that the current speaker cannot do any better and that he or she needs some help from his or her interlocutor.

There are differing functions for laughter across cultures. For instance, for many Africans and Chinese, laughter in a conversation may index nervousness or that the speaker is unsure about him or herself (Klopf & McCroskey 2007). The Japanese may use laughter to hide anger, embarrassment or confusion (Klopf & McCroskey 2007).

Differing conventions on laughter across cultures can lead to misunderstandings (Forman 2011). For instance, returning again to the shopkeeper extract at the start of this chapter, the African American's use of profanity and performance may be viewed as an invitation for his Korean interlocutor to laugh and share in the experience of the cold weather in Chicago. This is an invitation that the Korean shopkeeper does not take up. Davies (2004) notes that Germans view joking as a private affair and thus consider US Americans' frequent and public joking to be 'frivolous'. Language learners often find humour and appropriate laughter in their new language a difficult skill to master (see Bell & Attardo 2010; Forman 2011). In sum, laughter is one of among many conversational strategies individuals have at their disposal. A particular cultural group's strategies are often interpreted (and stereotyped) by others as that group's conversational style.

5.6   CONVERSATIONAL STYLES

Many researchers have shown how particular cultural groups use multiple conversational strategies that together may be viewed as conversational styles (e.g. Daun 2004 [1984]; Tannen 2004 [1981]; House 2010; Tulviste, Mizera & De Geer 2011; Goddard 2012). For instance, Germans tend to use fewer conversational routines (e.g. small talk) and tend to be less focused on conversation merely for social purposes (House 2010). The content- and task-oriented focus of German conversation has led German translators to omit small talk in their translations of the British *Paddington Bear* book series (House 2010). American conversational styles emphasise positivity, including the use of frequent compliments, conversational routines (e.g. extended greetings and small talk) and potentially disingenuous invitations (as noted above) (Pinto 2011a; Goddard 2012).

Conversational styles may be understood most clearly in relation to other conversational styles. In other words, individuals tend not to notice that they 'do' conversation in any particular way without comparing their way of doing conversation with another's. For instance, Daun (2004 [1984]) points out that Swedes were considered cold and quiet by many Europeans in the 1980s. The Swedish conversational style could be understood by measuring it against other Europeans' styles. Talking is considered a light pleasure in French culture whereas in Sweden it is considered a more serious and weighty affair (Daun 2004 [1984]). Swedes listen intently to a conversation and do not interrupt whereas in Germany interruptions and completing another's sentences show conversational engagement

(Daun 2004 [1984]). Tannen (2004 [1981]) argues that the 'pushy New York Jew' stereotype may be linked to differing conversational styles in the United States. Conversations among New Yorkers, especially Jewish speakers in New York, tend to be more fast-paced and consist of more overlapping talk than in other areas of the United States.

Social relations are advanced by conversational routines related to various topics in different societies. There can be significant differences in the way in which speakers engage with or carry out these routines. Béal (1992) describes the role of the question *Did you have a good weekend?* in workplace interaction in a French company operating in Australia, and indicates how such a simple question evokes quite different responses from Australian and French co-workers. Béal reports that Australian workers generally use the routine quite widely and view the question as a general expression of friendliness, and she further notes that the exchange is expected to be relatively short. By contrast, French co-workers tend only to ask such a question of individuals with whom they feel they have a good rapport, and treat the question as a sincere enquiry offering detailed responses, including the expression of opinions and feelings. Béal (1992, p. 25) observes that this difference of expectations results in tension:

> The Australians mentioned it as proof of the French tendency to be self-centred, forceful and insensitive to other people. The French in turn, mentioned it as a good example of what they perceived as the indifference and lack of sincerity of Australians.

Béal's research on workplace interaction in a French company operating in Australia (see also Béal 1990) is an excellent study based on naturally collected intercultural communication data, and follow-up interviews.

5.7 METHODOLOGIES: ETHNOGRAPHY AND S.P.E.A.K.I.N.G.

Some who explore conversation focus only on what can be observed in the conversation itself. In other words, they remain largely unconcerned with wider socio-cultural factors. The strictest adherents to Conversation Analysis indeed adopt this perspective. Others adopt a less stringent conversation-focused approach, and view ethnographic information as complementary data that may inform conversational observations (Auer 1998; Li Wei 1998). Still others again insist on adopting an ethnographic approach and working towards conversation as one of many human practices that serve to substantiate the human socio-cultural enterprise (e.g. Rampton 1995, 1998). In any case, ethnography plays in increased role in the study of human communication amidst globalisation (Blommaert 2010). As noted in Chapter 2, ethnography does not preconceive social practices or categories but rather 'discovers' them. However, ethnography need not be uninformed by prior work and thus here we introduce the dated but oft-cited model for ethnography of communication proposed by Dell Hymes.

Hymes (1972, 1974) devised **S.P.E.A.K.I.N.G.** as a generic grid for understanding the multifaceted nature of context. Hymes (1972, p. 59) drew on psycholinguistic findings that 'human memory works best with classifications of the magnitude of seven, plus or minus two' in devising S.P.E.A.K.I.N.G. Each of these letters makes reference to a fundamental element in the analysis of context. Hymes did not believe that S.P.E.A.K.I.N.G. had anything to do with the eventual formation of model or theory. He merely believed it to be a useful 'heuristic input' for ethnographic descriptions of communication (Hymes 1972, p. 58).

First, Hymes used 'situation' (S) to refer to both setting and scene. Setting refers to the physical circumstances of the speech act, including the time and the place. Scene is distinct from physical setting, referring more to the psychological setting. Hymes (1972, p. 60) illustrates this point with reference to the theatre: 'Within a play on the same stage with the same stage set the dramatic time may shift: "ten years later".' Next, (P) participants include the speaker (or sender or addressor) and hearer (or receiver, addressee or audience). This also includes a focus on the role of the participants (e.g. teacher, student) and how role may influence language. For instance, among the Apipon of Argentina, the suffix -*in* is added to each word if any participant is a member of the warrior class (Hymes 1972).

'Ends' (E) encompass a society's expected outcome of a speech event as well as the goals of participants within that event. For instance, for the Waiwai of Venezuela, the expected outcome of a meeting between prospective father-in-law and prospective son-in-law is a marriage contract (Hymes 1972). However, within such a meeting, the father-in-law and son-in-law have different goals in arriving at the marriage contract (e.g. dowry concerns) (Hymes 1972). The 'act of sequence' (A) overlaps with the notion of speech act and illocution, by referring to the relationship between form and content (discussed at length in Chapters 2–4). 'Key' (K) is used to refer to the tone, manner or spirit in which an act is done. For instance, you might say to a friend with a mullet haircut, 'I love your hair!'.

This utterance might be keyed as serious (e.g. I really do like mullets) or keyed as sarcastic (e.g. I don't like mullets and I am making fun of you). Individuals might key the utterance as non-serious by using a funny voice or making a face among other things.

'Instrumentality' (I) refers to the channel (e.g. email, oral, written) and/or code (e.g. language, dialect, register) that have been selected within a context. The 'norms of interaction' (N) refer to the unspoken rules that govern behaviour and interpretation of behaviour in talking. In other words, these are the expected rules of behaviour in a community. We become aware of cultural norms by observing the reactions shown by individual members of the community to ongoing behavior – approval or disapproval. For instance, it is understood that you should whisper in a church. Lastly, the (G) of Hymes' model stands for 'genres', which were discussed at length in Chapter 2 as a core component of the ethnographic approach as well as the study of intercultural communication more generally.

5.8   SUMMARY

There has been an increased call for studying lengthy stretches of text in order to understand intercultural communication (e.g. Hellerman & Cole 2008; Sifianou 2012). In this chapter, we have provided some of the tools for doing so and have shown what a focus on conversation as a co-constructed enterprise can reveal. We have considered a number of features of conversation, including greeting and leave-taking routines, and some ways in which laughter can be used in conversation, function and use of humour, and examined some features of turn-taking, including adjacency pairs, back-channelling and repetition. We have attempted to show the variety of dimensions along which cultural preferences can be found when communicating within and across cultures. In closing, we sought to provide a more sophisticated understanding of the ethnographic approach to human communication, an approach that will inform several of the remaining chapters.

5.9   REVIEW

1. **Key terms**
   Conversational routine, turn-taking, topic termination, leave-taking, contact termination, preference organisation, back-channelling, conversation openings, conversation closings, preferred and dispreferred turn structure, S.P.E.A.K.I.N.G.

2. **Key ideas**

Having read this chapter you should:

a. appreciate the ways in which routine conversations (such as answering the telephone and taking leave from someone) display conventionally determined patterns across different cultures

b. appreciate the role of turn-taking in both intra- and cross-cultural contexts

c. be able to analyse a stretch of recorded dialogue with reference to both turn-taking and the patterning of interruptions

d. be familiar with the concepts of preferred and dispreferred turn structure

e. appreciate the reason why feelings of ease or discord about an interaction are often related to the use (or non-use) of expected norms

f. be aware of the significance of different norms and conventions for intercultural communication.

3. **Focus questions**

a. Greetings and leave-takings

(i) As part of your daily routine, what kinds of greetings and leave-takings do you use? Describe the factors that affect the use of such aspects of conversation, including the social context, age differences, frequency of use, language factors, and formality vs informality of context.

(ii) If you know more than one language, how do the greetings and leave-takings and their usage differ from one language to the other?

b. Telephone conversations

The following extract is taken from the above text. Consider the extract and answer the questions:

Schegloff saw telephone openings as part of a broader category of summons–answer sequences – the telephone ring being the summons and the person picking up the telephone providing the answer, typically with *hello.*

(i) While Schegloff (1968) was describing the use of a fixed telephone, do you think the same may be said for the telephone behaviour when using a mobile phone? Provide reasons for your answer.

(ii) Sifianou (1989, p. 527) suggests that in England telephone behaviour appears to be *transactional* (serving to convey information) whereas in Greece it is *interactional* (serving to establish and maintain social relationships). In your own culture, which is the preferred telephone behaviour and is this the same for the fixed telephone and the mobile phone? Give examples and reasons.

(iii) Goddard (1977, p. 212) comments that this sequence is explicitly taught and children are instructed that when they ring to speak to a friend they should:

(1) check number
(2) excuse yourself
(3) name yourself
(4) ask for your friend.

When you were a child, did you learn the above sequence of answering the telephone? If so, do you continue to use this sequence in your daily life? If not, what sequence were you taught? How has it changed over time?

c. **Repetition in intercultural communication**

Identify how you use repetition as a strategy in your daily interactions and whether it is or has been useful as a strategy in intercultural communication. Provide examples for your answer.

4. **Research analysis**
Laughter
Consider the following extracts taken from Gavioli (1995, p. 374).

From English bookshop encounter:

Assistant:	Well, (laughter) yeah, there isn't anything in here at all! There's the *Basic writings on phenomenology*, but there is no – no S – I'm getting mixed up with Hegel I'm afraid.
Customer:	Ah: yeah (that's it).
Assistant:	We haven't even got anything listed as no longer stocked, or out of print or anything.
Customer:	Aha. It might actually be more than a year ago then I suppose.
Assistant:	Yeah. I think you can forget that one altogether quite frankly, and I don't think it'd be worth looking even in SLOV.
Customer:	Oh: could you tell me where it is anyway, just so I can have a look through it?

a. What is the function of this turn-initial laughter in the above example?

From Italian bookshop encounter:

Assistant:	No. I haven't got it then. Nothing doing (laughing)
Customer:	Because it was in the newspaper that –
Assistant:	that it had been published...
Customer:	That it is on sale on the...
Assistant:	Yes, erm, but we don't stock all the newest books so actually it is unlikely that we (laughing) stock it. If you want to try either at Muratori or perhaps at the Rinascita also.

    b. What is the function of the turn-final laughter in the above example?

    c. In your own language, is turn-initial or turn-final laughter the preferred response in initiating a remedy? Give an example and reasons for this preferred response.

    d. What do you think the consequences might be in an intercultural context when a person uses turn-initial laughter to initiate a remedy in a language where turn-final laughter is the preferred response?

    e. Have you ever been in or know of a situation in which you (or another) have laughed at an inappropriate moment? What were the consequences of such a dispreferred response? How was the situation remedied?

5. Research exercise adjacency pairs

    Record a conversation between yourself and another person, which lasts for approximately 30 seconds. Transcribe and analyse the conversation to identify the adjacency pairs. Identify the adjacency pairs using the examples given for Jane and Kate's conversation in section 5.2 (e.g. *summon–response, question–answer*).

SUGGESTED FURTHER READING

Revisit Conversation Analysis (CA) classics for a firm grounding in the structured and co-constructed nature of conversation (e.g. work by Sacks). Sidnell is a good overall introduction to CA and Tannen to conversation more generally. Béal's study of Australian–French interactions is revealing in terms of cross-cultural differences in conversational styles, as are Tannen's and Daun's respective pieces in the Kiesling and Paulston collection. While not dealt with in this chapter, many researchers have shed light on structure in multilingual conversations, including the papers in Auer (which often draw on but also critique the CA approach).

Auer P. (ed.) 1998 *Code-Switching in Conversation: Language, Interaction and Identity*. London & New York: Routledge, pp. 290–317.

Béal, C. 1992 'Did you have a good weekend? Or why is there no such thing as a simple question in cross-cultural encounters?' *Australian Review of Applied Linguistics*, vol. 15, no. 1, pp. 23–52.

Daun, Å. 2004 [1984] 'Swedishness as an obstacle in cross-cultural interaction'. In Kiesling, S. & Paulston, C. (eds) *Intercultural Discourse and Communication: The Essential Readings*. Boston, MA: Wiley Blackwell, pp. 150–63.

Sidnell, J. 2010 *Conversation Analysis: An Introduction*. John Wiley & Sons.

Tannen, D. 2004 [1981] 'New York Jewish conversational style'. In Kiesling, S. & Paulston, C. (eds) *Intercultural Discourse and Communication: The Essential Readings*. Boston, MA: Wiley Blackwell, pp. 135–49.

2007 *Talking Voices: Repetition, Dialogue, and Imagery in Conversational Discourse*. 2nd edn. Cambridge: Cambridge University Press.

6 | Positioning the self: role, power and gender

6.1 INTRODUCTION

Pᴇᴏᴘʟᴇ ғɪʟʟ a variety of roles in society and these roles come with certain expectations. For instance, medical doctors are expected to provide care for patients in medical contexts. The role 'doctor' is established by institutional conventions and societal expectations (Cordella 2004; see also Goffman 1959). Doctors also fill their role because they are more knowledgeable about the medical context. This knowledge includes knowledge of the topics at stake as well as the style of language used to discuss these topics. The role of the doctor, as well as the knowledge associated with this role, gives doctors some power over patients in the medical context.

Similar observations may be made about the respective roles of managers and subordinates in business contexts, legal professionals and clients in legal contexts, teachers and students in educational contexts, and so on. In sum, roles in society emerge because of institutional conventions, societal expectations and the possession of knowledge. Furthermore, many of these roles (e.g. doctors, legal professionals, teachers) are imbued with power over other contextually related roles (e.g. patients, clients, students). As social agents, we acquire these roles by gaining knowledge and these roles grant us certain powers over others. Historical circumstances often influence our ability to construct these roles. For instance, speakers of non-standard English varieties are often disadvantaged when entering the mainstream school system, which favours Standard English.

Role and power are not inflexible phenomena and often emerge through interaction. Hippocrates declared in his oath a desire to 'impart a knowledge' of the law of medicine to doctors and thus established them as 'authority figures' vis-à-vis their patients, traditional or otherwise (Cordella

2004, p. 5). Yet, Cordella (2004, p. 5) notes that for Hippocrates 'the onus was on the doctor to adjust his communication strategies in order to give instructions to the patient'. Failure to convey these instructions, in the face of traditional medicine or any other factor, would entail a failure to fill (or one might say socially construct) the role of doctor adequately.

Cultural differences in the perceptions of role and ways of speaking are important in understanding the social expectations and conventions that underlie language use and are used to interpret linguistic meaning in a given interaction. In this chapter, we examine role through a focus on two salient ways of speaking: power and gender. We show how social actors draw on stereotypically gendered and powerful ways of speaking to construct roles and accomplish goals across cultures. We begin by outlining the links between role and language (picking up on a topic first introduced in Chapter 2). We then introduce some of the rich intercultural research on power relations (e.g. Searle 1995; Fairclough 1989; Foucault 1978, 1980; Giddens 1982, 1993). We next introduce the notion of gendered ways of speaking. This lays the foundations for a subsequent discussion of the relationship of gender and power in constructing roles across cultures. In closing, this chapter introduces Critical Discourse Analysis, which has been an influential frame for studying power relations in society.

6.2   LANGUAGE AND ROLE

Roles on the one hand come with expected ways of speaking and on the other are constructed through particular ways of speaking. For instance, we generally expect that a lecturer in an Anglo university will use Standard English. We also expect that a book such as the one you are reading now will be written in a Standard English variety. Conversely, a gangster rapper would be expected to use a non-standard variety of English in a performance. However, these boundaries are sometimes blurred, for instance, when an academic such as H. Samy Alim (e.g. 2006) uses African American English styles to both ironise and challenge the hegemony of Standard English in the Anglo academic context. Alim uses language to construct a heterogeneous role as an academic (proficient in Standard English) and African American (proficient in African American Vernacular English). In doing so, he challenges dominant ideologies about how an academic should behave.

Social roles are often (if not always) heterogeneous and constructed through multiple 'voices' (see Chapter 2). For instance, Cordella (2004) finds that Chilean doctors construct the role of doctor by using three 'voices': doctor, educator and fellow human. So, like doctors more generally, Chilean doctors seek information, assess and review this information and align with authority when making recommendations (i.e 'doctor voice'). However, Cordella argues that Chilean doctors are also guided by a cultural schema known as *simpatía*, which favours cooperation, understanding and the avoidance of unpleasantness in asymmetrical power exchanges (see also Forbes & Cordella 1999). Thus, Chilean doctors often use an 'educator voice' to respond to patient discomfort or convey the inevitable and a 'fellow human voice' to facilitate patients' stories or create empathy. In short, there are many ways of speaking that go into creating or constructing a role like 'doctor' and these vary across cultures.

Linguistic features are critically important for constructing roles. Furthermore, some linguistic forms are more closely linked to role than others. For instance, linguistic forms that refer directly to persons are regarded as the most pragmatically salient to speakers and hearers (Errington 1985b; Woolard 2008). Errington (1985b) argues that forms referring to the self (e.g. first-person pronominal forms such as the English *I, me, my*) are particularly well suited for categorising the self and consequently asserting a role. For instance, Mendoza-Denton (2007) found that girls with gang affiliations pronounced the first-person pronoun *I* differently than other girls at a Northern California high school (i.e. with the tongue in a higher and posterior part of the mouth). Students who were particularly concerned with asserting their gang affiliation (i.e. 'iconic speakers') would emphasise this pronunciation.

Manns (2012) illustrates the use of self-referent forms to construct role by examining the pronominal choices of Indonesian youth in Java. Unlike many Indo-European languages, Indonesian offers speakers a range of choice in first-person pronouns. So, for instance, a young Indonesian in an informal context with friends would most typically select *aku* for 'I'. Yet, when functioning in a formal or professional context, that same speaker might select *saya* for 'I'. Islamic youth wishing to assert an Islamic identity might switch to the Arabic first-person form *ana* whereas speakers wishing to be playful or tough might switch to the Jakarta pronoun *gué* or *gua*. In any case, Manns (2012), drawing on previous research, likens these pronominal shifts to assuming, if for a moment, the voice (or role) of the perceived speaker in the context. As Englebretson (2007) notes, a Jakarta speaker is perceived to be tough, so selecting a Jakarta pronoun enables one to enact a stance of toughness if for a moment.

Of course, linguistic features other than pronouns are used to construct roles within languages and across contexts. For instance, many linguistic

Table 6.1 Stereotyped gender conversation styles

Feminine	Masculine
indirect	direct
conciliatory	confrontational
facilitative	competitive
collaborative	autonomous
minor contribution (in public)	dominates (public) talking time
supportive feedback	aggressive interruptions
person/process-oriented	task/outcome-oriented
affectively oriented	referentially oriented

(based on Holmes & Stubbe 2005, p. 574)

forms have been linked to femininity or masculinity (we will tease this point out further below). Table 6.1 contrasts oft-cited features of masculine and feminine conversational styles.

However, as we noted in Chapter 2, and as will be discussed throughout this chapter, there is nothing inherently masculine or feminine about any of these conversational styles. Gender is something that is socially constructed and males often adopt oft-cited 'feminine' styles just as females use oft-cited 'masculine' forms.

6.3   LANGUAGE AND POWER

Brown and Levinson (1987, p. 77) define **power** as follows:

> P (power) is an asymmetric social dimension of relative power, roughly in Weber's sense. That is, P (H, S) is the degree to which H [hearer] can impose his own plans and his own self-evaluation (face) at the expense of S's [speaker's] plans of self-evaluation.

This conceptualisation of power is based on the Weberian perception whereby power is seen to negatively influence others' behaviour or force people to perform acts that they wouldn't undertake by themselves.

Searle (1969, 1995) and Foucault (1980), however, argue that power relations exist as part of the social fabric of communication and should not be solely regarded as the negative forces of domination by those in powerful positions (e.g. the state, the police). Power should not only be seen in terms of inequity and domination, because 'power comes from below; that is, there is no binary and all-encompassing opposition between rulers and ruled at the root of power relations' (Foucault 1978, p. 94). Foucault emphasises that power is something that is not imposed 'from above', but is created through people interacting in a certain social context.

Giddens (1993, p. 116) further suggests that the concept of social action is 'logically tied to that of power'. He also conceives power as being contextually determined because it is regarded as a component of the discourse. Giddens suggests that the act of participation in an interaction can be sufficient to enable a person to acquire some level of control over the conversation. Giddens (1993) provides examples of extreme forms of social control that include an interaction between a prison guard and a prisoner. For instance, a prisoner can still maintain some level of social control even when in solitary confinement, by going on a hunger strike. Thus, even though there is an asymmetrical power relationship in favour of the prison guard, the prisoner can still exert some level of power within the interaction (see Giddens' 'dialectic of control'). Davidson (1986, p. 226) takes a similar perspective and suggests that power needs to be viewed 'as a netlike, circulating organization'. Power exists within the fabric of language and not outside of it, and is part of the interactional process. Therefore, the concept of power is not socially predetermined, but is dependent upon the context of the interaction.

Access to information and resources can directly influence the power relations between participants. Those who have access to information have more powerful positions in interactions. The differing degrees of symmetry in power relations and the relationship between power and discourse are the foci of research by critical discourse analysts. Many researchers (e.g. Fairclough 1989; van Dijk 1987, 1996; Wodak 1996; Fairclough & Wodak 1997; Teo 2000; Eades 2000; Cordella 2004) have attempted to identify and determine how access to information differs as a result of the socioeconomic, educational and cultural backgrounds of the participants and how this in turn impacts on the power relations in a given interaction and/or institution.

The access to information is central in an institutional context. The person with the greater access to information and resources is sometimes referred to as the **gatekeeper**, meaning that he or she possesses more power and thus controls the information flow in a given interaction (see Sarangi 1996; Sarangi & Roberts 1999). 'Institutions' or 'organisations' may be viewed as 'cultures with an emphasis on discourse and power' (Wodak

1996, p. 10). Sarangi and Roberts (1999) suggest that it is the setting (e.g. legal, educational, medical) that is important when studying institutional interactions. The roles of the participants and their access to information are continuously changing, which means that the power relations do not remain static. Given that, the power relations between participants depend on the particular context of the interaction, be it in a legal, educational, medical or media setting.

Power is emergent in interaction and both powerful and powerless roles may be challenged and redefined in interaction. For instance, some defence lawyers use their knowledge of the legal context to position rape victims as powerful and in control (Levinson 1992). Levinson (1992) illustrates how one defence lawyer uses this strategy to question the intentions and morality of an alleged rape victim in a cross-examination. Among other things, the lawyer uses the cross-examination to highlight the alleged victim's clothing, make-up, age and past sexual activities. Graham (2009) investigates the hospital context and reveals how there is a delicate negotiation of power among nurses, doctors, trainee doctors and social workers. Graham's study sought to address the concern of experienced nurses and social workers, who felt their opinions were not being respected by doctors and trainee doctors. In the following interaction, a social worker (SW) interrupts a doctor (MD), suggesting that a patient's mental issues aren't being adequately addressed in an impending discharge.

16	MD:	She came in with uh – GI symptoms. She's
17		probably a partial small bowel /obstruction/.
18		That's what we thought.
19		[. . .]
20		Um. She's been taking a lot of NSAIDs for
21		her pain so that was probably the root of most
22		of her GI problems.
23	SW1:	How about her mental status? *What's with the*
24		*mental status?* I mean – you know – I
25		understand that this is a confusing environment
26		. . . but she's not remembering what's happening.
27		She's very confused. I mean really confused.
28		Enough to be – make it bothersome.

(Graham 2009, pp. 22–3)

The social worker is careful about how the information is presented in light of the doctor's more powerful role in the hospital context. This includes the use of such hedges as *I mean* and *you know*, pauses and explicit respect for why the doctor has not been overly concerned with mental health (e.g. *I understand that*).

Schnurr, Marra and Holmes (2008) show how impoliteness (see Chapter 3) may be used to assert or challenge power roles in a meeting. In the following interaction, manager Serena arrives late to a fortnightly managers' meeting at an IT firm. The chair of the meeting, Tricia, challenges Serena about her tardiness. Tricia's personal assistant, Evelyn, also criticises Serena.

1	Tri:	good afternoon
2	Ser:	[in a light-hearted tone of voice]: sorry I'm late
3	Eve:	it's been noted
4		chocolates expected next meeting
5		[laughter]
6	Ser:	(that's right) cos I was considering whether you'd
7		notice if I didn't turn up
8		[laughter]
9	Tri:	[in a friendly tone of voice]: we noticed

(Schnurr, Marra & Holmes 2008, pp. 220–1)

Tricia asserts her displeasure in the opening line by ironically saying *good afternoon* in line 1. The meeting was scheduled for 10 am but by the time Serena arrives it is afternoon. Furthermore, Evelyn, who might be viewed as less powerful in terms of role, more overtly challenges Serena for her tardiness in lines 3–5.

The degree to which a role is considered powerful and the degree to which that power can be challenged both vary from culture to culture. This can, in part, be discussed in terms of Hofstede's power distance dimension, introduced in Chapter 1. This dimension relates to how accepting a particular culture is of power asymmetries. Hofstede posits that Latin American, Asian and African cultures are accepting of power asymmetries whereas Anglo and Germanic cultures are not. The acceptance or challenge of power asymmetries differs across these latter cultures. For instance, focusing on two cultures that are both accepting of power asymmetries, Japan and Mexico, acceptance is expressed in different ways (Dorfman et al. 1997). In Japan, workers value harmony, so before implementing a new policy, a Japanese supervisor will try to establish agreement with employees beforehand. Mexican supervisors, on the other hand, take an entirely autocratic approach.

6.4   LANGUAGE AND GENDER

Maleness and femaleness are closely linked to gender but they are biological whereas **gender** is a social practice, which is 'performed' (though not necessarily consciously) (Butler 1990; Cameron 2009). Certain practices (e.g. shaving conventions, wearing dresses) over time come to be linked to males or females and by consequence are viewed as masculine or feminine gender practices (Ochs 1992). To illustrate, the biological aspects of maleness and femaleness have remained the same over the past 100 years (and much longer, of course) but gender practices have certainly changed (Sorrells 2013). For instance, women have increasingly entered the workforce and taken up top roles within institutions in Western and Western-influenced societies. Moreover, as will be seen for the remainder of this chapter, males often adopt seemingly 'feminine' linguistic strategies and females 'masculine' strategies. In sum, the biological sense of male and female do not change (or do so at a slow evolutionary pace). However, what it means to be a male or female varies greatly throughout history and across cultures.

Gender differences have most often been conceptualised in two ways: separate worlds and cultural difference. The **separate worlds hypothesis** posits that adult gender separation can be linked to differing childhood play foci and ways of speaking (Lakoff 1975; Tannen 1990). Lakoff (1975) describes women's and men's language practices as kinds of registers. Tannen (1990) echoes this description by discussing male and female communicative systems respectively as genderlects (i.e. **gender** di**alects**). In other words, just as doctors or lawyers have ways of speaking (linguistic registers), so respectively do men and women. Tannen (1990) notes in a general sense that women's ways of speaking are oriented towards rapport, especially establishing and maintaining relationships. Men, on the other hand, see talk as a means for maintaining and negotiating hierarchy. Thus, Tannen (1990) concludes, male–female miscommunication often results from men and women speaking at crosspurposes.

Certain ways of speaking are more commonly linked to either men or women as a result of these 'separate worlds' and differing goals. For instance, literature has noted that women are more likely to pay compliments than men and, when they do, these compliments tend to address another's appearance (Coates 2004; Rees-Miller 2011). Conversely, men, when they do compliment, often address another's skills or abilities. Women's language has also been cited as more polite and cooperative than men's language (Holmes 1995; Mills 2003). This polite and cooperative style involves the increased use of certain language styles, such as hedges (e.g. *I think, I guess*), super-polite formulations (e.g. *would you please x, if you don't mind?*) and hyper-correct grammar (e.g. 'bookish' grammar and 'formal' pronunciation) (Joseph 2006). It also includes a reticence to interrupt or take the floor from another speaker (Holmes 1995). Conversely, men are seen as less likely to use such 'polite' language and more likely to interrupt or assert themselves in a conversation.

However, the two worlds hypothesis has been viewed as too polar and extreme by many (e.g. Holmes & Marra 2004; Cameron 2009). These researchers reject this hypothesis in favour of a more sophisticated discussion of **cultural difference**. Ethnographers have been particularly critical of the two worlds hypothesis (Goodwin 2005). These critiques have been especially aimed at the hypothesis' polarity and emphasis on gender segregation (Goodwin 2005; Cameron 2009). For instance, research on children's playground activities has refuted essentialist claims that girls are less competitive and more passive than boys (Goodwin 2005). In computer-mediated communication, different practices did emerge for male and female users (Herring 2005). However, it was also found that the minority sex (in terms of numbers) would adapt its behaviour in the direction of the majority (Herring 2005). In other words, men would adopt seemingly feminine practices when more women were involved in an online conversation and vice versa.

Differences between males and females also vary across cultures. For instance, Schofield (1982) and Corsaro (1997) have found that African American girls are much more independent and comfortable with boys than their white, middle-class counterparts (cited in Goodwin 2005). Kyratzis and Guo (2001, reviewed by Goodwin 2005) found that US American preschool boys are more assertive than their girl counterparts. However, in China they found the reverse to be true. Furthermore, context influenced the degree to which Chinese boys and girls were assertive. For instance, girls were found to be dominant in cross-sex conflict about courtship and boys more dominant in conflict involving work (Goodwin 2005).

Thus, as with power, gender is shown to be a fluid phenomenon, which is often emergent in conversation. For instance, businesses are increasingly commodifying language and this includes the commodification of seemingly feminine or masculine language features. Cameron (2000) describes how call centre workers draw on 'feminine' language features to facilitate '"emotional labour", involving the management of both the customer's feelings and the worker's own' (Cameron 2000, p. 339). Male call centre workers did not view the use of feminine style itself to be a problem. Rather, as with their female colleagues, they were more troubled by the need to

Table 6.2 **Gender and doctor–patient interruptions**

Gender of physicians	Number of interruptions	Physicians' interruptions	Patients' interruptions	*Number of patients*
Male	188	67%	33%	17
Female	59	32%	68%	4

(West 1998, p. 400)

use inauthentic and artificial language more generally to fill the role of 'call centre operator' (Cameron 2000).

6.5   LANGUAGE, POWER AND GENDER

A rich body of work has emerged which explores links between power and gender (Kiesling 1997; Lakoff 2005). At the extreme, some have proposed that differences between men and women should primarily be seen in terms of power rather than gender (Lakoff 2005). Suffice it to say, the degree to which speakers respect or orient to roles such as power and gender varies across culture. Furthermore, the degree to which styles perceived to be masculine and feminine may be used to assert or create power varies across cultures. In any case, it is clear that gender and power are linked and that associated practices emerge in interaction.

This is evidenced by West's (1998) study of male and female patient–doctor interactions. Focusing on interruptions (the rights of which are linked to power), West found that regardless of their patients' gender, male doctors interrupted patients twice as many times as they themselves were interrupted. Conversely, the reverse was found to be the case for females. Women are also shown to use more back-channelling devices than men in mixed-sex environments and this has been linked to power asymmetries (see Berk-Seligson 2009).

Speakers draw on both masculine and feminine styles when negotiating power in institutional settings (Holmes 2006; Mullany 2008; Schnurr, Marra & Holmes 2008; Ladegaard 2011, 2012). For instance, men use reputedly 'feminine' styles to manage face and discourses in business contexts. These feminine styles (e.g. hedges, modals) are used by a male in the following example from a business meeting (Schnurr, Marra & Holmes 2008).

Tricia and Noel are meant to be presenting on an issue at a meeting but do not agree on this issue. Tricia is the department director and Noel one of her subordinate managers.

```
1   Noel:    so Tricia and I might have a different story about that
2            of course you realise that +
3            //slightly different I mean we might\
4   Trish:   /[in a contestive tone of voice:] why would\\
5            we have a different story:
6   Noel:    well because I think the reason I think that we might
7            //just\slightly (veer) different
8   Trish:   /mm\\
```
                    (Schnurr, Marra & Holmes 2008, pp. 221–2)

Noel's utterance in line 1, though directed to a third party, represents a challenge to Tricia's authority. He immediately recognises this and attempts to mitigate his stance in lines 3, 6 and 7. Noel does this through the use of hedges (*well, slightly, just, I think*) and a modal (*might*). Women often use masculine styles to assert power within work contexts. For instance, some women are shown to use more aggressive or 'masculine' styles as they climb the corporate ladder (Tannen 1994). It has been posited that female managers have de-gendered the managerial role through the use of such styles (Holmes 2006). For example, it was noted above that 'interrupting' is often viewed in terms of a masculine behaviour. However, this is among the practices women use to assert power within the workplace context (Mullany 2008). For example, Sharon and David are managers within the same company and there is considerable tension between the two. These tensions emerge in the following exchange:

```
1   David:   So that's gone up from three something up
2            on the autumn side it
3   David:   [(.) side side                            ]
4            [((Sharon repeatedly whistles))] ((She waves
5            a piece of paper at David and then throws this
6            across the room at him))
7   David:   I'm SOOO sorry (.) ((picks up a different sheet
8            but not the one Sharon has thrown))
9            on page five of the autumn winter one
```
                                        (Mullany 2008, p. 242)

David opens with erroneous report information in line 1. Sharon interrupts David with whistling rather than speech to assert that she has the correct information. She follows by throwing the correct information at him. David responds with sarcasm, which is also often linked to 'masculine' practices. In short, both of these managers draw on masculine practices to assert power in unfolding discourse.

Although power is often linked to masculinity (e.g. Kiesling 1997), managers have been observed using more normatively feminine rather than masculine styles. Ladegaard (2011) finds that Danish CEOs, whether male or female, show a preference for indirect, 'normatively' feminine styles. Ladegaard finds the primary difference between these males and females can be found on two levels. First, male CEOs use a wider range of gender styles than their female counterparts. Notably, females are noted elsewhere reducing their pitch range (linked to gender) in order to present a steadfast image (see Cameron 2000). Second, and perhaps more importantly, there is a significant difference in the way in which subordinates respond to male and female CEOs respectively. The authority of male leaders is rarely if ever challenged in Ladegaard's study. However, female leadership authority is challenged several times.

Links between gender stereotypes and power have been examined and critiqued across cultures. For instance, Saito (2011) explores the interactional styles used by Japanese managers to deal with institutional conflict. Saito finds that managers draw on masculine and feminine styles to manage conflict and focus subordinates on institutional goals. Ladegaard (2012) finds that female managers in Hong Kong workplaces also draw on normatively masculine and feminine styles. For instance, females engage in jocular and rude humour to assert power in the workplace (see also Mullany 2004) and employees often have little recourse to respond. Thus, Ladegaard (2012) cautions that socio-cultural factors must be considered when observing gender and power. Ladegaard (2012, p. 1675) writes: 'Leaders in Hong Kong workplaces are assumed to act as benevolent autocrats, and employees are expected to demonstrate deference and filial piety'. This study, Ladegaard argues, shows that women should not be viewed as intrinsically more polite than men. Furthermore, it shows that the notion women are more polite will interact with a number of institutional and socio-cultural factors.

6.6 METHODOLOGIES: CRITICAL DISCOURSE ANALYSIS

The aims of a **Critical Discourse Analysis** (CDA) approach may be said to include understanding and analysing the influence of ideological loading in certain words and phrases in languages and the relations of power that underlie such linguistic forms, which are often not apparent to language users. CDA can also be applied to examine racist ideologies, discriminatory language or stereotyping in discourse (van Dijk 1987, 1996; Eades 2000; Teo 2000). It is used to address the different levels of access that members of a society may have to such resources based on their social class, education and cultural background. Fairclough and Wodak (1997) identify eight principles of CDA:

1. CDA addresses social problems
2. power relations are discursive
3. discourse constitutes society and culture
4. discourse does ideological work
5. discourse is historical
6. the link between text and society, between the micro and the macro, is mediated
7. discourse analysis is interpretative and explanatory
8. discourse is a form of social action.

These principles highlight the need to view power relations within and between societies in relation to a given interaction and in the context of social, political, historical, economic and linguistic ideologies and social practice. While Hofstede's dimensions (see Chapter 1) are useful in identifying the ideologies and social practice, Fairclough (1989) and Pennycook (2001) have both investigated the concept of ideology and power from the perspective of CDA. Fairclough proposes that language and power are affected by 'ideologies' that are 'implicit in the conventions according to which people interact linguistically, and of which people are generally not consciously aware' (1989, p. 2). Thus, when examining how power is used and manipulated, it needs to be analysed in terms of 'the ideological workings of language' (Heydon 2005). Pennycook (2001, p. 7) further suggests that when considering these ideological workings, one needs to '[turn] a sceptical eye towards assumptions, ideas that have become "naturalized", notions that are no longer questioned'.

The concept of social practice is also important in understanding the relationship between language and power. Fairclough (2000, p. 156) defines **social practice** as 'a particular area of social life which is structured in a distinctive way involving particular groups of people in particular relations with each other'. This means that language is identified as just one factor influencing the manifestation of power and ideologies in a given interaction. Language can be regarded as 'internalised' in discourse that exists as part of and is interrelated with the physical, sociological and psychological elements that also affect power relations in interactions, such as in institutional encounters (Heydon 2005).

Foucault (1980, p. 99) provides a succinct summary to the study of the relationship between power and language in that such a relationship should be analysed by:

starting... from the infinitesimal mechanisms, which each have their own history, their own trajectory, their own techniques and tactics, and then see how these mechanisms of power have been – and continue to be – invested, colonised, utilised, involuted, transformed, displaced, extended, etc., by ever more general mechanisms.

6.7   SUMMARY

Social roles are influenced by the underlying assumptions and ideologies embedded in people's beliefs and experiences. On the one hand, these concepts are somewhat static within and across cultures. For instance, as we introduced at the start of the chapter, we expect that a doctor has knowledge associated with the position. However, roles also emerge in interaction and this is seen perhaps most saliently through an investigation of power and gender. In this chapter, we showed how maleness and femaleness are biological but how the closely linked notion of genders are performed. These emerge through the use of certain linguistic practices. Masculine practices are often linked to power but we showed in this chapter how these links are often more nuanced than this. Furthermore, we did this by exploring the notion of managerial and leadership practices across cultures.

An awareness of cross-cultural role expectations and how social roles may be constructed in emergent discourse can reduce the possibility of communication breakdown. Such understanding may also be beneficial for better comprehending the social expectations and conventions underlying language use in different cultures in order to more successfully interpret linguistic meaning in a given interaction. In any case, as we noted in Chapter 2, language is often not directly linked to social roles (or identities) but rather indirectly linked. It is essential to understand cross-cultural understandings of indexicality wherever possible. Chapter 7 introduces names and terms of address, which are generally viewed as the most indexically salient linguistic forms for speakers, hearers and analysts.

6.8   REVIEW

1. **Key terms**
   Roles, social practice, cultural difference, two worlds hypothesis, interactional context, genderlect, masculinity, femininity, power, power relations, institutions, gatekeepers, ideology, Critical Discourse Analysis.

2. **Key ideas**

   Having read this chapter you should:

   a. understand how roles may be static or emergent in discourse

   b. be aware of the potential role of ideology, institutions and gatekeepers in the creation and perpetuation of perceptions of power

   c. understand the links between maleness and femaleness and masculinity and femininity respectively

   d. know how normatively masculine and feminine styles are mobilised for power goals in discourse

   e. be aware of the perspective of Critical Discourse Analysis in the discussion of power stereotyping and cultural differences

   f. appreciate the importance of interactional context to discourse power.

3. **Focus questions**

   a. **Language and power**

      Consider the following quote about in-group and out-group stereotypes: 'Dominant group members regularly engage in conversations about ethnic minority groups in society, and thus express and persuasively communicate their attitudes to other in-group members' (van Dijk 1987, p. 111).

      (i) Why is the dominant group referred to as the 'in-group'? In the above statement, which group is regarded as the 'out-group'? Give reasons.

      (ii) Based on what is current news in the mass media in your country, at a global level who (person or group) is regarded as the 'dominant group' and thus the 'in-group', and who is often negatively described as being on the outside, or the 'out-group'? Give reasons.

      (iii) In your own society, who (which group of people) would you describe as being part of the 'in-group' and who would be classified as being part of the 'out-group'? What do you think are the political, social, cultural, etc. reasons for such a grouping? What words or phrases are used to describe the 'in-group' and 'out-group' members?

   b. **Institutional power**

      Based on your own experience and language background, provide an institutional context, indicating the 'gatekeeper', the role of the participants and the setting (e.g. legal, educational, medical). Describe the power relations between the 'gatekeeper' and other participants in the context, and provide reasons as to whether the access to information changed or continues to change over time.

c. Power and meaning in newspapers

(i) How do the newspapers in your country or another with which you are familiar promote certain ideological constructions or stereotyping through the use of headlines, leads and generalisations (e.g. sexism, racism, relations between the in-group and out-group)?

(ii) What other examples of ideological bias or stereotyping have you read about in newspapers and on online news sites using such linguistic mechanisms (e.g. use of quotes, the types of people and their occupations quoted, use of adjectives and other words to describe events and/or people)?

4. Research analysis

a. Discriminatory language

Consider the following extract from Gottlieb (2006):

> Discriminatory language, and whether it should be regulated or not, have been hot topics in Japanese social debate for many years. The 1970s and 1980s in Japan saw an upsurge of protest from marginalised groups about the terms and stereotypes used to describe them in the language of public life, most often in the mass print and visual media. The Buraku Liberation League [the descendants of outcasts who were, and are still now, heavily discriminated against in Japan] and its forerunners had been active since the 1920s in rooting out and confronting any reported instance of derogatory language, subjecting offenders to a process of denunciation aimed at extracting both an apology for that particular instance and a promise of a more educated and serious approach in the future. Following their lead, disability activist groups, ethnic Korean resident groups and, to a lesser extent, women's groups mounted similar protests in the 1980s, energised by a wave of moral support offered by both international and domestic social changes occurring at the time. The International Year of Disabled Persons (1981), for example, provided the impetus for a change of terminology relating to disability in Japanese laws and statutes and for pressure to be brought to bear on media organisations about their use of language in this area.
>
> As a result of vocal protests from those groups affected, the Japanese media during this period drew up lists of words not to be used on any account [*kinkushū*] and lists of suggested substitute terms

[*iikaeshū*]. Many of these lists were in-house only and were not made public, although that of Japan's major public broadcaster, NHK, was. Other early ones may be found included as appendices in Japanese books on the subject. The motivation behind the lists and the consequent self-censorship of contentious terms was simple: to avoid the embarrassment of public protest (which could be very vocal indeed and occasionally spilled over into violence) and consequent loss of face.

(i) In the above extract, Gottlieb discusses numerous groups in Japanese society that have been subjected to discrimination and linguistic stereotyping. Using these groups as a basis, provide examples of discriminatory language that you have encountered in similar groups in your own social environment (e.g. sexist language, discriminatory language against people with disabilities or from certain cultural and ethnic groups, or people from certain socioeconomic groups). How has the usage of such discriminatory language changed over the past two decades and why?

(ii) Do you think that the substitutions of certain words and phrases can be effective in overcoming discriminatory language in the mass media? What strategies do you think could be successful in overcoming discriminatory language and linguistic stereotyping in your own country?

5. **Research exercise**

As more and more people from different linguistic and cultural backgrounds are coming into contact with each other, how can people address and overcome differing gender and power relations and cultural and linguistic stereotypes to successfully communicate in an intercultural context? Give three examples of strategies to ensure successful intercultural communication.

SUGGESTED FURTHER READING

Revisit Goffman's work for foundational discussions of role and society. Fairclough's work provides a firm grounding in power (albeit rather firmly from a CDA perspective). Bousfield and Locher's volume approaches more fluid notions of power from the perspective of impoliteness. Holmes' body of work provides a firm grounding in gender (as does the edited volume of Holmes and Meyerhoff). Barrett illustrates the fluid nature of role, gender and ethnicity through an investigation of African American drag queens.

Ladegaard's and Saito's respective works illustrate how seemingly 'gendered' practices come to bear on cross-cultural business contexts. Ochs' paper is among the first and most famous to tease out links between language and gender. Lastly, there are many works that deal with language and ethnicity, discussions of which would certainly complement this chapter. Harris and Rampton's edited volume is a great starting point.

Barrett, R. 1999 'Indexing polyphonous identity in the speech of African American drag queens'. In Bucholtz, M., Liang, A. & Sutton, L. (eds) *Reinventing Identities: The Gendered Self in Discourse.* Oxford: Oxford University Press, pp. 313–31.

Bousfield, D. & Locher, M. (eds) 2008 *Impoliteness in Language: Studies on its Interplay with Power in Theory and Practice.* Berlin: Mouton de Gruyter. pp. 127–54.

Fairclough, N. 1989 *Language and Power.* Harlow: Longman Group.

Harris, R. & Rampton, B. (eds) 2003 *The Language, Ethnicity and Race Reader.* New York & London: Routledge.

Holmes, J. 1995 *Women, Men and Politeness.* London: Longman.

Holmes, J. & Meyerhoff, M. (eds) 2005 *The Handbook of Language and Gender.* Malden, MA: Blackwell.

Ladegaard, H. 2011 '"Doing power" at work: Responding to male and female management styles in a global business corporation'. *Journal of Pragmatics,* vol. 43, pp. 4–19.

Ochs, E. 1992 'Indexing gender'. In Duranti A. & Goodwin C. (eds) *Rethinking Context: Language as an Interactive Phenomenon.* Cambridge: Cambridge University Press, pp. 335–58.

Saito, J. 2011 'Managing confrontational situations'. *Journal of Pragmatics,* vol. 43, pp. 1689–706.

7

Positioning the other: naming, address and honorifics

7.1   INTRODUCTION

In this chapter we turn our attention to how language may be used to position the other, with a focus on how address forms vary across cultures. Addressee reference forms have been shown to be a salient means of accomplishing goals related to politeness, power and conversational cohesion. For example, Rendle-Short (2009, p. 262) points out the address term *mate* 'works to emphasize the positive attitude of the speaker toward the hearer, adding a friendly tone to the interaction, orienting to the relaxed nature of the relationship'. In this capacity, *mate* is mobilised in a number of speech acts (e.g. greeting, leave-taking), especially those that are potentially face-threatening (e.g. advice-giving, requests), and to flag potentially problematic talk (e.g. disagreement, lack of clarity) (Rendle-Short 2009).

Such address forms, and the stances asserted with these forms, can contribute to a person's sense of identity and characterise 'an individual's position in his family and in society at large; it defines his social personality' (Mauss 1974, p.134; see also Wolfowitz 1991; Kiesling 2004, 2009; Agha 2007; Bucholtz 2009). Wolfowitz (1991) shows how Javanese speakers in Suriname use kin terms such as *ibu* ('mother') and *pak* ('father') for task-oriented utterances not unlike those noted for *mate* above. Javanese identity is critically linked to one's ability to select the appropriate kin term at the appropriate time and place. For instance, Manns (2011) shows how young Javanese university students in East Java are expected to select the kin terms *mas* ('older brother') or *mbak* ('older sister') with their more senior classmates. This is particularly the case when providing a dispreferred response in unfolding conversation (see Chapter 5). These forms and their use may be linked to the Javanese schema of *sopan* (in a very general sense, 'outward- and other-concerned politeness').

The nuances of naming and address vary widely across cultures. In this chapter, we explore some of these nuances. We begin with a discussion of pronouns of address. We show how these pronouns of address reflect culture-specific organisations of people and how these cultural organisations change over time. We then outline the complexities of naming systems across cultures and how these are mobilised for goals across cultures. Next, we extend our discussion of naming and address to another salient way in which speakers position the self and the other in society: honorifics. For instance, in English one might select the address term *sir* or *madam* when speaking to an individual of higher status than oneself or to index social distance. In some languages, such as Japanese or Javanese, one often must use an entirely different set of nouns and verbs when addressing that person, or indeed even talking about him or her, and these are known as honorifics. We close by reviewing some of the recent approaches posited for conducting research of computer-mediated communication.

7.2 PRONOUNS OF ADDRESS

Pronouns are markers of personal identity in relation to the group. Thus, pronouns of address serve to identify individuals within a given society and their daily usage reinforces personal and social identity. Pronouns are usually regarded as being primarily anaphoric devices, creating cohesion with grammatical structures, and their behaviour is believed to be governed by rules that specify which pronouns can 'replace' which other nominal constructions.

Mühlhäusler (1996, p. 300) points out that in addition to their grammatical and discourse cohesive functions, pronouns are important in the social context. He suggests that pronouns establish the divisions of personal space and the relations between one person and another. Therefore, pronominal systems portray the 'culture-specific organisations of people, space and its limits within which speakers can create speech situations' Mühlhäusler (1996, p. 300).

In most languages, the pronoun form of address has at least two second-person pronouns, such as *thou* and *ye* in early English. Examples of these second-person pronouns in contemporary languages include:

Italian: *tu* and *voi* (*lei* replacing *voi*)
French: *tu* and *vous*

Spanish: *tu* and *vos* (later *usted*)

German: *du* and *ihr* and then also *Sie* (third-person plural as a 'polite' form of 'you')

In many of these languages, the earlier second-person plural forms, for example, *vous*, *vos* and *Sie*, were also used as polite second-person forms, regardless of plurality. Some third-person plural forms, such as *Sie* (German) and *usted* (Spanish) are now used as polite forms of address.

Brown and Gilman (1960) and Brown and Ford (1961) argue that the use of **pronouns of address** is primarily determined by the relationship between the speaker and the hearer, and that this relationship may be interpreted in terms of two semantic dimensions: **power** (or 'status') and **solidarity** (or 'intimacy').[1] Brown and Gilman (1960) introduce the symbols *T* and *V* (Latin *tu* and *vos*) to differentiate the second-person pronouns that denote the 'familiar' (*T*, *tu*) and the 'polite' (*V*, *vos*). They suggest that in Western societies, during the nineteenth century, there was a shift in the 'power semantic' (i.e. hierarchical address system) towards the 'solidarity semantic' (i.e. greater equality between interactants).

T and V have now become generic symbols to designate a familiar (T) and a polite (V) pronoun in any language. In this sense address may be reciprocal or non-reciprocal and symmetrical or asymmetrical. Braun (1988, p.13) explains that:

> Address is reciprocal when two speakers exchange the same form of address (or equivalent ones)... Correspondingly, address is non-reciprocal when the forms used by the two speakers in a dyad are different (or non-equivalent)... All forms of address in a given dyad (interaction) being used reciprocally, the address relationship is symmetrical. When different forms are used, the address relationship is asymmetrical.

The power semantic is characterised by a non-reciprocal, asymmetrical relationship between the speaker and the hearer. Brown and Gilman (1960, p. 255) argue that 'power is a relationship between at least two persons, and it is nonreciprocal in the sense that both cannot have power in the same area of behavior'. The meaning of non-reciprocal V could be *older than*, *parent of*, *employer of*, *richer than*, *stronger than* and *nobler than*, implying a relation of 'more powerful than'.

---

[1] Brown and Gilman (1960, p. 253) define 'semantics' as the 'covariation between the pronoun used and the objective relationship existing between speaker and addressee'.

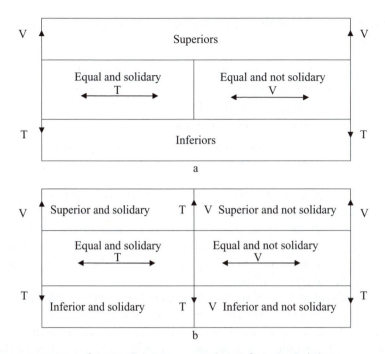

Figure 7.1 Use of T/V in relation to equality/inferiority/solidarity
(Brown & Gilman in Sebeok 1960, p. 259. © 1960 Massachusetts Institute of
Technology, by permission of The MIT Press.)

Brown and Gilman (1960, p. 257) also outline how the shift from a
power semantic to a solidarity semantic may have occurred:

> For many centuries French, English, Italian, Spanish, and German pronoun
> usage followed the rule of nonreciprocal *T-V* between persons of unequal
> power and the rule of mutual *V* or *T* (according to social-class member-
> ship) between persons of roughly equivalent power. There was at first no rule
> differentiating address among equals but, very gradually, a distinction devel-
> oped which is sometimes called the *T* of intimacy and the *V* of formality.
> We name this second dimension *solidarity*.

Brown and Gilman provide the schemas shown in Figure 7.1 to illustrate
the power and solidarity dimensions.

In these schemas, Brown and Gilman distinguish three levels of power:
superior, equal and inferior. In schema (a) the solidary dimension is shown
as only relevant between equals, whereas in scheme (b) solidary is shown

as relevant at each of the three levels of power, creating six categories of relationships:

1. a. superior and solidary: T (e.g. parent to child)
    b. superior and not solidary: T/V (e.g. employer to employee)
2. a. equal and solidary: T
    b. equal and not solidary: V
3. a. inferior and solidary: T/V (e.g. child to parent)
    b. inferior and not solidary: V (e.g. employee to employee).

Moreno (2002, p. 18) points out, with reference to the distinctions drawn by Brown and Gilman, that the T pronoun of solidarity 'can be produced by frequency of contact (if contact results in the creation or discovery of "like-mindedness", behaviour similarities, or affection), as well as by objective similarities of class, political membership, family, religion, profession, sex, or birthplace'.

Pronouns of address reflect the relationship between the speaker and the hearer. The V form (*vos, voi, vous, ihr*) is generally said to indicate formality, whereas the T form (*tu, du*) embodies intimacy. According to this two-dimensional semantic, T is a pronoun of condescension or intimacy and V is used for reverence or formality. Figure 7.2 illustrates the accepted directions of use of these pronouns of address between pairs of speakers in particular relationships.

The first row of dyads in Figure 7.2 exemplify relationships that allow both T and V alternatives to be used to inferior addressees but not vice versa, whereas the second three dyads exemplify relationships that allow both alternatives to superior addressees only. The final six dyads allow only one form, either formal or informal, depending on the relationship between members of the dyad.

The choice of pronouns in those languages with the T and V distinction may be sensitive to salient features of relationships, including respect, deference, intimacy and/or familiarity. In English, however, the distinction between the T and V forms has been lost and other features of the grammar need to be used to code deference and intimacy.

DIFFERING USAGE OF PERSONAL PRONOUNS

The above examples of the use of T and V forms illustrate how speakers of English, Italian, French and German may address each other by using

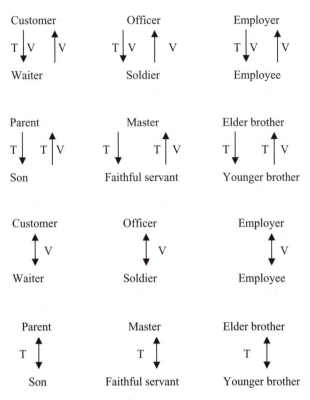

Figure 7.2 Use of pronouns of solidarity
(Brown & Gilman in Sebeok 1960, p. 260. © 1960 Massachusetts Institute of Technology, by permission of The MIT Press.)

second-person pronouns. In a given conversation, the speaker and the hearer change roles according to whose turn it is to speak, that is, who 'has the floor'. Such changes entail a shift in the use of the first- and second-person pronouns. At the beginning of the interaction, the speaker uses the first-person pronoun to denote him or herself; however, when the turn changes and the hearer becomes the speaker, the original speaker becomes the second person. Suzuki (1976, p. 261) suggests that this transfer between first- and second-person pronouns is a clear demonstration that the use of the first-person pronoun at root entails that 'The person who is speaking now is myself' (i.e. it is the linguistic expression of the speaker's role) while the second-person pronoun says to the addressee, 'You are the listener at this point in the conversation'. While this change in personal pronouns and perceived roles seems obvious to speakers of such languages as English, French and German, in Japanese the roles in a conversation and, therefore, the use of pronouns and forms of address, are often fixed. Suzuki (1976, p. 261) argues that:

> In fact, the reason why this class of words is called *personal* pronouns in European languages is that they are pronouns which possess the characteristics of a *persona*, or a player's mask. The interpersonal relationship visible in the interchangeable Latin 'ego' 'tu' transformation, or the English 'I' – 'you' transformation is correspondingly symmetrical.

Suzuki (1976) discusses ways in which formality and familiarity in the pronominal system can be expressed differently. She describes the Japanese method of address using a mixture of what she terms self-specifiers and other-specifiers (personal pronouns and kinship terms). Figure 7.3 is a description of certain specifiers in Japanese that are more complex than the T and V distinction. This figure is written from the perspective of a 40-year-old male teacher. What we see is that there is a variety of relationship terms that are typically used as an alternative to the use of pronouns.

Brown and Gilman's features of formality and intimacy are still very relevant in more complex systems of address, such as the Japanese system exemplified above. However, there are many ways to indicate personal and group identities besides the use of pronouns of address.

TERMS OF ADDRESS IN THE VIRTUAL WORLD

As in the 'real world', in the world of computer-mediated communication (CMC) the use of an incorrect or inappropriate address form can cause great offence and need redress (Usami 2002; Kretzenbacher 2005). For instance, Kretzenbacher (2005, p. 6) suggests that 'neither the T nor the V form *per se* can be said to be the "polite form", but only the form which is agreed upon to be the unmarked form in a particular situation by all participants in that situation'. Kretzenbacher (2005, p. 5) provides the following example taken from a newsgroup in which the administrator (*Christof*) admonishes a newcomer (*werbefrust*) for his or her use of the V form *Sie* instead of the T form *du:*

> *Zum Thema duzen: Im täglichen Leben im Internet ist es KEINE Unsitte sich zu duzen. Es ist sogar gänzlich normal.*
>
> *Andere Länder, andere Sitten, und das Internetist definitiv ein 'eigenes Land'. . . In Anlehnung an das englische 'you' hat sich im Laufe der Zeit im*

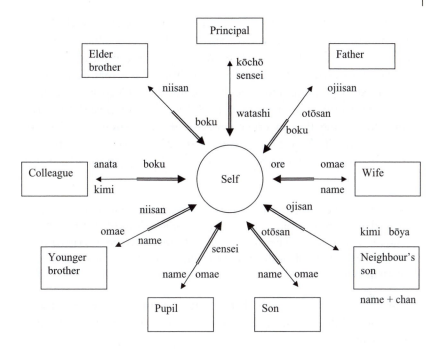

Terms used in Figure 7.3:

Self-specifiers

watakushi (I, formal), *boku* (I, informal), *ore* (I, intimate and vulgar), *ojisan* (uncle), *otōsan* (father), *sensei* (teacher) and *niisan* (elder brother).

Other-specifiers

Besides the second-person pronouns *anata (you,* formal), *kimi* (*you,* informal), *omae* (*you,* intimate and vulgar), we find as other-specifiers the person's name, *ojiisan* (grandfather/old man), *otōsan* and *niisan,* among others.

Figure 7.3 Interaction, communication and grouping
(Suzuki 1976, p. 257)

> *deutschsprachigem Internet durchgesetzt 'Du' zu sagen, unabhängig davon, mit wem man es zu tun hat.*

Regarding *du*-ing: In daily life on the Internet it is NOT bad manners to address each other as *du*. Rather, this is completely normal.

When in Rome, do as the Romans do, and the Internet definitely is 'a different country'... Following the model of English *you*, in the German speaking Internet it has become customary over time to address everybody as *du*, no matter who you are dealing with.

Kretzenbacher (2005) points out that much literature dealing with address in German on the internet, such as Schulze (1999), Bader (2002) and Hess-Lüttich and Wilde (2003), consider *du* as the universal form of address in CMC. However, Kretzenbacher's research illustrates that both *du* and *Sie* are used, depending upon the chat rooms and newsgroup. Based on the above example, the newcomer *werbefrust* did not accept Christof's argument, posting that in other newsgroups '*Sie* address is customary' (Kretzenbacher 2005, p. 5). Kretzenbacher (2005, p. 6) reaches the conclusion based on the research conducted with focus groups and network interviews that:

> in the case of the Usenet, we find a parallel to off-line communication in the coexistence of two systems, one tending towards unmarked *du*, the other towards unmarked *Sie*. These two possible situations have to be negotiated by newcomers, and often this is done on the basis of perceived degree of social distance.

It will remain to be seen whether, as internet use increases, the use of formal *Sie* stabilises or decreases over time, marking internet chat as a distinct genre.

7.3 NOUNS OF ADDRESS

Nouns of address are another means of indicating identity and personal relationships with others. Such forms of address can include:

- names   William
- kinship terms   Father
- titles (honorifics) Mr, Dr
- abstract nouns Your Honour.

NAMES

Each culture has its own naming system. Names and other terms of address may have different functions across societies. Wilson (1998, p. xii) suggests that in contemporary European and North American societies, the family name (or surname) attached to an individual indicates that he or she belongs to that particular family as a legitimate child, whereas the full name shows the 'place and roles within a family'. In contrast, in the languages of the Pacific region, calling a person by his or her name used to be viewed as giving power and/or possessing power over the named person (Mühlhäusler 1996, p. 56). This is also the case in Kyrgyz culture in which it was believed that a first name was 'loaded with power' (Hvoslef 2001, p. 87). Hvoslef also suggests that particular shamans could 'tell the future of an individual only by knowing his or her personal name'. In interviews with Javanese people, we have observed that in Javanese (as in other languages, i.e. Kyrgyz) the choosing of a name was very important to ensure the prosperity of the name bearer. The importance of naming practices is highlighted by Bateson (1980, p. 228) in the following quote concerning the Iatmul of New Guinea:

> The naming system is indeed a theoretical image of the whole culture and in it every formulated aspect of culture is reflected. Conversely, we may say that the system has its branches in every aspect of the culture and gives its support to every cultural activity. Every spell, every song... contains lists of names. The utterances of shamans are couched in terms of names... Marriages are often arranged in order to gain names. Reincarnation and succession are based upon the naming system. Land tenure is based on clan membership and clan.

Names may change as an individual progresses through life. For example, changes in names may occur at puberty, marriage, death of father or mother, or when there is a change in job. An individual may also be addressed differently depending on the context – such as the name employed by a close relative, a business associate, an acquaintance, by friends, in public, by spouses, and the list continues. Last names may also vary according to whether the referent is a female or male. For example, in Russian a man might have the last name of *Petrov*, while the woman would have the feminine *Petrova*. Another example of gender differences is found among Sikh Indians: men and women may have similar 'given' names, but their gender is marked by the use of 'Singh' for males and 'Kaur' for females. In Australia, however, 'Singh' is often adopted as a surname by Sikh Indians (males) and the general population views this as the last name of both the females and males.

The following example from Hvoslef (2001, p. 86) shows how the use of personal names may vary according to the culture and context. This example comes from the Kyrgyz Republic, one of the 15 new states that emerged after the dissolution of the Soviet Union:

> Dinara and Anara Khasanbaeva are, together with the driver, Asan Sartbai, heading towards the small village of Ensjilesj where the two girls were born

and raised some thirty years ago... [They are] meeting *tai ake* Toktobai ('mother's brother') and *tai ene* Burulusj ('mother's mother')... Toktobai turns toward Asan and asks him who he is and where his relatives come from. Asan... presents himself as *Kanat uulu Asanbek Sartbai* (*Kanat* = the personal name of his father, *uulu* = son, *Asan* = his own first name, *Sartbai* = the personal name of one of his ancestors). He continues telling that his relatives have their place of origin in a village near Naryn and that the name of his clan is 'Suksur' and the tribe 'Sajak'.

From the boy's name Toktobai can read that Asan is son of Kanat and that one of his forefathers probably had the personal name Sartbai.

In Kyrgyz society the personal name described an individual's relationships with others and some personal qualities. Traditionally, the Kyrgyz language didn't have a last name/surname as such, but in recent times the naming practices have changed under the influence of Russian, and the equivalent of a surname has now been adopted.

It is obvious from the above discussion that naming practices differ widely across cultures. The incorrect usage of a particular name or not being aware of differing naming systems could lead to miscommunication and ultimately insult and hurt.

USE OF FIRST NAMES

In an intercultural context, the inappropriate use of first names can cause great harm and offence. Bargiela et al. (2002, p. 1) argue that 'for many British and American (English) speakers informality is taken to be an indicator of ease of communication with strangers'. However in other cultures (Russian, Chinese, Italian and Arabic) such informality is seen as being overfamiliar and thus impolite, and instead distancing strategies in naming and addressing are employed to show politeness (e.g. use of first name plus an honorific). While Bargiela et al. (2002, p. 4) acknowledge that naming practices in different English-speaking countries such as Australia, Britain and America do differ, they indicate that 'the general rule in English speaking cultures is that you move to first name terms as soon as possible'.

Scollon, Scollon and Jones (2012) provide an example of how this English-speaking strategy of first name usage can cause problems when interacting with people from a Chinese language background. In the anecdote, an American, Andrew Richardson, introduces himself to a Chinese person by saying 'Call me Andy'. In response, the Chinese person gives his business card, which has the first name 'Hon-fai'. Andrew Richardson decides to call the man Hon-fai, based on his own English naming strategy of using the 'first name'. However, Scollon, Scollon and Jones (2012) observe that in this situation, the use of the name 'Hon-fai' is only for intimates, and not strangers. Consequently, instead of establishing a sense of rapport and friendliness, the use of such a 'first name' caused great embarrassment and discomfort due to the inappropriate use of an intimate form of address where distance, and not familiarity (non-reciprocal form), was regarded as a polite naming strategy.

Bargiela et al. (2002) further contrast Georgian and Russian naming practices and the use of first names and/or diminutive forms when addressing a person for the first time. The example given to illustrate this point is an exchange between a Georgian female patient and a young Russian female doctor in Moscow (in Russian). The Georgian female wants to show her familiarity and friendliness to the Russian doctor who is substituting for the professor/consultant at the hospital, so she asks whether she can address the doctor using a diminutive form of her first name (Bargiela et al. 2002, p. 5):

A[G]:   *mèzna j' vas budu nazivat' galicka?*
        (May I call you 'Galichka'?)[2]
B[R]:   *net, pèzaluísta*
        (No, please, don't.)

In Georgian, the use of this informal diminutive would have been appropriate; in Russian, however, such usage is regarded as not showing sufficient deference or respect. In Russian, the appropriate form of address would have been the first name plus a patronymic (Bargiela et al. 2002, p. 5). In this particular example, the rejection of the diminutive first name usage shows a conflict in the cultural values associated with the meaning of using the first name.

As may be seen in the above examples, Georgians, like the British and Americans, regard the reciprocal first name usage as indicating familiarity and friendliness. However, in other languages such usage may be interpreted as being overfamiliar and impolite. This is because in those languages (e.g. Russian) a level of deference is appropriate when asymmetrical power and status differences exist.

---

[2]   *Galichka* is the informal short form for the Russian first name *Galina*.

NICKNAMES

Nicknames serve numerous functions over and above that of the merely referential purpose of first names. Their usage may portray physical and personal characteristics of the name holders (e.g. *porky, dumbo*), place/heritage (*surgeon, Turk, American, Sweedy*) and emotion (*puppy, awks*), among other things (Starks, Taylor-Leech & Willoughby 2012). In general, nicknames develop spontaneously among people who know each other intimately and there is a high degree of familiarity between the interactants. Nicknames may be signs of endearment as well as of friendship and often signal a person's social and cultural position within a group. Affectionate nicknames may be diminutive forms of names such as *Sher* for *Sheryl* or *Billy* for *William*. Some nicknames, especially in English-speaking countries, are referred to as 'inevitable nicknames' in that individuals having certain last names are given a pre-existing nickname. These include *Thompson* becoming *Tommo* and *Webb* becoming *Spider* (Beale 1990).

De Klerk and Bosch (1997, p. 298) observe that diminutive forms with a final 'ee' sound (e.g. the sound at the end of *Katy, Lizzie*) are more frequent in English than for male nicknames (e.g. *Tommo* or *Dave*). In Australia name puns are an important source of nicknames. Heather Bowe recalls that her sister, Olwen, was called *Oboe* by close school friends, who then called Heather *Clarinet* ('sister of Oboe'). Furthermore, in Australia the acquisition of a nickname and its acceptance by people of non-English-speaking backgrounds (e.g. German and Chinese backgrounds) creates a greater level of familiarity and solidarity between people of differing language backgrounds and can help to more readily establish new identities within the wider Australian community.

Nicknames and their associated identities, in the emerging medium of computer-mediated communication (CMC), have also become an important means of identifying the participants in online chat rooms and newsgroups. Bays (1998, p. 11) observes that online, a nickname or *nick* 'can be anything from numbers and punctuation to a highly personal and/or evocative name' and potentially contains numerous sociological cues (e.g. gender, approximate age, music and sports interests). Examples may include *camel66, musiclover33, Iamsohot1* and *Birdie_sunneyman*. She further points out that 'the nickname is the first sign of individuality when one encounters another participant. It serves as a first impression and shows the aspect of *face* that the participant wants to present on-line' (1998, p. 11). In addition, a nickname has the function of beginning a person's *line*, which is followed by other verification process attempts to discover the authenticity of the nickname adopted and the information contained in the *line*. Bays (1998. p. 11) comments on the relationship between the virtual and physical world of nicknaming practices:

> The criteria for the construction of the online identity diverges from that of the physical person . . . with each successive nickname one can assert a new individuality and recreate the limits of his 'self', whereas in the physical world one is technically less able to change his identity with such malleability . . . the (online) participant technically can question his identity on a physical, superficial, social level each time he connects. In contrast, because the referent is less changeable, in the physical world the connection between one's name and one's physical identity is much stronger.

However, while it may appear that in a virtual world there is no end to the great diversity and flexibility in the adoption of nicknames, Schiano (1997) argues that as the majority of online users develop a sense of 'CMC maturity', 'the perceived anonymity of early days develops into pseudonymy, where participants reciprocally recognize each other' and a more stable and set identity is adopted (Bays 1998). Consequently, nicknames used in cyberspace act as a marker or representative that individualises its name holder or, in this case, the online participant, just as in the physical world.

KINSHIP TERMS

Kin terms relate to blood relations or are extensions of these blood ties. Agha (2007, p. 263) calls the latter metaphorical kin terms, noting that there are 'cases where the persons performatively related to each other through the use of kinterms [sic] are known to be non-kin'. For instance, in English a male friend of one's parents' generation may be called *uncle* and a female *aunt* or *aunty*. Kinship relationships are of great importance to intercultural communication. In some cultures such as the Japanese, Korean, Vietnamese and Chinese, kinship relationships reflect the hierarchical social structure. The use of kinship terms reinforces the importance of the relationships they code. Suzuki (1976) uses the concept of kinship as the basis of her description of forms of address in Japanese society. She characterises terms of address in terms of distinctions between self and other, and intra- and extra-familial, as shown below.

Self-specifiers: these terms are used to denote the speaker (personal pronouns) (see above discussion). The choice of self-specifier is determined

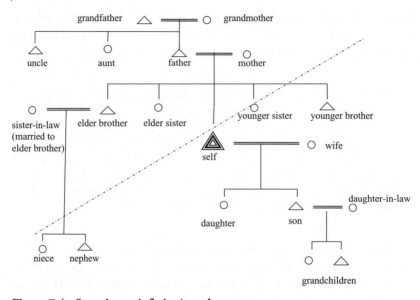

Figure 7.4 Superior vs inferior/equal status
(Suzuki 1976, p. 257)

by the relationship between the speaker and the hearer. A choice of self-specifiers reflects power differences and gradations of social distance.

Other-specifiers: these terms are used to denote the hearer or third person.

Intra-familial self-specifiers and other specifiers: Suzuki proposes five principles to account for the ways in which a speaker may refer to self and others, according to whether the 'other' is in the group of superiors or inferiors (see below for details).

Extra-familial self-specifiers: Japanese speakers expand the five principles of intra-familial specifiers to the community at large. **Societal specifiers** are used in place of the familial terms but the superior–inferior relationship is maintained.

Suzuki (1976) argues that these self- and other-specifiers are similar to personal pronouns (see above discussion of T and V forms). However, unlike pronouns, these terms are based on kinship relationships. As a result of the hierarchical nature of kinship relations, the use of these terms may be reciprocal or non-reciprocal and symmetrical or asymmetrical, similar to that of the use of T and V pronouns. Suzuki provides an example of the intra-familial self-specifiers and other-specifiers to explain the address system in Japanese. Figure 7.4 is taken from Suzuki (1976), and is used in her explanation of the five principles that relate to the 'boundaries of superior and inferior relations... among members of a family or relationship group'.

The relationships in Figure 7.4 are shown from the perspective of a 40-year-old teacher. Those above the diagonal broken line are treated as superiors and those below are regarded as either being inferior or equal in relation to self. Suzuki's five principles are:

A. The speaker (self) cannot address other relatives above his locus in the family by means of personal pronouns. He is not permitted, for example, to address his father as anata (you formal) or kimi (you informal), and the same strictures apply when he addresses, say, his elder brother.

B. The speaker addresses people above his station in the family, as a rule, by use of terms denoting their relationship to him. But he does not address people below himself by the terms for those relationships. He would not, for example, call his younger brother vocatively with a phrase like, 'Hey! Ototo (younger brother)!' nor would he ask pronominally his daughter, 'Where is Musume (daughter) going?'[3]

C. The speaker may not address people located above himself by their names alone (unless suffixed by an appropriate kin term), but may so address those located below him.

D. Speakers, especially female speakers, may, in addressing people above themselves, use their own names as self-specifiers, but may not do so in conversation with people located below them. Thus, Yoshiko (daughter) may say to her mother, 'Momma, Yoshiko hates that,' but her mother may not use her own name in a similar situation in conversation with her daughter.

E. In conversation with relations below himself the speaker may use as a self-specifier the term indicating his own relationship to the addressee, but a junior speaker may not do this in speaking to a senior one. In a conversation between brothers, for example, then, the brother may specify himself by saying 'niisan', but the younger brother may not use 'ototochan' to indicate himself.

(Suzuki 1976, pp. 257–8)

7.4   HONORIFICS

Honorifics (or more accurately honorific language features) are used in a general sense to convey honour or respect to an addressee (Agha 1998).

---

[3] A parent doesn't refer to a child as 'daughter' but would either use a pronoun or the child's name.

English speakers most commonly use abstract nouns in titles as *honorifics* (e.g. *Your Honour*). Titles themselves may be prefixed or suffixed to names, terms of occupation or they may just be free (e.g. *Mrs* and *Mr* in English). The honorific registers in languages are traditionally viewed as a means of showing respect and deference or to convey honour. However, Agha (1998, p. 153) argues that honorific speech also serves other roles, such as 'control and domination, irony, innuendo, and masked aggression'. Honorific discourse is usually associated with both linguistic and non-linguistic elements (e.g. gesture, dress, or bodily posture of the interactants).

Agha (1998, p. 153) suggests that 'every language contains some items that conventionally possess honorific value; for example, every language contains honorific titles'. Examples include *Herr/Frau/Fräulein* in German, the first name and the patronymic in Russian, and *Mr/Mrs/Miss/Ms* in English. In Japanese, the equivalents of such titles are suffixes attached to an individual's first or last name, such as *-sama*, *-san*, *-kun* and *-chan*, as shown below:

-sama	the formal version of *-san*, and is used primarily in addressing persons of much higher rank and in commercial and business settings to address customers. It is also used to address or speak of persons or things for which the speaker wishes to show deference, *kami-sama* (spirits or deities). It is also found following a person's name in addresses on envelopes and frequently appears in business emails.
-san	(e.g. Yoshida-*san*): used for both single and married people and when attached to the last name/family name conveys a greater degree of formality. (It is never used as a self-specifier.)
-kun	(e.g. Takahiro-*kun*): used when addressing people of equal or lower status. It is also commonly used for boys of primary and secondary school ages, whereas *-san* is the equivalent for girls.
-chan	(e.g. Yoko-*chan*): used to express intimacy and familiarity between close friends and for children.

Agha (1998, p.153) points out that different languages use different methods to indicate honorific language. These may consist of the use of titles and terms of address as well as honorific forms, including pronouns, nouns, verbs and adverbs. The use of the honorific register often marks a social relationship of respect among the interactants.

Honorific abstract nouns in English include *Your Honour, Your Grace, Your Majesty, Your Highness* and *Your Excellency*, and all occur with possessive pronouns. English also contains such nouns of address as *Ladies and Gentlemen* to address a group and the nouns *Sir* and *Madam* to address individuals. Occupational terms, such as *doctor*, can also be used in English either as an honorific title such as *Dr Murphy*, or as an honorific (e.g. *Doctor, could you please...*). In Japanese, other occupational terms such as *sensei* 'teacher' are also used in these two ways: *Yoshida sensei* or just *sensei*. Koyama (1992, p. 46) points out that the term *sensei* 'is often employed as a general term to refer to a person of higher status – a teacher, a doctor or even a politician'.

HONORIFIC LANGUAGE USE

The Javanese speaker may use a number of pronominal, lexical and prosodic codes to index his or her relationship vis-à-vis an interlocutor (e.g. Geertz 1960; Kartomihardjo 1981; Errington 1985a, 1988; Siegel 1986; Keeler 1990; Kurniasih 2006). In order to understand these speech levels, Geertz (1976, p. 173) uses the metaphor of a protective barrier to explain the levels of politeness and formality in behaviour in traditional Javanese culture. The features of this barrier depend on the people involved in a given language context. These levels differ as a result of obligatory distinctions according to differences in status, rank, seniority and degree of regular acquaintance between the addresser and addressee (Errington 1985a, pp. 10–11). Each speech level is a metonym for social situations in traditional Javanese society. If a Javanese person fails to use a speech level correctly in a given situation, he or she may be called *durung njawani* ('not yet Javanese'), which implies a level of immaturity or being 'less than fully human'. The proper behaviour of Javanese people depends first on the control of the proper forms of linguistic expression, and second on the ability to choose the appropriate etiquette pattern by properly determining the social relations.

The Javanese speech styles are varyingly described as having three to 12 different levels. However, most discussions refer to the speech styles in terms of a continuum of Low Javanese (*ngoko*) at one end and High Javanese (*krama*) at the other. *Ngoko* is the 'basic' language people use to speak to intimates or inferiors, express anger and humiliate their superiors. *Krama*, the honorific register, is employed to show a level of respect and honour when addressing people who are older, unfamiliar and superior (Koentjaraningrat 1989, pp. 16–18). The differences in the speech level are outlined by Kurniasih (2006, p. 6) (with reference to the medial *madya* style):

Ngoko:	Bu Kusmi	arep	lunga	pasar	tuku	jarik
Madya:	Bu Kusmi	ajeng	kesah	peken	tumbas	sinjang
Krama:	Bu Kusmi	badhe	tindak	peken	mundhut	nyamping
English:	Mrs Kusmi	is going	to go	market	to buy	a skirt

(Kurniasih 2006, p. 6)

The basic semantic meaning of these three sentences is the same. However, a speaker will vary his or her lexical choices based on such considerations as age, sex, status by birth, financial or educational attainment, family and marital connections, and intimacy (Kartomihardjo 1981). In other words, a speaker addressing an intimate friend may use the word *pasar* ('market'), but when addressing an individual of higher status must select *peken* though the referred to market has not changed. In traditional Javanese culture, every person needs to be aware of his or her position in society and act accordingly. Thus, if the social behaviour and the use of the correct speech level are inappropriate, the addresser or addressee is not at all well regarded.

Japanese is another language example that uses a complex system of linguistic features for honorific purposes (e.g. Koyama 1992; Burdelski 2013; Cook 2013; Geyer 2013). Koyama (1992) gives the example of Tom, an exchange student who has been living with a Japanese host family for nearly one year. One day, Tom gives his host sister Yoko a birthday present. However, Yoko appears to become quite angry when Tom uses the verb *yarimasu* ('to give') when addressing her. Her response is *So you think I'm inferior to you, do you? After all, you're younger than me* (in English). According to Koyama, this example illustrates the problems using the appropriate language register in Japanese society.

The use of particular word forms depends on the age and status (power vs solidarity) of the interactants – that is, the superior–inferior relationship. In Japanese 'to give' could be expressed using *yarimasu*, *agemasu* and *sashiagemasu*. The use and meaning of these verbs are as follows:

yarimasu:	used by a superior speaking to an inferior
agemasu:	a neutral form used with a hearer of equal status (i.e. between friends)
sashiagemasu:	an honorific form used with a hearer of equal status in a distant social relationship or by an inferior speaking to a superior

(adapted from Koyama 1992, p. 33)

The appropriate use of such forms is essential in successfully communicating in the Japanese context. In Japanese culture the roles between interactants are generally fixed and dependent on age, social distance and the status between the people in a given conversation. We have observed while living and researching in Japan that the strict usage of honorific forms is changing in modern Japanese society. However, the misuse of such forms can still lead to offence and discomfort, and result in the addresser or the addressee being poorly regarded.

Thus, honorific discourse is part of a complex interactional system that uses both linguistic and non-linguistic elements to convey respect, deference and solidarity. As illustrated above, all languages and cultures use honorific forms whether they be honorific titles or a more complex system of pronouns, nouns, verbs and adverbs.

7.5   METHODOLOGIES: COMPUTER-MEDIATED COMMUNICATION

Computer-mediated communication (CMC) presents a series of new challenges to researchers concerned with language and intercultural communication. At the onset, it has led theorists to ask such broad questions such as 'Does the Internet have a culture?' (Macfadyen, Roche & Doff 2004, p. 12). Most relevant to intercultural communication, researchers have sought to understand how CMC's symbolic resources overlap with or differ from those of the 'real world'. For instance, CMC consists of a style of language that is neither spoken nor written (Crystal 2006). Furthermore, prosodic and paralinguistic cues (e.g. intonation, facial expressions) are unavailable in CMC and this has led to a range of alternative strategies (e.g. creative orthography, emoticons). In any case, researchers remain highly polarised about what CMC means for language and culture and how the medium should be approached methodologically (Macfadyen, Roche & Doff 2004).

Many researchers have sought to understand how patterns of interaction unfold in CMC (Harrison 2003) and what implications these have for intercultural communication (Sugimoto & Levine 2000). Identity, of course, is a nebulous concept in CMC (e.g. Kitalong & Kitalong 2000; Miller & Slater 2001). Some propose that the internet marks a domain of anonymity where one may assume any identity without impunity (see Christopherson 2007). Still others propose that group identity becomes even more salient within CMC. For instance, the Social Identity Model of

Deindividuation Effects (SIDE) has been applied to the CMC context and been used to show that individuals are even more apt to conform to social norms and value a discernible group identity in CMC than in face-to-face interactions (Lea & Spears 1991; Haines & Mann 2011).

Researchers have often found traditional 'spoken language' methodologies such as ethnography (e.g. Miller & Slater 2001), systemic-functional linguistics (e.g. Belz 2003) and Conversation Analysis (e.g. González-Lloret 2011) to be useful for framing CMC. However, these methodologies sometimes need to be modified in light of CMC's differing conventions. For instance, Miller and Slater (2001) conducted an ethnography of Trinidadian diaspora identity in both the CMC and real-world contexts. That said, some researchers have proposed new and innovative approaches for CMC. For example, Bucher (2002), reviewed by Macfadyen, Roche and Doff (2003, p. 30), posits 'a more meaningful approach to understanding the relationship between Internet and communication and culture needs to shift the focus away from the communicator and onto the "power of the audience"'.

7.6   SUMMARY

Pronouns, names and terms of address are important for identifying individuals and their role in society and their use serves to maintain social cohesion. Names and terms of address can also influence the individual's perception of self and relationships. The linguistic choice of forms of address can be sensitive to the age of the speaker and hearer, the medium of communication (physical and virtual worlds), social status (i.e. power vs solidarity), social distance (superior–inferior relationships or equals) and even someone's physical and personal attributes (especially for nicknames). Each culture and language has its own differing norms for the correct usage of forms of address. Clyne and Platt (1990, p. 46) suggest that when dealing with differing forms of address across cultures:

> the most appropriate strategy is to be alert, to enquire and not to be surprised about differences from the English language system.

To close this chapter, we briefly reviewed some of the issues encountered by researchers concerned with CMC as well as how they coped with these issues. See Macfadyen, Roche and Doff (2003) for a bibliographical review of intercultural research related to CMC.

7.7 REVIEW

1. **Key terms**

   Forms of address, pronouns of address, semantics of pronouns of address, T and V, honorifics, speaker, addressee, power, solidarity, superiors and inferiors, group styles, nicknames, self-specifiers, other-specifiers, intra- and extra-familial, roles.

2. **Key ideas**

   Having read this chapter you should:

   a. understand the significance of the (unspoken) rules that lie behind such practices as the assignment of nicknames, the employment of special forms of address, and the ascription of honorific titles

   b. understand, and be able to critique, in the light of inter- and cross-cultural evidence, the 'universality' claims relating to systems of address

   c. appreciate how naming practices are employed in particular cultures.

3. **Focus questions**

   a. Pronouns of address

   (i) Using Brown and Gilman's (1960) dyads in Figure 7.2 to identify the T and/or V distinctions, describe what would be the appropriate pronouns of address in the following situations:

   – between a second-year undergraduate student and a department head at university

   – between fellow classmates in a mathematics class at high school

   – between a customer and a customer service person at a big department store (e.g. Wal-Mart or Kmart)

   – between an undergraduate student and an administrative officer at university.

   If you speak a language other than English as your first language, or if you are very familiar with another language, then also consider your answer using that language.

   (ii) What are the salient features that influence your choice of T and V forms of address? As in the above question, if you speak a language other than English as your first language, or if you are very familiar with another language, then also consider your answer using that language.

   b. Nicknames

   Nicknames serve numerous functions over and above that of the merely referential one of first names.

   (i) What nicknames, if any, have you personally acquired? What are the functions of these nicknames?

   (ii) What is the meaning associated with these nicknames and the social contexts of their use?

c. Nicknames online

In CMC the use of a nickname and/or *nick* may be used to provide anonymity and pseudonymy.

   (i) What examples of a nickname have you encountered in your experience in online chat rooms and newsgroups?

   (ii) Does the use of such nicknames online differ from those used in the physical world?

d. Use of first names

Do you agree with the statement by Bargiela et al. (2002) that 'the general rule in English-speaking cultures is that you move to first name terms as soon as possible'? Provide two examples to illustrate your opinion. Try to use examples in which the interactants are from different language backgrounds. If you speak a language other than English as your first language, or if you are very familiar with another language, then consider your answer from the perspective of that language and cultural group.

4. Research analysis

a. Avoidance of naming

Consider the following extract taken from Bargiela et al. (2002, p. 12) describing a naming strategy employed by British people.

> Many British people have adopted the strategy of not using names at all in certain circumstances to avoid the difficulty of finding the appropriate form of address. For example, it used to be relatively acceptable to summon a waiter in a restaurant by calling out 'Waiter'; however, this is a very rare practice now, and saying 'Excuse me', gesturing or trying to catch the waiter's eye is now far more common. This avoidance of naming is also made more complicated by not knowing what is the correct name for someone because of changes in the way that women, in particular, name themselves. Thus, it is not self-evident that the wife of Mr Jones will be called Mrs Jones. Nor will it be clear whether a woman wishes to be called Mrs, Miss or Ms. First name use for women has been identified as problematic, since it is far more frequently used in relation to women than to men and may be considered demeaning, overly familiar and even infantilising. Thus, a frequent strategy in Britain, when meeting people for the first time, is either to wait until they have introduced themselves or have been introduced, before using a name, or to use no name at all.

(i) Have you ever encountered a naming practice, such as that described in the above quote, or employed one yourself in order to avoid any offence or misunderstanding? Besides the example contexts given, in what other contexts do you think such a naming practice would be acceptable in the English-speaking world?

(ii) In cultures where the preferred naming strategy is to use a name or an honorific to show deference and respect, what would be the consequences of avoidance of naming in an intercultural context? To illustrate your opinion, provide three examples of cultures in which such a naming practice might be considered impolite.

(iii) If a person intends to show solidarity and friendship with their interlocutor, what would be the most appropriate naming strategy to use? If a person wants to show deference, what would be the naming strategies he or she would use? How would social differences such as age, education and job status affect such naming practices? If you speak a language other than English as your first language, or if you are very familiar with another language, then also consider your answer using that language. Provide at least two different language examples.

b. **Use of T and V forms**

Consider the following consumer opinions of the use of the German T and V forms of address in corporate/business situations reported by Kretzenbacher (2005, pp. 10, 12) in response to the questions 'Have you ever been addressed with a form you didn't expect? When, by whom?'

Consumer 1:

Wenn es förmlich ist, wenn es um einen Vertrag geht, kann ich es überhaupt nicht leiden, wenn man sich mit du anspricht, weil man dann in so eine unformale Ebene fällt, wo es immer ganz schwer ist, seine Interessen durchzusetzen. Ein Beispiel ist, ich wollte ein Auto kaufen, da kam der Mann zu mir und sagte, was für ein tolles Auto es war und du... und so... das war in diesem Moment extrem unpassend. Das war ein seriöses Geschäft, da möchte man sich nicht duzen... ich hab ihn zurückgesiezt, aber er hat mich geduzt. Das war ein eigenartiger Mensch. Das war unangenehm.

[In a formal situation, if it is about a contract, I don't appreciate it at all if one is on a *du* basis, because it moves one to such an informal level at which it is always very difficult to see to one's own interests. One example is, I wanted to buy a car, and this man approached me and told me what a brilliant car it was... and addressed me as *du*... and so... that was extremely inappropriate at that moment. That was a serious business transaction, one does not want to be on a *du* basis there... I returned a *Sie* address, but he addressed me as *du*. That was an odd person. It was unpleasant.]

Consumer 2:
Sogar im aktuellen Ikea-katalog wird man neuerdings geduzt, und das obwohl die seit jahren ihr studi-image erfolgreich hinter sich gelassen haben. Befremdlich.

[Even in the new IKEA catalogue one is addressed as *du* now; even though they have succeeded in leaving behind their student image for years. Disconcerting.]

(i) In the above examples, why do you think the use of the T form of address *du* caused such annoyance? Give reasons.

(ii) Based on the above consumer responses, why is there such reluctance in accepting the *du* form by consumers in consumer advertising in German? From the consumer's perspective, what is the meaning associated with the use of the T form *du*, instead of the V form *Sie*?

(iii) Why do you believe that IKEA has adopted the use of the T form in its advertising? What advantage is there for IKEA to use the T form instead of the V form in its marketing strategy?

(iv) From the perspective of the customer what would have been the most appropriate form of address for the car salesman to use with consumer 1? Why do you think the salesperson used the reciprocal pronoun of address (T form), even after the customer used the non-reciprocal *Sie* form?

5. **Research exercise**
Within your own extended family, what names, pronouns and other forms of address are used to address your family members from an inter-generation perspective (e.g. those forms of address used between grand-child and grandparent, child and parent, between siblings, between husband and wife).

SUGGESTED FURTHER READING

As with earlier chapters, we recommend revisiting the classics for a firm theoretical grounding in pronouns and terms of address. For pronouns, this means looking at Roger Brown's work with colleagues. For terms of address, the text by Mühlhäusler and Harré makes a good starting point, as does Braun. For more recent work on pronouns, Indonesian scholars such as Djenar have done excellent work shedding light on that language's complex pronominal system. For more recent work on address terms, we recommend Bucholtz, Kiesling and Rendle-Short. Lastly, indexical salience and its relevance to communication has been raised a few times in this chapter and the previous one. Errington's foundational paper on indexical salience (based on the Javanese speech styles) is worth a read, as is Woolard's reflections on indexical salience's relevance to the contemporary sociolingusitic endeavour.

Braun, F. 1988 *Terms of Address: Problems of Patterns and Usage in Various Languages and Cultures.* Berlin: Mouton de Gruyter.

Brown, R. & Ford, M. 1961 'Address in American English'. *Journal of Abnormal and Social Psychology*, vol. 67, pp. 375–85.

Brown, R. & Gilman, A. 1960 'The pronouns of power and solidarity'. In Sebeok, T. A. (ed.) *Style in Language*. New York: Technology Press of MIT.

Bucholtz, M. 2009 'From stance to style: Gender, interaction, and indexicality in Mexican immigrant youth slang'. In Jaffe, A. (ed.) *Stance: Sociolinguistic Perspectives*. New York: Oxford, pp. 146–90.

Djenar, D. N. 2006 'Patterns and variation of address terms in colloquial Indonesian'. *Australian Review of Applied Linguistics*, vol. 29, no. 2, pp. 22.1–22.16.

Errington, J. 1985b 'On the nature of the sociolinguistic sign: Describing the Javanese speech levels'. In Mertz E. (ed.) *Semiotic Mediation: Sociocultural and Psychological Perspectives*. London: Academic Press, pp. 287–310.

Kiesling, S. 2004 'Dude' *American Speech*, vol. 79, no. 3, pp. 281–305.

Mühlhäusler, P. & Harré, R. 1990 *Pronouns and People. The Linguistic Construction of Social and Personal Identity*. Oxford: Blackwell.

Rendle-Short, J. 2009 'The address term mate in Australian English: Is it still a masculine term?'. *Australian Journal of Linguistics*, vol. 29, no. 2, pp. 245–68.

Woolard, K. 2008 'What dat now?: Linguistic-anthropological contributions to the explanation of sociolinguistic icons and change'. *Journal of Sociolinguistics*, vol. 12, no. 4, pp. 432–52.

8 | Cultural differences in writing

8.1   INTRODUCTION

V ARIATION IN THE organisation of writing across cultures has been studied from a number of perspectives. Givón (1983) developed a quantitative model for cross-language discourse analysis to measure topic continuity (thematic, action and topic/participant continuity) in a number of languages. Kaplan (1966, 1972, 1988) pioneered research in the area of contrastive rhetoric (also known as contrastive discourse analysis) by examining variation in the organisation of writing by writers from different language/cultural traditions (see also Connor & Kaplan 1987). Connor (2008, 2011) and Connor, Nagelhout and Rozycki (2008) have introduced the term 'intercultural rhetoric' to underscore the global orientation of their recent research in this area.

Research in the field of genre analysis (Swales, 1990, 2004; Bhathia 1993, 2004) and corpus analysis (Johansson 1998) has also recently started to include writing produced by researchers writing in a second language as a means of global communication.

The field of discourse analysis has developed in other important ways over the past three decades, emphasising the importance of social context, including variables such as audience and purpose; processes such as revision and collaboration; and interactional aspects of writing, such as expectations of a particular discourse community, the latter explored in the work of Fairclough (1992), Gee (1999, 2005) and Hyland (2000, 2004, 2005, 2009). Analysis of the use of particular textual elements has also developed fresh perspectives – for example, the studies reported in Hyland and Sancho-Guinda's (2012) edited volume *Stance and Voice in Written Academic Genres*. Fløttum (2012, pp. 218 ff.) reports on a selection of other research on cross-cultural academic discourse with a focus of stance and voice, including Mauranen (1993), Vassileva (2000) and the work of the Norwegian KIAP project[1] (Fløttum et al. 2008; Fløttum 2010).

The transition from the comparison of writing from different cultures to the analysis of writing produced in intercultural contexts has called for new writing corpora. Connor (2011, p. 47) emphasises the importance of assembling comparable corpora of L1 (first-language) and L2 (second-language) writing. Pérez-Llantada's (2012) study, *Scientific Discourse and the Rhetoric of Globalization*, is a good example of the kind of intercultural research Connor is calling for. Pérez-Llantada provides a comprehensive study of intercultural writing, drawing on cross-linguistic and intercultural corpora in the field of academic discourse to provide comparative text analysis as well as a complementary ethnographic analysis of the writing context.

In this chapter, we examine some of the research based on Kaplan's contrastive rhetoric approach, including Hinds (1980) on Japanese and Clyne (1987) on English and German. We also examine research on writing in the intercultural context, in the section on letter writing (8.7) and in the section on academic writing in the global context (8.8). The latter includes Pérez-Llantada's (2012) research, which compares academic writing from three sub-corpora: L1 English scholars, L1 Spanish scholars and scholars of Spanish-speaking background who are writing in L2 English. Pérez-Llantada illustrates the development of hybridity in written discourse in the practice of intercultural/global communication by L2 writers.

8.2   LINEARITY: A KEY PRINCIPLE OF ENGLISH WRITTEN DISCOURSE

Kaplan (1966, 1972) contrasted various discourse types with the **linear** structure of English writing, most typically exemplified in English expository prose. Key features of the English expository style are taken to include:

- a clear, concise and defined thesis statement that occurs in the first paragraph of the essay
- clear and logical transitions between the introduction, body and conclusions
- body paragraphs that include evidential support

---

[1] KIAP is a Norwegian acronym for Cultural Identity and Academic Prose, a research project involving analysis of research articles (from the disciplines of economics, linguistics and medicine) written in three languages (English, Norwegian and French), which is coordinated by Kjersti Fløttum.

- a conclusion that does not simply restate the thesis, but readdresses it in the light of evidence provided
- relevance is advocated as the primary virtue to be striven for in the construction of an essay
- repetition is deemed undesirable.

In English-speaking countries, the expectations of expository prose, including linearity, are directly taught through the education system, at secondary schools, and in the United States through a required first-year subject taught in most universities. In the global context, such conventions are taught in English as a second language/English for specific purposes classes.

The comparison of English writing conventions with those from other language traditions continues to be of interest, as seen, for instance, in the following brief account by Fløttum (2012):

> Mauranen (1993)... compares the style of Anglo-American and Finish scholars, and her chief finding is that the English scientific style is more explicit and direct than the Finnish one. More specifically, Anglo-Americans usually start their papers with their main point(s), whereas the Finns prefer to reserve them to the end. This directness and explicitness of scientific English in contrast with other languages has been substantiated by Vassileva's stylistic study (2000) of English, Romance and Slavic, and by that of Fløttum et al (2006) of English French and Norwegian.
>
> (Fløttum 2012, p. 219)

Pérez-Llantada (2012, pp. 127 ff.), in her research on scientific discourse in the global context, refers to the awareness of the Anglophone normative model expressed by writers and reviewers of academic articles. Of journal referees from a North American university Pérez-Llantada reports: 'their comments as reviewers made it clear that clarity and simplicity of style are a must'. She reports similar comments made by L1 Spanish academics about their own writing:

> In [English] we use long sentences and paragraphs, sometimes too pompous, and this is totally different from the more straight-to-the-point, short sentences in English academic writing.
>
> (Pérez-Llantada 2012, p. 129)

Pérez-Llantada (2012, p.129) further reports that the majority of the University of Zaragoza scholars in her study explicitly described their L2

English writing style as 'dense, elaborate and non-synthetic' – very much resembling the L1 Spanish intellectual style that she described in her analysis chapter (Pérez-Llantada 2012, ch 4). Some of the scholars explicitly stated that 'adhering to the standardized simplicity and conciseness style in prestigious English-medium publications was particularly difficult due to their ingrained culture-specific intellectual tradition and way of thinking'.

8.3   NON-LINEAR DISCOURSE STRUCTURES

Based on an analysis of English essays written by foreign university students in the United States, Kaplan (1966, 1972) reported four kinds of discourse structures that contrast in different ways with the English ideal of 'linear texts'.

These may be summarised with some typical exemplars as follows:[2]

1. Parallel constructions, in which the first idea is completed in the second part (*Semitic*, Arabic).
2. Circling organisation/multiple perspectives approaches ('indirection' in Kaplan's terms). Here the topic is looked at from a variety of different tangents, but the subject is never looked at directly (*Oriental*, e.g. Indonesian, Indian, Chinese, Japanese, Korean).
3. Freedom to digress and to introduce 'extraneous' material (*Romance*, Central European – German, Italian, Spanish, Latin American; less of French).
4. Similar to 3, but with different lengths, parenthetical amplifications of subordinate elements, and no 'rounding off' (*Russian*, Eastern European variant of 3).

PARALLEL CONSTRUCTIONS: EXAMPLES FROM ARABIC

Arabic discourse is influenced by the ancient Semitic oral tradition, which Kaplan (1972, p. 250) suggests is based on a complex set of parallel constructions, both positive and negative. This kind of parallelism is evident in the English translation (King James version) of the Old Testament of the Bible. Clyne (1994, p. 172) points out that this ancient Semitic rhetorical

---

[2] This listing largely follows Clyne (1994, p. 161). Kaplan's language types are given in italics and Clyne's cultural grouping, giving more specific language exemplification, is given as well.

tradition is also evident in the Koran, and in the New Testament verses of the Lord's Prayer and the Beatitudes.

We exemplify this parallelism from the first part of the Beatitudes (Matthew 5, 3–5):

> *Blessed are the poor in spirit; for theirs is the kingdom of heaven.*
>
> *Blessed are they that mourn; for they shall be comforted.*
>
> *Blessed are the meek; for they shall inherit the earth.*
>
> *Blessed are they which do hunger and thirst after righteousness for they shall be filled.*

Parallelism in the above example is illustrated by the two-part structure of each sentence (*'Blessed are xxx, for xxx'*) and by the four-line structure, the last line of which is longer than the others.

Clyne (1991a, p. 213) provides the following examples of such parallelism from a letter of inquiry from an Egyptian university student:

> *My Dear respected Master xxx University*
>
> *Good morning or after Good Night*

We can see the parallelism in the double greeting structure, and also in the complementarity of the second line, *Good morning or after Good Night*. Some of these features are also found in the intercultural letters discussed in section 8.7.

8.4 MULTIPLE PERSPECTIVES: THE EXAMPLE OF JAPANESE

Japanese is one of the Oriental languages identified by Kaplan (1966, 1972) as having a discourse structure he characterised as 'an approach by indirection', meaning topics are looked at from different tangents. Other languages described as having this structure include Indonesian, Indian (Pandharipande 1983; Kachru 1988), Chinese, and Korean (Eggington 1987).

Hinds (1980) reviews two expository prose styles in frequent use in Japan. Hinds (1980, p. 132) briefly discusses one style that reflects the classical Chinese organisation of poetry. Hinds (following Takemata 1976) describes this style of prose in terms of the four characters: *ki, shoo, ten* and *ketsu* (here represented in Pin Ying, the Chinese adopted use of the Roman alphabet). These characters describe the development of a classical Chinese poem. Hinds (1980, p. 132) provides their respective meanings as defined by Takemata (1976, p. 26):

(*ki*)	First, begin one's argument
(*shoo*)	Next, develop that
(*ten*)	At the point where this development is finished, turn the idea into a sub-theme where there is a connection, but not a directly connected association (to the major theme)
(*ketsu*)	Last, bring all of this together and reach a conclusion.

Hinds comments that while this style is common, it is not the sole means of organisation afforded to the Japanese author. In the body of his article, Hinds (1980) goes on to illustrate a second style of discourse organisation he calls 'Return to Baseline Theme'. He examines two articles from a Japanese–English bilingual fan magazine published in Honolulu, Hawaii, each written in English and in Japanese. Hinds (1980, p. 150) identifies the characteristics of Japanese expository prose as follows:

1. Paragraphs are organized by means of the return to a theme at the initiation of each perspective.
2. The theme of an article is continually reinforced, although the theme may never be explicitly stated.
3. Information in each perspective frequently maintains a loose semantic cohesiveness, although this cohesiveness is subordinated to the reinforcement of the theme.
4. Perspectives are structured paratactically: there will be (a) an introduction which reinforces the theme, (b) directly or indirectly related comments, and (c) an optional generalization, a summation, or both.
5. Grammatical reflexes of paragraph structuring are weak, but suggestive.

These features can be seen in the following literal translation of one of the Japanese texts presented by Hinds (1980, pp. 138–40). Hinds also provides the Japanese text in Roman script with morpheme glosses (1980, pp. 141–4), although this is not reproduced here.

The article about May Yokomoto is from the magazine *Kokiku* (May 1977), published in Hawaii, which contains articles about popular television, movie and recording stars. Typically, two articles appear on the same page, one in Japanese and the other in English. Some of these articles are translations from one language to the other, and some are original compositions in each language based on the same set of notes. The English article on May Yokomoto is presented further below so that the difference between the Japanese discourse style and the English discourse style can be seen.

MAY YOKOMOTO (JAPANESE TEXT)

This is a literal translation of the Japanese article:

(1) 'I hosted a program called "World Circus" with Masai Sakai. The film of the show came from London, and I had to do things like dress up like clowns, and fly on a trapeze in a large studio. I'm happy.'

(2) The parents of May Yokomoto keep a close eye on this modern girl who speaks Japanese fluently.

(3) She is fresh as a young sweet-fish splashing on the water.

(4) When she speaks of Japan, she continually uses the word tamoshi (happy).

(5) Some examples of her happiness are:

(6) When she appeared twice on Sanshi Katsura's program 'Let's Get Married,' she was paired with two of her fans, and she ended up winning both times; and now she has two tickets for a Hawaiian vacation.

(7) She now lives in an apartment near Tokyo Metropolitan University by herself, and since she cannot read Japanese, she has difficulty with the trains.

(8) However, many strangers recognize her on the street and help her.

(9) She has traveled in her work from Hokkaido to Kyushu, and has been able to sample a variety of local foods etc.

(10) 'Well, there are bad things too, but I forgot those.'

(11) She is perfectly open and friendly.

(12) Because of this she is loved by everyone.

(13) 'However, when I don't grasp the meaning of the songs I sing it's terrible. There are lots of words that don't appear in the dictionary. At those times I think back on all the help with the language I used to get from Mr Urata when I was in Hawaii.'

(14) She began hula lessons at five, and at seven she began singing lessons with Harry Urata.

(15) She began with a song something like 'The Doll with Blue Eyes.'

(16) The TV programs she appears on frequently are singing shows like Star-Tanjo.

(17) Last year she had a 2.5 hour radio program on Radio Kanto called 'Teach Japanese to May'.

(18) The last program at the end of March was done via international telephone from Hawaii.

(19) This time she has returned home in conjunction with an appearance on Star-Tanjo in Waikiki, and for a magazine frontispiece picture session with Sakiko Itoh.

(20) May Yokomoto, who was elected two years ago as Hawaii's new star on Star-Tanjo, is a lucky girl whose looks and talents were noticed, and who has been sought after for commercials for leading companies, for magazines, and for TV after her debut in May of last year.

(21) She has released her third record called 'Anata chance yo'.

(22) Her real name is Cid Akemi Yokomoto.

(23) She graduated from Roosevelt High School.

(24) She is a pure Hawaiian product, and was runner-up in the Miss Teenage Hawaii contest in 1974.

(Hinds 1980, pp. 138–40)

Hinds represents the structure of this Japanese text as in Figure 8.1.

MAY YOKOMOTO (ENGLISH TEXT)

Hinds (1980, pp. 124–6) provides a parallel text, written in English from the same bilingual magazine. The more linear discourse structure of this article will be more familiar to English readers.

> May Yokomoto returned to Hawaii recently to appear in the Star Tanjo. In addition, the friendly eighteen year old was kept busy by photo sessions with Sakiko Ito. They had numerous pictures taken of them on the beach for *Myojo* magazine in Japan.
>
> She is having a good time in Japan doing commercials, television and radio work. For example, she appeared on the TV game show 'Kekkonshimashoo' (Let's Get Married), where she won two trips to Hawaii, which she is saving for future use. May also appears on 'Sekai no Circus' with her favourite actor, Masai Sakai. On this program, May had to dress up like a clown and even swung on a trapeze. She also had a radio program on Radio KANTO called 'Teach Japanese to May'.
>
> May has her own apartment in Tokyo, but still has a hard time getting around on trains. Recently, though, people have begun to recognize 'May-chan' and help her find her destination. She says living in Japan is not easy, but is fun most of the time.

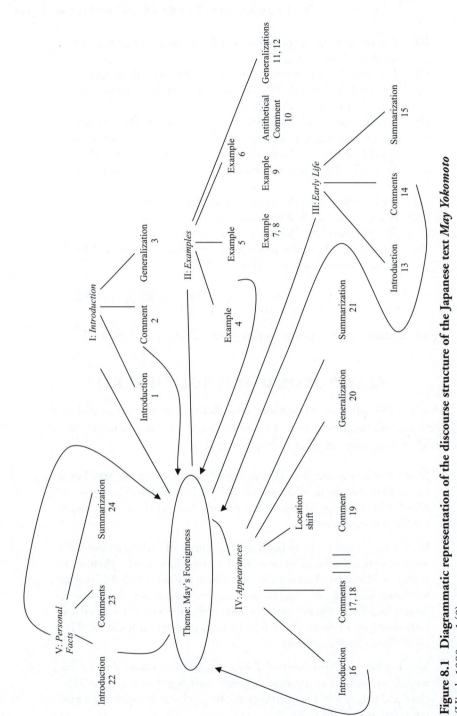

Figure 8.1 Diagrammatic representation of the discourse structure of the Japanese text *May Yokomoto* (Hinds 1980, p. 149)

May's parents are pleased that her Japanese has improved so much, but says she still has a hard time understanding some of the songs.

May says 'While in Hawaii, my teacher Harry Urata always explained everything to me. He made it seem easy.'

May has travelled all over, from Hokkaido to Kyushu. In the process, she has learned all about Japanese gourmet foods.

Two years ago May was the winner of the 'Star Tanjo'. Last year, she made her debut in Japan and is already a popular talent.

May began studying hula at the age of five, and started music lessons with Harry Urata at the age of seven. She was runner up in the Miss Teenage Hawaii contest in 1974. Her real name is Cid Akemi Yokomoto. She is a graduate of Roosevelt High School.

In these two texts from Hinds (1980) we can see how the same content can be presented using different methods of textual organisation depending on the cultural preference. The Japanese text is a clear example of the circling organisation (indirection in Kaplan's terms) identified above.

8.5 'DIGRESSIVENESS': GERMAN ACADEMIC REGISTER

Clyne (1987, p. 213) lists the following four features of the German academic register, which have been observed by various researchers, and which students entering German universities are in the process of acquiring (e.g. papers in Bungarten 1981; Clyne 1991a). Clyne (1994, p.164) exemplifies the first two of these observed features.

1. Agentless passives and impersonal reflexive constructions, e.g.
   'Selection error <u>must be regarded</u> as a defect'
   '<u>One</u> can assume that there was competition for the best job.'
   'There <u>it is obvious</u> that returnees are underprivileged.'
   es zeigt sich 'it shows itself'
   es fragt sich eben, ob nicht 'it asks itself if not . . .'
2. Hedged performatives using modals *kann* 'can', *muss* 'may' and *darf*, parenthetical verbs, the equivalent of 'seem, appear, guess' and passive infinitives 'it is to be hoped . . .' e.g. 'Thus it seems unnecessary to discuss a new model here.'
3. A large number of nominalisations and compound nouns.
4. Syntactic complexity.

Clyne's (1987) research also identifies a fifth feature, 'digressiveness', which had not been previously described in the literature. 'Digressiveness' may include a separately labelled section called the *Exkurs* ('excursus' or 'excursion'). Clyne (1994, p. 163) provides the following summation of 'digressions':

> 'Digressions' generally fulfil particular functions in German academic texts. In our corpus, 'digressions' enable writers to add a theoretical component in an empirical text, a historical overview, ideological dimension, or simply more content, or engage in a continuing polemic with members of a competing school... these are all crucial aspects of German intellectual style and German culture. The presence of one or more sections labelled *Exkurs* (excursion 'digression') in most good dissertations in German speaking universities confirm that linearity is not a prerequisite of academic writing in German.

8.6   THE FORM/CONTENT DISTINCTION

The linear/non-linear distinction proposed above may be better understood as a form/content distinction. Clyne (1994, p. 186) suggests that although all cultures could be expected to apply a combination of formal and content criteria to determine the structure and progression of a piece of discourse, some cultures, such as English-based ones, more strongly foreground form while others are more content-oriented. The following points illustrate this distinction.

- Content orientation often appears to be associated with a cultural idealisation of knowledge and the authority of the academic or intellectual work. For instance, if a text can be readily understood, then, from a German perspective, it may be seen to be dubious and unprofessional.
- From the perspective of content-oriented cultures, the English linear structure might be considered simplistic, due to its high usage of advance organisers and its emphasis on the careful presentation of thought structures and strategies of expression.
- In Japanese and Central European cultures, the onus falls on the reader to make the effort to understand the text produced by the knowledgeable, and therefore, authoritative person; rather than the writer seeing it as his or her job to present the material in a well-organised and understandable way, as is the case for English-based cultures.

Such differences are likely to cause difficulties for readers and writers with different expectations of written discourse and may pose particular challenges for international students (see also Connor 2003; Noor 2001).

8.7 LETTER WRITING

Although there are many differences between spoken and written language, letter writing sits somewhere between the two, because a letter is typically part of a communication exchange. Letters are distinct from other forms of writing in that they typically contain a greeting and a closing sequence. In addition, business letters usually contain at least one of the following 'speech acts' (see Chapter 3):

- requests for information
- directives
- complaints
- threats
- promises
- social comments.

In a study of letters of request by Mandarin speakers from China to the China Section of Radio Australia, Kirkpatrick (1991) found that native speakers of Chinese prefer to place requests towards the end of letters, and that a typical scheme for a Chinese letter of request includes salutation, preamble (facework), reasons and then the request (Kirkpatrick 1991, p. 183). Kirkpatrick reports that while the request and the reason may occur in either order in both Mandarin and English, his research shows that there is a strong preference by Mandarin writers to put the reason before the request, rather than the reverse, which he suggests is more typical in English. Kirkpatrick sees the reason–request sequence as an instance of the more general *because–therefore* sequence.

In a sample of 20 letters of request from South Asian students requesting university application information, comprising 11 letters from Indians, seven from Pakistanis, and one each from a Bangladeshi and a Sri Lankan, Clyne (1991b, p. 209) found that the main speech acts performed were request, introduction and expression of interest. Clyne found that nine out of the 20 letters followed the sequence introduction + expression of interest + request, while seven went directly to the expression of interest followed by the request. We note that this preference for the request to come towards the end of the letter is similar to what Kirkpatrick reports for Mandarin.

In a sample of 20 similar letters of request from Arabic-speaking students, consisting of 11 letters from Egyptians, two from Syrians and one each from a Jordanian, a Kuwaiti, a Lebanese, a Libyan, an Omanian, a Moroccan and a Saudi Arabian, Clyne (1991b, p. 211) found far more individual variation and creativity. However, in most cases the request also tended to be towards the end of the letter.

Other research on letters is addressed in Bowe and Martin (2007, pp. 130 ff.), including discussions of salutations and opening sequences, honorific features, forms of deference, parallel constructions, expressions, closings. What we see from the research in Bowe and Martin (2007) and that referred to above is that although there are common themes expressed within letters from different cultures, it is the relative ordering of different segments of the letters that may differ cross-culturally. Other cultural specific features, such as the Middle Eastern preference for parallelism, are also examples of cross-cultural differences found in intercultural letter writing.

8.8 ACADEMIC WRITING IN THE GLOBAL WORLD

Academic writing is one of the fastest growing genres of intercultural written discourse, and the field of English for academic purposes has spawned a great deal of important research.

In a comprehensive study of scientific discourse in the global context, Pérez-Llantada (2012) provides a text linguistic analysis of academic articles written by native English speakers writing in English (L1 English), native Spanish speakers writing in Spanish (L1 Spanish) and native Spanish speakers writing in English (L2 English). Pérez-Llantada interprets aspects of this text analysis in terms of the rhetorical styles identified by Kaplan (1966) and Connor et al. (2008). The text analysis drew on Coxhead's (2000) Academic Word Lists, nominal compounding (e.g. Matthiessen 1995), lexico-grammatical features (e.g. Hyland & Tse 2005); Biber et al. (1999); Hyland (2008). Pérez-Llantada complements the text linguistic/rhetorical analysis of her three sub-corpora with an ethnographic account of the disciplinary research practices and procedures of her subjects, which provides a rich account of the context in which the writing was produced. Her data is drawn from the Spanish English Research Article Corpus (SERAC) compiled at the University of Zaragoza, Spain.

Pérez-Llantada found that there was broad equivalence across the three sub-corpora in terms of the frequency of occurrence of a range of lexical items, grammatical and function words and a common pool of word sequences associated with the typical communicative purposes of scientific prose. While she did find that a few sequences were unique to particular sub-corpora, it was at the level of argumentation structure that Pérez-Llantada found the greatest variation across the three sub-corpora.

Pérez-Llantada's findings (2012, pp. 81–3) are summarised below:

1. Equivalent words and phrases found frequently across all sub-corpora
   (a) Frequently occurring lexical content words across the three subcorpora (e.g. *data/datos, study/studio, work/trabajo, analysis/análisis, research, informayion/información, results/resultados*).
   (b) Grammatical categorisation of lexical and function words (e.g. V modals, such as *can, may, will, would, could/puede, pueden*).
   (c) Word sequences associated with the typical communicative purposes of scientific prose:
   – in the provision of factual evidence (e.g. *the presence of/la presencia de, the fact that/el hecho de*)
   – reader signposts (e.g. *in this study/en este studio, the other hand/por otro lado*)
   – conveying impersonality (e.g. *the results of/los resultados de*).
2. Sequences unique to each subcorpus
   (a) L1 English corpus
   Expressions of probability (e.g. *more likely to, likely to be, the likelihood of*).
   (b) L1 Spanish subcorpus
   Higher occurrences of relative clause constructions than complement clauses and linking phrases.
   (c) L2 English corpus
   Expressions of probability (e.g. *it is possible, it can be, it should be, seems to be*). Also higher uses of passive constructions, past participle clauses and metadiscourse expressions.

At the level of argumentation structure, Pérez-Llantada (2012, p. 100) found greater variation across the three subcorpora. Her findings may be summarised as follows:

The L1 English texts:

- display a more simplified syntax than the other two subsets
- use a linear intellectual style and display an overtly critical stance
- in discussions/conclusions withhold full commitment to the claims they make in the article for persuasion purposes.

The L1 Spanish texts:

- are syntactically dense (involving coordination, subordination and complementation constructions)
- exhibit long sentences, verbosity and wordiness
- feature the digressive style of Romance languages.

The L2 texts (written by Spanish speakers):

- resemble the syntactic digressiveness of the L1 Spanish subset of texts
- exhibit wordiness and abundant clausal elaboration.

Pérez-Llantada characterises the L2 academic research texts in terms of discourse hybridity. She states:

> Compared to the L1 English subset of texts, the L2 English texts show convergence regarding the preferred patterns and discourse uses of standardized phraseology but divergence in terms of syntactic elaboration and formal argumentative style, indicating that 'two sets of values are simultaneously at work in the writing of a scientific report: those common to the academic community and those held in esteem in the writer's national culture'.
>
> (Pérez-Llantada 2012, pp. 101 ff.)

Pérez-Llantada (2012, p. 102) points out that the resultant hybridity of the L2 English texts has been identified by other scholars, such as Mauranen with Finnish (e.g. Mauranen 2005),[3] Clyne with German (e.g. Clyne 1994), Duszak with Polish (e.g. Duszak 2005), Giannoni with Italian (e.g. Giannoni 2008) and Bennett with Portuguese (e.g. Bennett 2011), to name a few. The term 'hybridity' is used as a cover term by Pérez-Llantada, whereas some others, such as Clyne (1994), use the term 'interlanguage'. Pérez-Llantada concludes that differences between L1 and L2 English texts lie in differing culture-specific intellectual styles and scholarly traditions. In summary, she restates the main thesis from the introduction to Clyne's 1994 monograph, on intercultural communication in the workplace (in Australia):

> the discourse level of language is inseparable from cultural behaviour and . . . except in individuals with a high degree of biculturalism as well as bilingualism, this will determine a great deal of inter-lingual transfer at the discourse level.
>
> (Clyne 1994, p. 6)

---

[3] The reference details given here in parentheses were not provided by Pérez-Llantada in this context, but were sourced by the present authors from elsewhere in Pérez-Llantada's monograph.

In order to better understand the discourse production identified above, Pérez-Llantada (2012) provides an ethnographic analysis of the research environment, practices and procedures identified by a representative group of Spanish academics and an equally representative group of scholars from a North American context. As Pérez-Llantada (2012, pp. 105–6) indicates, the data consisted of interview-based protocols to examine:

- the scholars' attitudes towards research production in the globalising landscape, with a special focus on the role of English as a lingua franca for scientific dissemination
- the scientists' discourse practices in an English medium research world, into the specific research procedures of sub-disciplinary communities, and into the extent to which the nature of knowledge affects the actual discourse practices of the scholars
- the scientists' awareness of the standard discourse and rhetorical conventions of scientific English
- processes of acquisition of academic literacies within the scientists' community practices and procedures for interaction, as well as the scientists' perceptions of the most problematic aspects of writing up science and presenting it in English to both English-native and non-native peer scientists.

Pérez-Llantada (2012, pp. 108 ff.) reports that scientific communication was unanimously described by both University of Michigan and University of Zaragoza senior and junior academics as 'the main means of disseminating scientific knowledge and having an intellectual conversation with people working on related topics'. As well as the satisfaction of engaging in scholarly interaction in their chosen field of research, subjects identified the importance of international publication as a measure by which they, as scholars, are valued, paid and promoted. Pérez-Llantada found that the 'publish (in English) or perish' imperative was more keenly reported by the non-native English scholars, who saw publication in highly valued academic journals as a crucial step towards their international research profile. These subjects reported that their writing was shaped by the publication guidelines of Anglophone journals and publishers and by subsequent referee reports. The Anglophone norms of 'clarity' and 'brevity' were among the most recurrent features commented upon by all scholars in Pérez-Llantada's study.

Another interesting aspect of the ethnographic study was description of different processes involved in multi-party authorship. Pérez-Llantada (2012, p. 119) covers a variety of contexts, from the two-party mentor/mentee writing process involving successive revisions to the multi-party writing more often found in 'experimental and problem-solving-oriented fields'. Junior researchers in these fields often have the responsibility of 'drafting the scientific observation, experimentation and validation of research' whereas the senior researchers 'routinely took responsibility for writing up interpretations, anticipating audience reactions and framing the science in a wider context'. In the case of multi-location research sites, including transnational collaboration, scholars from differing levels of experience and from different traditions reported that electronic communication and digital technologies facilitate both the informal exchange of ideas and the writing task as they shape and reshape the texts they create (Pérez-Llantada 2012, pp. 191–21).

While accepting that many of the norms and standards of scholarly academic writing reproduce Anglo-American models, Fløttum (2012, p. 228) suggests that scholars from non-English-speaking countries may want to resist these norms when writing in their own language, so that national writing conventions may be maintained and developed. She writes:

> The dilemma often felt by the Norwegian researcher is, on one the hand, to position him/herself at the international research front, and on the other, to cultivate and develop academic Norwegian through publication in this language, but only researchers from Scandinavian countries would have access to it. In addition, there are political questions involved, depending on the recognition a country gives to national and international publishers. Whether or not 'the use of English by non-native English speakers' represents a threat for local identities and scholarly traditions (Mauranen, Pérez-Llantada & Swales 2010, p. 646) is an issue which still needs investigation.
>
> Fløttum (2012, p. 228)

8.9 METHODOLOGIES: INVESTIGATING WRITING

CROSS-CULTURAL OR INTERCULTURAL DATA

By far the most significant distinction in relation to cross-cultural and intercultural studies of written discourse is the matter of whether the studies examine actual writing produced in the intercultural context, or whether the studies are contrasting writing from different cultures. Kaplan's (1996, 1972) seminal study was, in fact, based on intercultural data (English essays written by foreign university students in the United States). Many subsequent studies in this field have been studies of writing produced by native speakers of the languages being studied (i.e. L1 speakers).

More recently, researchers such as Connor (2011) have advocated for the importance of intercultural texts under the banner of 'intercultural rhetoric'. Clyne's (1994) monograph made a significant contribution to the field of intercultural communication research based largely on spoken and written language collected in multicultural contexts. We see researchers such as Pérez-Llantada (2012) making a three-way comparison of second-language writing, in her case L2 English, L1 English and L1 Spanish. Other similar research includes that of Giannoni (2008) with Italian, Bennett 2011 with Portuguese, Mauranen (2005) with English and Finnish, Duszak (2005) with English and Polish, and other contributors to the collection edited by Cortese and Duszak (2005).

'TOP-DOWN' AND 'BOTTOM-UP' APPROACHES

Another methodological contrast is that of 'top-down' approaches as compared to 'bottom-up' approaches. Hind's 1980 analysis of Japanese and English texts, discussed in section 8.3 above, exemplifies a top-down approach, in which the focus is on the macro arrangement or organisation of the text. This method of analysis was adopted by Kaplan (1966, 1972).

Genre analysis may also be seen as a top-down approach, in that it identifies text types in terms of macro purpose and context, and only subsequently proceeds with other levels of analysis, some of which may be regarded as bottom-up levels of analysis.

While corpus linguistics has typically involved computer-assisted analysis of texts, and is well suited to bottom-up analysis of word lists, lexical collocations (lexical bundles) and grammatical features, genre analysis has had an effect on this field and so we now see the compilation of specialised corpora (Flowerdew 2004, 2012), thus creating a top-down starting point.

Clyne (1994) also takes a top-down approach in his methodologies, following Kaplan in his chapter on writing. (In his analysis of English as a lingua franca in Australian workplaces, Clyne adopts the speech act as the main unit of analysis; this is a productive level of analysis for conversation, which is closer to a top-down approach than a bottom-up one.)

MULTIFACETED APPROACHES

Other significant dimensions are the methodological traditions, by which the text is collected and analysed. Pérez-Llantada's (2012) study is multi-faceted. The text analysis, using lexical and grammatical counts, had no contextual reference and might be criticised in the absence of other analysis. This study could have been enriched by a more top-down analysis of text organisation (e.g. following Kaplan 1966, 1972 or Hinds 1980).

To undertake her study, Pérez-Llantada drew on an existing corpus of English research articles written by Anglophone L1 and Spanish L1 scholars respectively. This data was further compared with academic articles written by Spanish scholars in Spanish (Spanish L1), part of the SERAC (Spanish English Research Article Corpus) databases compiled by the InterLAE research group at the University of Zaragoza (Pérez-Llantada 2012, pp. 73–4).

The ethnographic dimension of Pérez-Llantada's study did not involve the same individuals whose writing formed part of the SERAC database. For the ethnographic study Pérez-Llantada assembled a representative group of subjects from a university in Spain and one in the United States. This is one of the compromises that are sometimes necessary in research practice. An interesting part of the ethnographic study was the issue of non-native speakers of English needing to publish in international English academic journals. It explored the attitudes and experiences of the L2 academic writers, and the perspective of English journal referees (which provides an explanation for the privileged position of Anglo norms) in the context of academic research articles.

8.10 SUMMARY

In this chapter we have examined research on variation in the organisation of written discourse from cross-linguistic and intercultural perspectives. This has included academic writing and other forms of expository prose as well as a section on letters. We have found that, as with spoken discourse, the organisation of writing may be influenced by culture-specific norms, which may give rise to negative evaluations in intercultural contexts. The growing dominance of English in scholarly publications is an issue for non-native English speakers. Many of them regard it is a necessary challenge of globalisation, though some are concerned for the negative impact this may have on national scholarly traditions.

8.11   REVIEW

1. **Key terms**

   Rhetorical features, linearity, digression, circling, parallelism, textual symmetry corpus studies, corpora, genre analysis. Note the overlap in the use of these terms: contrastive rhetoric/discourse, cross-cultural rhetoric/discourse, intercultural rhetoric/discourse.

2. **Key ideas**

   Having read this chapter you should:

   a. appreciate that different preferences for the organisation of written texts are culturally determined conventions

   b. be aware of the significance of written discourse conventions for international cultural interaction.

3. **Focus questions**

   a. Analysis of written discourse

   (i) Based on Kaplan's (1966, 1972) analysis of discourse, categorise your own language's written discourse (e.g. linear, digressive). Give at least three reasons for your choice.

   (ii) Which discourse structure do you feel the most comfortable with in writing essays? Give reasons for this.

   b. Japanese

   (i) Based on the description and analysis of Hinds (1980) of an article about May Yokomoto, do you think that such phrases as *multiple perspectives* and *circular* accurately describe the Japanese written discourse?

   (ii) How does this discourse structure differ from the linear written style (i.e. English)? Provide at least four examples.

   c. Content-oriented and form-oriented cultures

   Consider the following statement from earlier in the chapter:

   > From the perspective of content-oriented cultures, the English linear structure might be considered simplistic due to its high usage of advance organisers and its emphasis on the careful presentation of thought structures and strategies of expression.

   Based on your own language background, do you agree or disagree with the above statement? Give reasons for your choice.

4. **Research analysis**

   Regional discourse patterns

   Consider the following table taken from Precht (1998, p. 260) in which letters of recommendation were analysed. The table summarises some of the features of such letters:

American	German	British	Eastern European
Linear	Linear	Linear	Digressive tendency
Symmetrical	Asymmetrical	Symmetrical	Symmetrical
Integration of data	Data not integrated	Integration of data	Integration of data
Early advance organisers	Few advance organisers	Some advance organisers	Some advance organisers

- **a.** How does Precht's research on digressiveness/linearity, textual symmetry and advance organisers agree or disagree with Clyne's (1987, 1994) categorisation of German and English academic written discourse? Analyse the above table.
- **b.** What do you think the reasons are for these different findings?
- **c.** Do you think that a US American employer would negatively or positively regard a letter of recommendation with a digressive tendency (i.e. Eastern European) instead of a linear writing style? Give reasons for your answer.
- **d.** What interpretation do you think a German employer would have of a letter of recommendation using advance organisers at the beginning of the text (i.e. US American English)?
- **e.** In your own experience, how have your letters of recommendation (those written for you) been structured and organised? Have the structure and organisation of information differed according to the language used and/or the language background of the writer? Use the above table as a guide for your description and analysis.

5. **Research exercise**
   Letters and emails
   Find six examples of written letters (three samples) and emails (three samples) that cover the same topic and serve the same purpose (e.g. personal communication to a friend, business correspondence) and compare and contrast their contents and form. In your analysis address such questions as:
   - **a.** How has the advent of email affected the style of letter writing (i.e. salutations and opening sequences, honorific features)?
   - **b.** Using the discussion of the differences in letter-writing styles across cultures, describe and analyse the similarities and differences between letter writing and emails in the same language.

SUGGESTED FURTHER READING

The study of writing is a burgeoning topic in the area of intercultural communication. Furthermore, computer-mediated communication further complicates how we communicate across cultures. Clyne's and Kaplan's respective works do much to provide foundations for understanding differences in writing across cultures. We have drawn heavily on Pérez-Llantada here, and this provides a wonderful overview of the complexities of intercultural communication in this era of globalisation. We also recommend dipping into some of the literature on computer-mediated communication, which often spans the boundaries of spoken and written communication. Crystal and Danet explore these questions quite well in their respective works, as do the references noted in Macfadyen, Roche and Dorff (introduced at the end of Chapter 7).

Clyne, M. 1987 'Cultural differences in the organisation of academic discourse'. *Journal of Pragmatics*, vol. 11, pp. 211–47.

1994 *Inter-cultural Communication at Work: Cultural Values in Discourse*. Cambridge: Cambridge University Press, pp. 160–75.

Connor, U. & Kaplan, R. B. (eds) 1987 *Writing Across Cultures*. Reading, Massachusetts: Addison-Wesley.

Crystal, D. 2006 *Language and the Internet*. 2nd edn. Cambridge: Cambridge University Press.

Danet, B. 2001 *Cyberpl@y: Communicating Online*. Oxford: Berg.

Hinds, J. 1980 'Japanese expository prose'. *Papers in Linguistics: International Journal of Human Communication*, vol. 13, no. 1, pp. 117–58.

Kaplan, R. B. 1966 'Cultural thought patterns in intercultural education'. *Language Learning*, vol. 16, no. 1, pp. 1–20.

Macfadyen, L., Roche, J. & Doff, S. 2004 *Communicating across Cultures in Cyberspace*. Münster: Lit Verlag.

Pérez-Llantada, C. 2012 *Scientific Discourse and the Rhetoric of Globalization: The Impact of Culture and Language*. London, New York: Continuum International Publishing Group.

Precht, K. 1998 'A cross-cultural comparison of letters of recommendation'. *English for Specific Purposes*, vol. 17, no. 3, pp. 241–65.

Part III
Professional communication across cultures

9 | Translating language and culture

9.1   INTRODUCTION

Linguistic and cultural 'brokers' such as family members, friends and professional translators play a critical role in facilitating intercultural communication. For instance, Bolden (2012) demonstrates how family members serve as language brokers for Russian immigrants to the United States. Bolden finds these family members play a particularly valuable role in mediating miscommunication. We have shown extensively by now how intercultural communication often leads to miscommunication due to a lack of shared cultural conventions. This chapter marks a shift from a discussion of non-shared systems to how brokers in professional and non-professional contexts cope with non-shared systems and reduce miscommunication wherever possible.

Thus, it seems appropriate to begin our applied discussion with the linguistic and cultural brokers who have made a career out of conveying linguistic and cultural differences: interpreters and translators. Interpreting and translating involve rendering information and ideas from one language to another. Interpreters are concerned with the spoken word and translators are concerned with the written or recorded word. That said, many use translation as a blanket term for referring to the activities and responsibilities of professional brokers of both the spoken and written word. In any case, perhaps more than any other professionals, interpreters and translators are at the heart of the intercultural communication process. In addition, most individuals engaging in intercultural communication find themselves playing an interpretive role of some sorts.

Leanza (2007, p. 14), reviewing Jalbert (1998), notes that interpreters and translators not only facilitate the communication process but also act as cultural informants, cultural mediators and advocates. Leanza (2007, p. 14) writes on the medical interpreter's role as cultural broker or cultural mediator: 'The interpreter is a Cultural Informant but also a negotiator between two conflicting value systems or symbolic universes.' This chapter explores the processes of interpreting and translating, how interpreters and translators cope with the complexities of these processes and how this might inform readers' work as linguistic and cultural mediators. We begin by discussing the processes and problems inherent in interpreting and translating. We then delve into how these processes and problems are dealt with by language professionals in a variety of contexts.

9.2   TRANSLATING AND INTERPRETING: AN OVERVIEW

TRANSLATING AND INTERPRETING

Crystal (2010, p. 354) writes: 'Translation is often used as a neutral term [for interpreting and translating] when the meaning expressions in one language (the 'source' language) is turned into the meaning of another (the 'target' language).' There are three basic kinds of translation in the neutral (and very general) sense: word-for-word, literal and free; see also the 'word-for-word' and 'sense-for-sense' dichotomy (e.g. Munday 2001). Crystal (2010) illustrates these three dimensions with reference to the English idiomatic expression *It's raining cats and dogs*. A **word-for-word translation** entails providing a word-for-word translation of a source language into a target language. So, for instance, this idiom would look like this:

| Il | est | pleuvant | chats | et | chiens. |
| It | is | raining | cats | and | dogs. |

The word-for-word French translation carries little semblance to the original semantic meaning of the English idiom. More so, this word-for-word rendering is grammatically incorrect in French. A French speaker does not use the form *est pleuvant* for 'it is raining' but rather *il pleut*. Furthermore, a French speaker would use the plural article *des* before both cats and dogs respectively.

A **literal translation** aims to replicate the general structure of the source language in the target language. However, the translation 'is normalized according to the rules of the target language' (Crystal 2010, p. 354). Hence, the grammatical errors noted for French above would be tended to in a literal translation: *Il pleut des chats et des chiens*. Yet, the idiomatic sense of 'heavy raining' is still not attended to by this literal translation. Thus, in a **free translation**, the translator ignores 'the linguistic structure of the source language . . . and an equivalent is found based on the meaning it conveys' (Crystal 2010, p. 354). A free translation of the idiom *It's raining cats and dogs* would either make explicit reference to 'heavy rain' or use its French equivalent, *Il pleut des cordes* (literally 'It's raining ropes').

Translators and interpreters encounter a number of difficulties in rendering a source language appropriately in a target language. Most relevant to the current discussion, as Bassnett (1998, p. 82) notes, 'Cultural difference manifests itself during the task of translating, and frequently looms up as an unforeseeable difficulty'. The English word *cousin* has eight corresponding forms in Arabic, which, among other things, designate the gender and lineage of the cousin (Thomas 1998). Similar issues are encountered when rendering T/V languages such as French or Swedish (see Chapter 7) into a language without this distinction, such as English. Arabic translations of popular Western fiction and literature sometimes exclude alcohol for the benefit of their Islamic readers (Amin-Zaki 1998). As noted in Chapter 5, German translations of the British Paddington Bear series sometimes leave out 'small talk' to cater to the German distaste for 'empty verbiage' (House 2010, p. 569).

TRANSLATORS AND INTERPRETERS

Translators and interpreters respectively encounter differing constraints in rendering a source's symbolic meaning interpretable in the target language. As noted above, translators most typically deal with written or recorded texts. Therefore, on the one hand, written translation may be viewed as an 'easier' discipline in the sense that one has more time and resources on which to draw. For instance, the topic is normally well known ahead of time (e.g. a popular book, a speech) and there are fewer social variables with which to deal (e.g. multiple co-present participants). However, written and recorded translation also presents certain difficulties in that the audience is less explicit (Crystal 2010) and often more numerous, heterogeneous and complex. In any case, a good translator can translate up to 1000 words per hour for popular texts and more technical texts can be translated at 400 words per hour (Crystal 2010).

In the spoken realm, there are three main types of interpreting used in the world:

- **Simultaneous interpreting**, typically used at international conferences where personal headphones are used, and interpreting is conducted into numbers of languages simultaneously, each with a different interpreter. In such circumstances, delegates often present prepared papers and these can sometimes be made available to the interpreters ahead of time to assist in their preparation. However, this is not always the case. Simultaneous translation is not used very often in Australia.

- **Chuchotage**, a term used to refer to the kind of interpretation produced by an interpreter 'whispering' simultaneous translation to a single client.
- **Sequential translation**, the type of translation most widely used for community and business purposes.

In all types of interpreting, the interpreter is expected to represent what the speaker says and to speak in the first person: for example, *I went to the city* and not *He says that he went to the city.*

Interpreters face a number of challenges in rendering the source language into the target language. On the one hand, interpreters generally face less uncertainly about the target audience than translators of the written and recorded word. However, unlike translators, interpreters are normally expected to handle spontaneous and dialogic conversations about varied topics (Crystal 2010) and this can make interpreting tricky in its own right. The ear-to-voice span is normally 2–3 seconds for an interpreter but it can last as long as 10 seconds due to a number of complicating factors (Crystal 2010). For instance, a longer ratio may result from more difficult texts and/or if a speaker increases his or her speed. Furthermore, certain linguistic idiosyncrasies and differences may impact difficulty and ear-to-voice times. For instance, many languages (e.g. Farsi) place the verb at the end of a sentence (e.g. *I the baby fed*) and these can take longer to translate into verb-medial (SVO) languages such as English.

PRIMACY OF THE MOTHER TONGUE

Best practice suggests that translators and interpreters should preferably translate and/or interpret into their mother tongue. For example, if you want something translated from English to Mandarin, a native speaker of Mandarin would probably be better for the job, whereas if you wanted something translated from Mandarin to English, a native English speaker would probably be better; all other things being equal. It is generally possible to make such choices for translating and for simultaneous conference interpreting. However, interpreting often involves conversation between two parties, and would therefore require two interpreters to be present if an interpreter worked into the mother tongue only. In contexts such as this, where interpreting is between individuals or small groups, then interpreters are typically required to work into both languages, and are expected to act with impartiality so as not to prejudice either party to the conversation.

9.3 PRAGMATIC EQUIVALENCE AND IMPARTIALITY

The basic aim of translators and interpreters is to provide something approaching pragmatic and semantic equivalence (Crystal 2010). However, Crystal (2010, p. 355) notes 'this is nigh impossible in terms of rhythm, sound symbolism, puns and cultural allusions'. This issue is known as the incommensurability problem, and refers to the degree to which conceptual categories and symbolic systems differ across cultures (Foley 1997). From the position of translation theorists and anthropologists, the bridging of these differences can be difficult but certainly not impossible. Anthropologists assert that 'there is a broad background of shared beliefs and understandings common to us all by virtue of being a human person' (Foley 1997, p. 173). This enables us to establish a 'bridgehead' even when meeting an entirely 'alien' human system (Foley 1997, p. 173).

The tradition of translation theory identifies the complexity of the task facing translators (and interpreters). Translation theorists have identified 'dynamic equivalence' (Nida & Taber 1974, p. 200) or 'pragmatic equivalence' (Widdowson 1978, p. 54) as being the key objective of successful translation (see Hatim 2001; Munday 2001, among others, for histories of translation theory). Widdowson emphasises that translation not only involves correspondence between formal pattern and cognitive meaning, but also correspondence in the situation of use. Dynamic equivalence means showing a concern that 'the message of the original text [will be] so transported into the receptor language that the response of the receptor is essentially that of the original receptors' (Nida & Taber 1969, cited in Hatim 2001, p. 19). Such a translator is not only concerned with accurate conveyance of ideas but also the omission of information/text where this information/text would be 'alien' or 'incomprehensible' to a receiver (Hatim 2001, p. 20). For instance, a translator concerned with dynamic equivalence would delete alcohol in Arabic texts or small talk in German texts, as we noted above.

This inspires, of course, debates revolving around cultural appropriateness, creative licence with another author's work and, when the translated work emerges from a less dominant cultural group, power. For instance, a process of **domestication** dominates the Anglo-American tradition of translation (Munday 2001). This entails reducing 'the foreign text to... target-language cultural values' (Venuti 1995, cited in Munday 2001, p. 146) with the aim of 'translating [it] in a transparent, fluent, "invisible" style in order to minimize the foreignness of the [target text]' (Munday 2001, p. 146). For instance, in Indonesia, urban Parisian French television programs have been dubbed into urban Jakarta Indonesian for the benefit of Indonesian viewers (Loven 2008). Domestication contrasts with the process of foreignisation, which aims to bring the reader closer to the writer's words rather than the other way around (Munday 2001). **Foreignisation**, as Venuti (1995, cited in Munday 2001, p. 147) describes it, places pressure on the target language's cultural 'values to register the linguistic and cultural differences of the foreign text, sending the reader abroad'. To return to the Indonesian example above, foreignisation would aim for translation that maintained a distinctly French rather than Indonesian feel.

In any case, Larson (1984, p. 33) claims that to be faithful to the original text a translator must communicate not only the same information, but must also attempt to evoke the same emotional response:

> In many ways, the *emotional tone* of a passage is the key to real communication effectiveness. The author may wish to create a feeling of urgency, persuasiveness, tentativeness, exuberance or despondency. Whatever the *tone* of the source text, built into it by choices of tense, mood, voice and choice of the main action verbs, it is important that this same emotion be communicated in the translation. For an effective transfer of the text, the translator must be well acquainted with both the source and receptor language and culture.
>
> (Larson 1984, p. 425)

The re-creation of the *emotional tone* of the source is particularly difficult for interpreters, who are expected to interpret *impartially* for two parties. Given that *pragmatic equivalence* involves re-creating a new utterance with all the nuances of the source utterance, this must surely involve unpacking any implications that could conventionally be intended by the first party and rendering the complete message to the second party. Unless an interpreter is a consummate actor, and has outstanding pragmatic competence in both languages, it may be difficult for interpreters to convey the *emotional tone* or *pragmatic equivalence* of the spoken word for both sides of a negotiation in an ongoing way. For business negotiation, therefore, it might be more reasonable to engage an interpreter or bilingual professional to act as a dedicated advocate for a single party rather than expect a single interpreter to serve both parties.

Pragmatic and semantic equivalence may also be a problem where the senses of words and phrases differ or do not exist across the source and target languages. For instance, in Indonesian there is a word, *jera*, that means 'to be so frightened by a past experience that one would not try this thing again' (de Boinod 2007). In the Tsonga language, the word *rhwe* means to 'sleep on a floor without a mat, normally drunk and naked' (de Boinod 2007). English cannot convey either of these ideas in a single word. Moreover, one might get thrown off by false friends in presuming equivalence. For example, the Spanish word *idioma* and the French *idiome* equate to 'language' in English rather than 'idiom'. The Irish *fear* equates to the English 'man' and the German *also* equates to 'therefore' in English. A Spanish friend with whom one of the authors lived in Indonesia complained that upon returning to Spain her friends found her to be rude and abrupt. This is because she continued to use the Indonesian *ya* ('yes') in Spain. In Spain, *ya* means 'already' rather than its pervasive Indonesian function as a minimal response (see Chapter 5).

9.4 TRANSLATORS/INTERPRETERS AS INSTITUTIONAL GATEKEEPERS

Translators and interpreters may act as institutional gatekeepers in a number of contexts (e.g. Davidson 2000) and this isn't always best practice. Davidson (2000) reports a study conducted in the outpatients unit of the Riverview General Hospital in Northern California where about 40 per cent of outpatients requested an interpreter. Davidson (2000, p. 385) approached the study as a political, social and linguistic enterprise with an eye towards answering the following questions:

- What is the role of the interpreter within the goal-oriented, learned form of interaction known as the 'medical interview'?
- What is the 'interpretive habit' and how does one engage in the practice of interpreting?
- If interpreters are *not* neutral, do they challenge the authority of the 'physician-judge' and act as patient 'ambassadors' or 'advocates' (as Haffner 1992 suggests) or do they reinforce the institutional authority of the physician and health-care establishment? Should we create a model for the 'interpreter-judge'?

From the analysis of interactions recorded in 1996, Davidson found that the interpreters in the study tended to adopt the role of 'institutional gatekeeper' by selective non-reporting of aspects of the patients' discourse, partly as a consequence of perceived time constraints, and partly due to their own sense of the relevance of the patient's input. Out of 33 patient-generated questions (from 10 interpreted visits) only 15 were passed on to the doctor, while 18 were not passed on at all. Seventeen out of the 18 not passed on to the doctor by the interpreter were actually answered by the interpreter with no reference to the doctor (2000, p. 391). A qualitative analysis of the data suggested that some material that was not passed on was in fact relevant to the diagnosis. Implied criticism of the doctor or of past diagnosis was one class of patient comment that tended to be expunged by the interpreters (Davidson 2000, p. 398). Davidson concluded that:

> The linguistic data, both quantitative and qualitative, points strongly away from a conclusion that interpreters are acting as 'advocates' or 'ambassadors' for interpreted patients, but are acting, at least in part, as informational gatekeepers who keep the interview 'on track' and physician on schedule. While the interpreters do in fact convey much of what is said, they also interpret selectively, and appear to do so in a patterned (non-random) fashion.
>
> (Davidson, 2000, p. 4)

Davidson noted that the interpreters at Riverview were professional in the sense that they were paid employees of the hospital, but that the training given to these interpreters was scant. There was no requirement of any formal degree in interpreting or translation. The only requirements for becoming an interpreter at Riverview were a good grasp of both English and Spanish, and the ability to translate 50 medical terms on a test with complete accuracy. There was no training in discourse processes, and the training for how medical interactions worked was on the job. Davidson reports that the physicians, for their part, received absolutely no training in how to use interpreters, beyond being told how to summon them.

Davidson's research is of interest in that it is based on actual data on the use of translation in medical encounters in a context that he suggests is broadly representative (at the time at least) of widespread practice in the United States. Unfortunately, as he points out, it is far from best practice.

9.5 TRANSLATING/INTERPRETING IN THE WORKPLACE

Linguistic and cultural knowledge is increasingly becoming a commodity in this globalised world (Cameron 2000; Heller 2010), as is the ability to translate this knowledge across cultures. Translators and interpreters are perhaps more relevant than ever in a number of workplace contexts. In this section, we provide an overview of the need for translators and interpreters in these contexts as well as some of the issues these linguistic and cultural brokers encounter.

LEGAL CONTEXTS

Courtroom interpreting is becoming increasingly important in the twenty-first century, with increased migration in the wake of globalisation (Eades 2006). Interpreters and translators are provided free of charge to non-English or low English proficient individuals in many countries where English is the dominant language (e.g. Australia and the United States). However, the quality of these translators and interpreters varies (Berk-Seligson 2001). Furthermore, interpreting and translating in the courtroom presents a unique set of problems, even for the most experienced and skilled professionals. For instance, participants in the legal process may produce inexplicit, ambiguous and confused speech and this has been presented as particularly problematic for language professionals (Lee 2009).

The translation of certain linguistic features from one language to another can be problematic and impact how legal professionals and juries view an utterance (Lee 2009). For example, discourse markers (e.g. *well, you know*) are translated variably, inconsistently and sometimes not at all by court interpreters (Hale 2004; Leung & Gibbons 2009). Many Asian languages frequently omit subjects (e.g. *go to store* rather than *I go to the store*) and lack certain grammatical features present in English (e.g. subject–verb agreement) (Lee 2009). Conversely, English lacks the rich series of expressive discourse markers present in many Asian languages (see. Leung & Gibbons 2009). Even where English and Asian languages share similar discourse markers, English speakers often use them less. For example, Wouk (1998) finds that Indonesian speakers use the utterance-final *kan* ('you know') five times more frequently than English or Swedish speakers would use the equivalent discourse marker in their respective languages.

Many individuals who find themselves in the legal process hail from lower socioeconomic or educational backgrounds. These individuals often speak non-standard language varieties (e.g. African American Vernacular English, Puerto Rican Spanish). This presents interpreters with the dilemma of how such language should be rendered in a context that favours standard (or even hyper-standard) English. Berk-Seligson (2001, p. 599) illustrates this point with the following Spanish to English courtroom translation:

Interpreter:	Qué edad tiene usted?
	'How old are you?'
Witness:	Veinte años.
	'Twenty years'.
Interpreter:	I am twenty years old.

(Berk-Seligson 2001, p. 599)

The interpreter in this case favours formal (and even hyper-formal) English and Spanish. This is even the case when rendering the witness' casual response. In Spanish, the pronoun is often omitted in casual conversation and by witnesses in courtroom discourse (Berk-Seligson 2001; Angermeyer 2005). The witness here rarely uses the pronoun *yo* ('I') to refer to himself in any of the exchanges. However, the interpreter always includes this pronoun in the English translation as well as uses the formal *usted* ('you') when speaking to the witness.

Linguistic decisions such as these may unduly advantage or disadvantage a witness or an accused in a legal context. For instance, Berk-Seligson (1988) found that courtroom interpreters would often translate the Spanish *señor* ('sir') and *señora* ('madam') directly into English. These forms are more readily used in Spanish than in English and this led English-speaker jurors to view witnesses as more polite than was arguably merited. Courtroom translations might also impact whether or not a witness feels like they are required to answer a question. For instance, Hale (2004, p. 58) shows how the following request for information was rendered as a polar yes/no question for one witness:

Question:	Yeah, can you tell the court to the best . . . to the best of your recollection, to the best of your memory?
Interpreter:	¿Pero algo recuerda usted? 'But you remember something?'

(Hale 2004, p. 58)

Polar questions such as these can influence witnesses' memory (Loftus 2001), so it is essential that the nuances of such questioning not be lost in translation.

INTERNATIONAL BUSINESS CONTEXTS

Many studies have shown by now that linguistic and cultural knowledge are valuable resources within international business contexts. Such knowledge enables a company to establish stronger relationships with overseas companies as well as to increase sales in overseas markets. With regard to the latter, Ferraro (2002, p. 47) points out:

> a knowledge of a customer's language has distinct sales value . . . the American businessman who can speak the foreign tongue fluently and who can make intelligent comments on the art and literature of the country will gain not only the business but also the respect of the person he is dealing with.
> (Ferraro 2002, p. 47)

For example, Ferraro (2002) notes that the British automobile manufacturer Jaguar in 1983 began an in-house language program for the learning of German. *The Economist* later linked the establishment of this centre to a 60 per cent increase in Jaguar sales against strong competition from local competitors Mercedes and BMW (Ferraro 2002).

It is not enough to have a basic understanding of the language. It is important in dealing with local markets and local businessmen and women to have a sophisticated understanding of the subtleties and connotations of language (Martin & Nakayama 2004). For instance, the German CEO of Rover has been noted remarking 'When the British say that they have a "slight" problem, I know that it has to be taken seriously' (Martin & Nakayama 2004). When a British business person indicates an issue is to be 'tabled', this means it is to be brought up for discussion and consideration (Martin & Nakayama 2004). However, when an American business person uses this word, it means the issue is to be withdrawn and no longer considered.

Linguistic and cultural knowledge is viewed by many businesses to be a 'soft skill' and thus not prioritised over 'harder skills' such as accounting and mathematics (Ainsworth 2012). Therefore, many businesses tend to rely on interpreters and translators when working in overseas markets. Victor (1992, pp. 38–45) outlines a number of useful tips for addressing translation and interpreting issues in the international business context.

These tips touch on many of the topics we have reviewed above (e.g. literal vs free translation; pragmatic equivalence). For instance, Victor (1992) highlights that care must be taken with the selection of translators and interpreters – one must consider reputability, experience, dialect familiarity, and expertise with business terminology. Victor (1992, p. 41) reports that when General Motors entered the Belgian market it mistranslated its slogan 'Body by Fisher' into 'Corpse by Fisher' (Ricks 1983, p. 83). Victor suggests that choosing a reputable translator reduces the likelihood of similar blunders.

Victor (1992) also recommends adjusting untranslated communication so that idiomatic speech, slang and colloquialisms are avoided. He reports a famous example of the failure of idioms to translate: this involved Pepsi's 'Come alive with Pepsi' campaign, in which the popular English language advertisement was mistranslated into German as 'Come out of the grave' and in Asia as 'Bring your ancestors back from the grave' (Ricks 1983, p. 84). Victor also insists that a company should personally review translated documents. Victor (1992, p. 42) suggests that even if a business person does not understand the target language, he or she can review errors in the spelling of the names of key personnel, company names, brands and trademarks, and check that layout and print quality are appropriate.

Victor notes that companies should pay attention to the pronunciation of names and important terms. He also flags that companies should be aware of different customs concerning the sequencing of names and differing conventions concerning family names. Victor (1992, p. 43) reports that, for example, almost 10 per cent of the population (i.e. well over 100 million people) in the People's Republic of China are named Zhang, and in Korea, half of the population has one of four names: Kim, Lee, Park or Choi (Demente 1988, 1989). Victor suggests that in such countries it is imperative to remember the full names and usually the titles and company sections of business associates.

Victor also recommends that companies double-check translations using established and reliable means such as back-translation. Victor (1992, p. 44) suggests that the most reliable means of discovering translation errors is the system called **back-translation**. This is a process involving the following:

- First have the document translated into the new language.
- Then have the document translated back into the original language.
- Then compare the original manuscript with the back-translated document to determine errors or discrepancies.

You may find it interesting and fun to try doing this with an internet translation tool.

Victor (1992, p. 40) suggests a number of strategies for speaking English to an audience for whom English is a second language. Among other things, he recommends

- rephrasing frequently
- repeating key ideas in different words
- using written support because most people's written knowledge of a foreign language exceeds their spoken knowledge for that language.

Of course these principles would be of benefit in all intercultural communication to minimise interference from differences in pronunciation, rhythm and stress placement.

ADVERTISING CONTEXTS

Language and culture are frequently mobilised as a 'value-add' in advertising (Heller 2010). This has implications for how and the degree to which foreign languages are translated and/or integrated into local contexts. On the one hand, one finds English on T-shirts throughout the non-English speaking world (Heller 2010). On the other, one finds English speakers with Chinese tattoos and Anglo-based companies using the French language or French accents in advertisements to index romance or sophistication (see Heller 2010). Martin (2007, p. 170) writes: 'advertisers create a panoply of border-crossing experiences, encouraging their audiences to view these messages from their own cultural perspective.'

Yet, as noted above in relation to Victor, translating and interpreting advertisements across cultures presents certain challenges. For example, Weller (1992) reports the difficulties inherent in the translation of an advertisement for cat food from English into Spanish and Portuguese. Her comments are based on a research project involving third-year undergraduate students from Mexico City and Rio de Janeiro.

The task was to translate the advertisement in Figure 9.1.

Weller reports that translation of the English word 'juice' is not straightforward because the closest equivalent more typically refers to fruit juice in Mexico (even though you can say *jugo de carne* ('meat juice'), and even more so in Brazil, where *molto* ('sauce') or *caldo* ('broth') are more commonly used with dinner food. The term 'crunchy nuggets' also proved difficult. Another problem was how to handle the brand name, 'New Chef's Blend'. Weller reports that many students kept the brand name in English

---

NEW Chef's Blend – made with real meat juices!

NEW MEAT TASTE

Chef's Blend

Now you can turn on your cat with the real taste of meat! because the New Chef's Blend is made with real meat juices for real meat taste. Each crunchy nugget gets its taste from real beef, chicken, liver and turkey juices. Cats will love the real meat taste. 100% nutritionally complete Chef's Blend Dry Cat Dinners. Turn on your cat to the New Chef's Blend with real meat taste from real meat juices!

Figure 9.1 Pet food advertisement
(Weller 1992)

(perhaps to take advantage of the novelty of something foreign), whereas others chose to translate it in part (*Nueva Chef's Blend*) or translated it in full (*Nueva Receta del Chef*).

Some student translators took advantage of the fact that imperative, diminutive and augmentative suffixes can express endearment (-inho/ão in Portuguese and -ito/ón in Spanish) and used these to create extra appeal. Examples are words such as *pedacinho* (little morsel) for nugget, *gatinho* (little kitten) or *gatão* (big cat or 'hunk' in colloquial American English) and *gostinho* (special flavour), among others.

Weller (1992, p. 149) reports that further research, using the same advertisement, was conducted in Mexico by Murillo (1989). Murillo consulted with several advertising agencies and reported that these agencies thought that the translation students' versions were not creative enough and felt that in this case a whole rewrite was necessary, including the presentation of the product for a Mexican audience. In a culture where people feed their cats with table scraps, such advertising would need to introduce the concept of 'pet food'.

Language has increasingly become commodified within the travel experience (e.g. Bowe & Zhang 2001; Thurlow & Jaworski 2003; Jaworski & Thurlow 2009). Bowe and Zhang (2001) examined travel advertising in Chinese newspapers and found it drew heavily on images of the beauty of the vista and the changing seasons, and health and happiness deriving from the travel experience. Chinese travel agencies have names that also draw on similar themes: for instance, 'Spring and Autumn Travel Agency', 'Golden Bridge Travel Agency', 'Health and Splendour Travel Agency' and 'Golden Sea Travel Agency'.

The focal points in one of the advertisements examined by Bowe and Zhang (2001) include 'romantic journey', 'comfortable journey', 'unforgettable journey', 'sweet journey' and 'healthy journey'. At the centre of the advertisement there are two large overprints of the Chinese characters for happiness, with the meaning 'Double Happiness'. Another advertisement contains famous lines from an ancient Chinese poet describing the natural beauty of the Mongolian region, referring to the vast sky, boundless wilds, cattle and sheep, low grass and (gently) blowing winds. One advertisement incorporates a western heart symbol with a more traditional invitation along the lines of 'Put my sincere heart into your palm and dissolve your confidence into my sincere heart'. In none of the Chinese advertisements is price or value mentioned at all.

These advertisements contrast with travel advertising in newspapers in Western cultures, which tends to involve price discounts and inclusive packages. In glossy magazines beauty is often highlighted through photographic images rather than descriptive language, but health and happiness do not generally rate a mention. (Glossy magazines have not been widely affordable in China so no parallel can be drawn with them.) It is clear that cultural practice will determine, to a large extent, what is appropriate in an advertisement, although aspects of Western cultural practice are being incorporated as a result of globalisation.

9.6   REGULATING TRANSLATING AND INTERPRETING

In order to measure and maintain standards, institutions, governments and commercial entities around the world have sought to regulate language skills, translating and interpreting. Employers and the public more generally tend to be most familiar with English-language exams created by commercial enterprises. For instance, the three most well-known exams for English proficiency testing are arguably the commercial TOEFL (Test of English as a Foreign Language), TOEIC (Test of English for International Communication) and IELTS (International English Language Testing System). Less well known are tests and standards such as Interagency Language Roundtable scale (ILR scale) used by the US Foreign Service and the Common European Framework of Reference for Languages (CEFR) used in

Europe. However, the latter has certainly gained in popularity beyond Europe in recent years.

A full discussion of language testing and standards is vast and beyond the scope of this book. However, in light of the topic at hand, it is worth focusing on one system that serves to examine the skills of interpreters and translators. Interpreting and translation services developed in Australia to cater for the needs of a growing migrant community after World War Two. Some training was needed to improve the ad hoc interpreting provided by younger family members and earlier migrants who had acquired some English skills. In their early phase, the interpreter-training services sought to provide minimal training for migrant staff already employed in support roles in the health, legal and social security areas, were asked to act as interpreters from time to time. By the 1970s Australia had become fully professional in the provision of interpreting and translating services for migrant settlement purposes, having introduced a national telephone interpreter service and established the National Accreditation Authority for Translators and Interpreters (NAATI) (see Gentile 1991).

The ongoing effects of globalisation have resulted in Australia becoming increasingly oriented towards international engagement and overseas markets and there is a growing demand for business and conference interpreting of all types. Australia continues to have a special need for adequate interpreting services for Aboriginal and Torres Strait Islander people, notably in the legal and health areas. The provision of Auslan interpreters for the deaf has also become a matter of priority, as part of an expectation of equity of access to services for all citizens.

9.7   SUMMARY

This chapter has explored key issues relating to the practice of translating and interpreting and related these to the broader issues of intercultural communication. As noted at the start, interpreters and translators play a key role as mediators of linguistic and cultural meaning. Such linguistic brokers are faced with the complexities of conveying semantic and pragmatic equivalence. They also need to know that they may end up as gatekeepers in multilingual or multicultural affairs and must be sure to act impartially and convey all relevant information wherever possible. In any case, interpreting and translating is a growing field in professional and non-professional realms in this increasingly globalised world. In the next chapter we broaden our focus beyond translation and interpreting to a discussion of intercultural communication in the workplace.

9.8   REVIEW

1. **Key terms**

    Interpreter, translator, simultaneous interpreting, chuchotage, sequential translation, pragmatic equivalence, impartiality, bilingual professional, language aide, adjustment of untranslated communication, back-translation.

2. **Key ideas**

    Having read this chapter you should:

    a. appreciate the difference between interpreting and translating

    b. be able to make appropriate decisions in the selection and employment of translators and interpreters, based on standard criteria

    c. appreciate the need for sensitivity to cross-cultural differences in the organisation and presentation of spoken and written material designed for international communication.

3. **Focus questions**

    a. Semantic equivalence with pronouns

    In Chapter 7 we discussed the fact that in some cultures formal pronoun forms are widely used in public contexts and informal forms are reserved for close personal acquaintances, whereas in other cultures informal forms might be widely used in public discourse, and the use of formal forms reserved for extreme formality and for coding extreme social distance.

    (i) Given that the task of an interpreter is to render a client's speech into a second language, without changing the meaning, explain why it might be necessary when interpreting between certain languages for interpreters not to use the grammatically equivalent pronoun form, but to change from a formal form to an informal form.

    (ii) What reasons might an interpreter offer for not making such a switch?

    b. Business interpreting

    (i) In the business context, it might be advantageous for each of the negotiating parties to employ their own interpreter, rather than just use one. Explain why this might be so.

    (ii) What disadvantages might accrue from the two parties sharing the same interpreter?

    (iii) Explain why it might sometimes be in the business interests of a company for an interpreter not to be impartial. How can this ethical issue be resolved?

    c. Employing staff with foreign language skills

      (i) If a hotel was seeking to employ customer service personnel with foreign language skills, what level of skills might be required to handle the following:

        – an enquiry about the location of a suitable restaurant

        – a complaint about the use of disrespectful language by a hotel employee

        – a major emergency at the hotel such as a large explosion.

      (ii) What skill level would be appropriate to this role?

      (iii) How might organisations such as international hotels best plan for the provision of interpreting and translation needs?

4. Research analysis

Explain exactly what went wrong with each of the following mistranslations:

  (i) When entering the Belgian market General Motors mistranslated its slogan 'Body by Fisher' into 'Corpse by Fisher'.

  (ii) In Pepsi's 'Come alive with Pepsi' campaign, the popular English language advertisement was mistranslated into German as 'Come out of the grave' and in Asia as 'Bring your ancestors back from the grave'.

5. Research exercise

  a. Locate a pair of magazines published in English and also in another language.

  b. Compare a text or advertisement in each language in terms of the features discussed in this chapter. (If you are comparing longer texts, you may need to also refer to the discussions in Chapter 8 on cultural differences in writing.)

This exercise is suitable for bilingual students, or for students with complementary language skills working in pairs.

SUGGESTED FURTHER READING

Crystal provides an excellent and accessible introduction to translation and Munday to the study of translation. Ferraro's well-cited book, now into a seventh edition (with newly added co-author Elizabeth Briody), outlines some 'wonderful' (mis)translations in a business context. Though not necessarily translation- or interpreting-focused, many works by Heller, Thurlow and Jaworski speak to the commodification of language(s) and provide a valuable resource to those engaged in international business. The legal context is fraught with linguistic difficulties, as shown in this chapter and the next one. Berk-Seligson's and Hale's respective bodies of work are excellent starting points for understanding the valuable role of translators/interpreters as cultural brokers. Furthermore, their work illustrates how the successful or unsuccessful accomplishment of this role can have powerful consequences for those engaged in intercultural communication. Lastly, *Target: International Journal of Translation Studies* is not dedicated to issues of intercultural communication. However, these issues are often dealt with in its pages.

Berk-Seligson, S. 2009 *Coerced Confessions: The Discourse of Bilingual Police Interrogations.* Berlin: Mouton de Gruyter.

Crystal, D. 2010 *The Cambridge Encyclopedia of Language.* 3rd edn. Cambridge: Cambridge University Press.

Ferraro, G. 2002 *The Cultural Dimension of International Business.* 4th edn. Upper Saddle River, NJ: Prentice Hall.

Hale, S. 2004 *The Discourse of Court Reporting. Discourse Practices of the Law, the Witness and the Interpreter.* Amsterdam: Benjamins.

Heller, M. 2010 'The commodification of language'. *Annual Review of Anthropology*, vol. 39, pp. 101–14.

Munday, J. 2001 *Introducing Translation Studies: Theories and Applications.* London and New York: Routledge.

Pym, A. 2004 'Propositions on cross-cultural communication and translation'. *Target: International Journal of Translation Studies*, vol. 16, no. 1, pp. 1–28.

Thurlow, C. & Jaworski, A. 2003 'Communicating a global reach: Inflight magazines as a globalising genre in tourism'. *Journal of Sociolinguistics*, vol. 7, no. 4, pp. 581–608.

10

Intercultural communication in the workplace

10.1   INTRODUCTION

I N T H I S chapter, we survey important workplace communication research, with the aim of showing how a combination of methods and theoretical concepts may contribute to intercultural understanding and smoother working relationships. The 1990s saw a series of key workplace communication studies, with many of these originating from the Australian context. Michael Clyne (1994), in particular, building on the seminal work of John Gumperz, played a major role in spearheading studies of intercultural communication in the workplace. In recent years, there have been growing numbers of workplace studies in the United Kingdom, the United States and beyond. We review some of these studies here to demonstrate how workplace research has evolved in recent years. In any case, a survey of intercultural communication in the workplace shows how research may highlight the causes of miscommunication and how such miscommunication may be resolved.

This book has noted a few times by now that within the intercultural communication field there has been an increased focus on ethnography, naturally occurring conversations and constructivist approaches in the past few decades. Thus, in this chapter we begin each section with a review of some of the seminal 1990s studies of workplaces. We use these as a foundation for discussing more recent and more ethnographically and constructivist-driven approaches. In doing so, we introduce a few more useful theoretical concepts for understanding workplace culture. Of particular note, monolithic, homogenous and nationalistic accounts of workplace cultures have been shown to be reductive. Thus, we show how the Community of Practice, devised in the field of education and used extensively by sociolinguists, provides a useful frame for understanding workplace culture(s).

This chapter begins with a general discussion of workplace culture, focusing firstly on the work of Clyne and his contemporaries, and secondly on the Community of Practice. We then survey workplace studies in a series of workplace cultures, namely business, medical and legal. Business presents a sophisticated and fluid context in which intercultural communication or miscommunication can severely impact a company's profit margin. Medical and legal contexts are interesting foci because Western approaches to medical and legal practice are very reliant on question and answer pairs. Our earlier discussion of speech acts comes to bear on these contexts. In any case, each of these subsections includes a discussion of some of the seminal works on workplace cultures as well as more contemporary works.

10.2 WORKPLACE CULTURES IN CONTACT

Studies of intercultural workplaces owe much to a series of projects in the 1970s and 1980s. For instance, the German Heidelberger Forschungsprojekt Pidgin-Deutch (1975) explored best practice for the investigation of industrial communication (Clyne 1994). Yet, John Gumperz and his contemporaries are considered to have done the pioneering research on intercultural communication in the workplace. Gumperz, Jupp and Roberts, among others, explored intercultural communication in the 1970s and 1980s as part of the British National Centre for Industrial Training (e.g. Gumperz, Jupp & Roberts 1979; Gumperz 1982). Gumperz's study of Londoners born in Pakistan, India and the West Indies led him to lay the foundations for interactional sociolinguistics (Tannen 2011). Interactional sociolinguistics informs many if not most contemporary approaches to naturally occurring discourse in the workplace. On the one hand, Gumperz was a humanist and social activist who used sociolinguistic theory to shed light on employment discrimination in the workplace (Tannen 2011). On the other, Gumperz dedicated himself to an objective approach using naturally occurring data, with a focus on how such interaction might shed light on cultural difference (Heller 2013). Heller (2013, p. 395) notes: '[Gumperz] was concerned about the effect of historical conditions on real people in real time with their lives . . . and [p]erhaps his greatest insight was the recognition that social difference and social inequality get made in communicative practice.'

Gumperz inspired a series of 1990s studies that illustrated the complexities of workplace cultures in context. Of particular note, there was a proliferation of intercultural workplace studies in Melbourne, Australia. A major demographic shift occurred in Australia from the 1940s to the 1990s. Post–World War Two industrial expansion led to waves of migration from Europe, Latin America and the Mediterranean regions of the Middle East. The conflict in South-East Asia led to another wave of migration, in the late 1970s and early 1980s. In the wake of a changing Australia, Michael Clyne emerged as a champion of its multilingual and multicultural potential (see Pauwels 2011). The work of Clyne and his PhD students, colleagues and contemporaries highlighted cultural difference in the Australian workplace and how such difference could be overcome.

Clyne (1994) investigated a series of workplaces with diverse ethnolinguistic composition in Melbourne, Australia. This work drew heavily upon as well as revised Speech Act Theory and Grice's maxims (see Chapter 2). Clyne's work focused on two car factories, one of American origin and one of Japanese origin; a textile factory of Australian origin; an electronics factory of German origin; the catering section of a migrant hostel; two government offices; and meetings of a multicultural parents' group. In all, a total of 182 hours of audio recordings were analysed. Clyne's monograph contains an excellent account of theoretical perspectives underpinning the methodology and analysis of a wide range of features of intercultural communication.

Of a total of 26 instances of communication breakdown in the corpus, Clyne reported that 18 of them were resolved through negotiation of meaning. Six of the instances involved problems in understanding the content and/or context or the communication, seven involved vocabulary or grammatical decoding difficulties and another six were discourse problems related to cultural background. The example discussed in Chapter 4, of an apology offered by a Polish female operator taking considerable time to gain the acceptance of her workplace supervisor of Malaysian–Chinese background, is an instance of the last type.

Several of the instances of miscommunication were those in which the addressee did not understand 'small talk', which was intended by the speaker as friendly phatic communication but, perhaps, due to it referring to activities and people outside the context of the workplace, was not understood at all. One instance was the result of intolerance of a longer pause than met the expectations of the communication partner. Clyne observed (1994, p. 147) that the resolution of most of the instances of communication breakdown in the corpus, and the attempted resolution of all of them, speak for the intercultural expertise that has been acquired in Australian society and the Australian workplace.

Béal (1990) investigated a Melbourne workplace context in which native speakers of French and native speakers of Australian English worked together. This part of her study related to differences in the ways in which French and Australian co-workers behaved when it came to requests and how the two sets of sociolinguistic rules could clash. There has been considerable work on cross-cultural differences in requests (see Chapter 4). In Béal's study, we see examples of how such differences are actually played out within a single intercultural workplace. In particular, Béal identifies differences between speakers as to which politeness strategies they prefer to use when making a request, differences between speakers in the assessment of what constitutes a 'face-threatening' act, and clashes between 'face wants' and other wants (Béal 1990, p. 16).

Using Brown and Levinson's notions of positive politeness (aiming to satisfy the interlocutor's desire to be acknowledged and approved of) and negative politeness (minimising a potential threat to territory, privacy or freedom of action (Brown & Levinson 1987)), Béal found that French and Australian speakers tended to choose different conventionalised forms to minimise the threat to the face of the hearer when making a request. Unfortunately, in both directions, interlocutors misinterpreted the negative politeness strategies of their co-workers.

In French, negative politeness is accomplished most of the time by the use of an impersonal verb such as *il faut* (literally, *it has to be* + past participle). In English one would typically use an indirect speech act such as *could you possibly (do such and such)*. Béal (1990, p. 20) recounts the case of a young French employee who had only been in Australia for a few months having a rather serious falling out with one of the secretaries. In discussion with Béal after the incident, the employee exclaimed:

> honestly, I don't understand what I did wrong, I said 'this has to be done immediately', you know, 'Il faut le faire toute de suite', 'il faut': 'this has to be done' (toute de suite means 'immediately') . . .

Béal observes that the explanation showed that the employee was carrying communication conventions from French to English and by insisting that she had correctly translated 'Il faut' she was emphasising the French rationale for choosing this particular strategy, which carries the idea 'this is not me asking, the order comes from above us – it is me and you versus the system'. To a native speaker of English, this form comes across as very abrupt because it lacks any personal touch. In contrast, Béal reports that the English habit of asking 'Would you mind doing this for me', which may be regarded as acknowledging a personal debt (another instance of negative politeness), annoyed some of the French people; for them making requests in the workplace personal was inappropriate and they interpreted the 'for me' as a case of 'me and the system versus you'.

More generally, Béal found that the French employees were more likely to use positive politeness strategies – through the use of in-group terminology, directness and turn overlap – to emphasise their shared group affiliation. They therefore tended to interpret the conventionally indirect request forms used by Australian employees as deliberate attempts to keep social distance.

Béal (1990, p. 31) suggests that her data identifies the need to reassess, to some extent, the accepted current models for the description of politeness phenomena. In her view, tying up the notion of politeness almost exclusively to the notion of face represents an essentially Anglo-centric approach that regards positive face strategies as 'less polite'. By ranking negative politeness as more polite than positive politeness, Béal argues that the fundamental difference between positive and negative politeness is obliterated or becomes blurred, and the theory cannot account easily for examples such as those in which French speakers feel insulted by tactful Australian negative politeness strategies.

Béal (1990, p. 31) observes three basic differences between positive politeness and negative politeness. She suggests that positive politeness is global, rather than related to speech acts; long term, rather than immediate; and escalating, rather than stable. Béal's point exemplifies our observations in Chapter 3, that positive politeness, which relates to the acknowledgment of another person's worth, can be achieved not only by refraining from criticism of the person, and by building up solidarity through the use of shared colloquial expressions and other informal linguistic in-group behaviour, but also by overt acknowledgement of the accomplishments of the individual, which may be expressed formally in many circumstances. As Béal points out, these gestures form part of an ongoing process of creating relationships. On the other hand, negative politeness, which relates to the management of face-threatening acts (FTAs), refers to the particular situation of use, and to particular speech acts, that may involve FTAs. Of course, the impact of negative politeness will also be sensitive to what different people regard as FTAs.

The work undertaken by researchers such as Gumperz, Clyne and Béal laid the groundwork for later, more sophisticated accounts of language in the workplace. Recent research has sought to mobilise constructivist and ethnographic methodologies for understanding workplace culture.

→ whom do you socialize with? (workplace)

The **Communities of Practice** (CofP) concept has been a particularly valuable tool for understanding workplace cultures in recent years. Eckert and McConnell-Ginet (1992, p. 464) define a CofP as:

> an aggregate of people who come together around mutual engagement in an endeavour. Ways of doing things, ways of talking, beliefs, power relations – in short, practices – emerge in the course of this mutual endeavour. As a social construct, a Community of Practice is different from the traditional community, primarily because it is defined by its membership and by the practice in which that membership engages.

CofPs are primarily discussed along three dimensions: mutual engagement, a jointly negotiated enterprise and a shared repertoire. Thus, the CofP is well suited to studying workplace contexts. Workplace culture by its very nature entails mutual engagement in a jointly negotiated enterprise. Furthermore, as Schnurr (2009b, p. 4) points out, 'Groups that work together for a long time often develop a shared repertoire of behavioural and linguistic norms'.

Numerous studies have drawn on the CofP to study workplace contexts in recent years (e.g. Mullany 2004; Schnurr, Marra & Holmes 2007; Schnurr 2009a, 2009b; Angouri 2010; Angouri & Marra 2011). For instance, Schnurr, Marra and Holmes (2007) use the CofP to illustrate how leadership strategies differ in New Zealand between Māori and Pākehā (white European) contexts. In a general sense, many business norms may be understood in terms of the dominant Pākehā culture. However, the CofP approach enables the analyst to understand how the local Māori business, as a CofP positioned within wider Pākehā society, conducts business practices in local and distinctly Māori ways. For instance, among other things, a Māori meeting generally opens with formal greetings or prayers, whereas Pākehā openings are less formal (Schnurr, Marra & Holmes 2007). Complaints in the Pākehā business context are often conducted through administrative means (e.g. official paper notices), whereas in the Māori CofP they are shown to be accomplished through humorous banter (Schnurr, Marra & Holmes 2007).

Workplaces have been a rich domain for studies of intercultural communication for a number of reasons. First, they mark a key testing ground for theoretical concepts used to understand intercultural communication. Second, workplaces are increasingly seeing the financial benefits of intercultural training (see Chapter 11). Third, and perhaps the most important reason, globalisation has led to increasingly diversified workplaces. We are more likely than ever to encounter someone unlike ourselves in the global workforce, be it as a co-worker or a client. In the following sections, we review three workplace contexts: business, medical and legal. Each workplace presents its own challenges. Negotiation is key to business contexts. Information seeking and presentation are critical in the medical and legal contexts.

10.3   BUSINESS CONTEXTS

Negotiation is a fundamental human practice. Ferraro (2002, p. 125) points out: 'We negotiate with our spouses, children, co-workers, friends, bosses, landlords, customers, bankers, neighbors, and clients.' Yet, negotiation can be particularly stressful where the financial stakes are high and cultural values and symbolic systems aren't shared. Ferraro (2002, p. 125) writes: 'different values, attitudes, morals, behaviors, and linguistic styles... can greatly affect the process and outcome of our negotiations.' This is particularly problematic in the twenty-first century; as Angouri (2010, p. 206) writes:

> the international nature of socio-economic activities is reshaping workplace settings and creating the need for large numbers of employees to perform successful communicative acts with a wider range of interactants than in the past, often using a language other than their mother tongue.

This section reviews how cultural differences come to bear on business interactions, especially those involving negotiation.

To start with, negotiation has been shown to be problematic at the level of Hofstede's national cultural differences (see Chapter 1). For instance, Ferraro (2002) notes that cultures that favour individualism (e.g. US American) may run into problems when negotiating with those that favour collectivism (e.g. Japanese). For instance, US Americans are more likely to focus on self-interest in negotiations whereas Japanese are more likely to suppress self-interest in favour of the interests of the group (Ferraro 2002). Each strategy may be viewed as inappropriate by the other side. Differing norms as to directness/indirectness may also be problematic. For instance, the Japanese might find the US American style to be unintelligent because it lacks subtlety (Ferraro 2002). Conversely, the US Americans might find the Japanese style to be 'sneaky and covert' (Ferraro 2002, p. 126)

A number of studies emerged in the 1990s and early 2000s that investigated the language of business negotiations (e.g. Marriott 1990; the edited volume by Firth 1995; Spencer-Oatey & Xing 2003). Marriott (1990) investigated a business encounter between a Japanese businessman and an Australian businessman meeting for the first time. This study shows that miscommunication occurs significantly when the parties have different expectations of the particular phase of the negotiation. Marriott uses the term **norm discrepancy** to refer to the observation that the two parties each assume the negotiation will proceed in certain (but quite different) ways according to the norms of their respective cultures.

Marriott's methodology involved videotaping the actual business encounter between (J), the senior Japanese representative of a Japanese company located in Melbourne, who had been resident in Australia for two and a half months, and an Australian businessman (A), who was the managing director of his own, recently established, small cheese company. Marriott also conducted follow-up interviews with each participant during which the videotape was replayed segment by segment. These interviews and all comments by the participants were audio-taped. Marriott's use of follow-up interviews followed the approach advocated by Neustypný (e.g. Neustypný 1985) and proved to be of significant value.

Marriott (1990, p. 40) reports that an examination of the discourse of the business negotiation and of the follow-up interviews revealed that the Australian and the Japanese interactants held disparate views on the function of their first interaction. The Australian's objective was clearly to introduce his product and to obtain from his Japanese addressee an indication of interest in proceeding to a further stage of the negotiation. The objective of the Japanese businessman, on the other hand, was to obtain information about the Australian company and of its intention relating to future cooperation.

In the follow-up interview, Marriott (1990, p. 47) reports that J declared that the purpose of his first meeting was to procure information about A's company and its plans. Simultaneously, he raised two socioeconomic problems. One concerned the lack of the Australian company possessing a patent. The other related to the small size of the Japanese cheese market for such specialised cream cheese as that manufactured by A's company. However, J did not explicitly refer to the difficulties of entering into a cooperative arrangement with the Australian as the purpose of that meeting was just to gather information for reporting to head office.

Marriott suggests that although it could be argued that the Japanese businessman's behaviour was motivated by the desire to express politeness by avoiding an explicit display of disinterest, as is frequently contended in the popular literature, there is a much stronger case for arguing that his conduct was due to different norms concerning the function of the interaction. The cultural norm of the Japanese businessman certainly did not require him to make any commitment at this stage or even venture his own individual evaluation. Marriott concludes that the disparity of the norms in this regard was particularly strong, and since it was the Australian businessman who, using his own native norm, noted and negatively evaluated a deviation in the conduct of the Japanese businessman, it was he who was frustrated at the outcome of the negotiation.

Spencer-Oatey and Xing (2003) report on two Chinese–British business meetings held by the same British company to welcome groups of engineers from a Chinese company with which they had been doing business for some time. Spencer-Oatey and Xing (2003, p. 38) report that despite many similarities between the meetings, both the British and the Chinese were very satisfied with the first meeting, while the Chinese were very annoyed with the second meeting. The seating arrangements were interpreted as conveying a negative 'status' message. The Chinese Delegation Leader expressed his concerns as follows:

> it shouldn't have been that he was the chair and we were seated along the sides of the table. With equal status, they should sit along this side and we should sit along that side . . .

In other words, the Chinese felt that since the two teams were of equal status, they should have sat on opposite sides of the table, with the heads of each side sitting in the middle.

Spencer-Oatey and Xing also report two difficulties relating to the welcome speech offered by the British chairman. First, the Chinese felt that the British chairman's comments on the Sino-British relationship were not weighty enough. Spencer-Oatey and Xing (2003, p. 39) explain that the Chinese had heard on the grapevine that the British company was in serious financial difficulties, and they believed it was the Chinese contracts that had saved them from bankruptcy. This was expressed by a Chinese sales manager in the following terms:

> It is understandable for them to praise their own products, but by doing so they in fact made a big mistake. Why? Because, you see, because for a company when they haven't got new orders for their products for several years it is a serious problem for them, but they didn't talk about it . . . he should have said that you have made great efforts regarding [the sale of] our products, right? And hope you continue. They should have said more in this respect. He didn't mention our orders. So in fact this is a very important matter. It is not a matter of just receiving us . . .

Spencer-Oatey and Xing conclude that the British were not strong enough in their compliments towards the Chinese, and in the degree of gratitude they expressed.

Recent research on business contexts is largely driven by authentic interactional data (see Drew & Heritage 1992). Much of this research has been concerned with how leadership is accomplished in workplace settings (e.g. Holmes 2005; Schnurr, Marra & Holmes 2007; Schnurr 2009a, 2009b; Angouri & Marra 2011; Schnurr & Chan 2011; Schnurr & Zayts 2011). Superiors in business contexts draw on a range of strategies to accomplish leadership (Rogerson-Revell 2011). Furthermore, subordinates respond to these strategies in varied ways across cultures. Humour, teasing and self-denigration are among the key strategies used to accomplish leadership across cultures. The use of humour in international business contexts can lead to miscommunication. For instance, the Australian willingness to joke and tease in a business context can make Asians uncomfortable (Mulholland 1997, cited in Rogerson-Revell 2007). However, in many if not most instances, it may be noted that there are similarities and differences in the way in which leadership is accomplished.

For example, Schnurr and Chan (2011) investigate how employees in New Zealand and Hong Kong companies do and respond to teasing and self-denigration. In New Zealand, managers are more likely to engage in self-denigration, as is seen in the following exchange. A manager, Jill, has just returned from seeking IT assistance. She shares her experience with another, lower ranking manager, Lucy:

1	Jill:	[comes back]
2		he just laughed at me
3	Lucy:	[laughs]: oh no:
4	Jill:	he's definitely going to come to my aid
5		but () he just sort of laughed at me
6	Lucy:	[laughs]
7	Jill:	(and then) I've got this appalling reputation
8		of being such a technical klutz and //()\ sometimes
9	Lucy:	/[laughs]\\
10	Jill:	look it's not ME + I work with what I've got + //()\
11	Lucy:	/I know\\ It's the tools you've been prov//ided\
12	Jill:	/that's\\ right +++

(Schnurr & Chan 2011, p. 31)

Jill downplays her higher status and face by categorising herself as a 'technical klutz' in line 8 (Scnurr & Chan 2011). However, this is meant to be taken lightly as playful self-denigration and this is partially acknowledged by Lucy's laughter.

Similar self-denigration is noted in the Hong Kong context as in the following interaction where a boss, Liu, is annoyed at a subordinate, Benjamin, for taking a phone call. Liu makes this point in part by teasing Benjamin for his impoliteness with the caller, his father:

9	Liu:	/talking to your father\\ in such an impolite manner
10		how//can you do this\
11	Some & Ben:	/[soft laughter]\\
12		[Benjamin smiles through Liu's utterance]
13	Liu:	{you} can be impolite to your boss
14		{you} can't be impolite to your father
15		//don't you know\
16		it's hard to be a father +
17		do you understand
18	Some:	/[louder laughter]\\
19	Benjamin:	Mm

(Schnurr & Chan 2011, p. 28)

The boss Liu engages in self-denigration in lines 13–4 where he indicates that one can be impolite to their boss but not to their father. This is clearly meant as a joke within the Hong Kong context, where it is unlikely that one will be impolite to their boss (Schnurr & Chan 2011). This self-denigrating joke is acknowledged with laughter by others present at the meeting.

Schnurr and Chan find that individuals use teasing and self-denigration in similar ways in New Zealand and Hong Kong. However, there are some differences in the way in which subordinates react to the teasing and self-denigration. For instance, subordinates in New Zealand generally play along with the teasing, shift responsibility onto others, tease back or laugh. In Hong Kong, however, the strategies are more varied and complex. Subordinates would most typically sigh, plead for the teasing to stop or attempt to shift the blame. This is seen in the following exchange, in which the Hong Kong boss Liu teases manager Richard for a sudden trust in an employee, Anthony. Richard had often questioned Anthony, a relatively new hire, until recently. Liu notes this:

1	Liu:	no need to take a look
2		he trusts him now
3	Richard:	[sighs]

4	Liu:	{he} suddenly has so much confidence in (him) +
5	Richard:	[sighs] {i've} already got used to {it}
6	Liu:	already got used to {it}
7		good (.)

(Schnurr & Chan 2011, p. 25)

Schnurr and Chan (2011) attribute the differing responses of New Zealand and Hong Kong employees to socio-cultural norms. Hierarchy is more important in Hong Kong, so employees will be more reticent to question hierarchies. Subordinates in New Zealand, which emphasises a more egalitarian culture, would be more apt to tease back.

Schnurr and Chan (2011) note how individual and local CofPs may orient to wider socio-cultural norms. In other words, local CofPs may on the one hand reaffirm cultural norms, as is the case in the New Zealand company's CofP. Subordinates of this CofP have a local repertoire that permits them to tease their superiors to an extent. This is unsurprising in light of wider socio-cultural norms in New Zealand that favour egalitarianism. However, other CofPs in other companies may not approve of this behaviour. In Hong Kong, we see the case of a CofP within a company that arguably does not reaffirm cultural norms to a degree. The Hong Kong CofP, a sales and production team, permits some teasing of individuals whereas other, more hierarchically focused business CofPs may not.

Thus, in approaching international business, one must take into account local socio-cultural norms. However, one must always realise that local practices, while embedded within wider socio-cultural norms, are ultimately driven by the CofP within which one is operating.

10.4   MEDICAL CONTEXTS

Communication also unfolds in varied ways within medical contexts across cultures. Consequently, globalisation has meant a growing concern for intercultural competency by medical practitioners (Cole 2004; Lamiani 2008). Schouten and Meeuwesen (2006, p. 21) note: 'Culture and ethnicity have been cited as barriers in establishing an effective and satisfying doctor-patient relationship.' This has led some medical practitioners to discuss health-care delivery in terms of cultural safety (Phiri, Dietsch & Bonner 2010). Cultural safety results from sophisticated cultural awareness and a cultural sensitivity that legitimises cultural differences of the 'other' within the medical context (Phiri, Dietsch & Bonner 2010).

Cultural safety evolved as a result of Māori patients' dissatisfaction with the Pākehā medical system (Phiri, Dietsch & Bonner 2010).

The doctor–patient relationship may be influenced at the macro level by national cultural difference (see Chapter 1). For instance, for nations that favour a larger power distance, consultations are shorter and unexpected information is less likely to be exchanged. Furthermore, rapport is less likely to be built in nations with higher uncertainty avoidance (Meeuwesen, van den Brink-Muinen & Hofstede 2009). Along these lines, doctors in such cultures are less likely to make eye contact. In Europe, migrants from non-Western contexts have been shown to be more cooperative patients than those from Western contexts (Schouten, Meeuwesen, Tromp & Harmsen 2007). Among other things, migrant patients are less engaged with the consultation in a symmetrical way than their Western counterparts. They are also less likely to 'put on the breaks' in a consultation where there has been a misunderstanding (Meeuwesen, van den Brink-Muinen & Hofstede 2009).

Language and speech acts are of course critically important in the doctor–patient relationship (e.g. Suurmond & Seeleman 2006; Cordella & Spike 2008; Cordella & Musgrave 2009; Cordella 2012; Lingard 2013). For instance, requests for information are critically important to assessing a patient's wellbeing and for obtaining their medical history. Davidson (2000, p. 383) characterises medical interviews as a type of verbal and physical investigation:

> a matching of unorganized experiences against familiar patterns and processes of human vulnerability to disease. The overt elaborated goals of the medical interview are: (1) from the data provided, determine what, if anything, is wrong with the patient; (2) elaborate a plan of treatment for the ailment; and (3) convince the patient of the validity of the diagnosis so that treatment can be followed.

Davidson suggests that the 'creation' of medical 'facts' through medical practice is heavily influenced by a social evaluation of the meaning and importance of whatever facts are uncovered or created (Foucault 1963; Waitzkin 1991). Davidson (2000, p. 383) thus sees diagnosis as an 'interpretive process in which the patient's physical and verbal data is passed, by physicians, through a grid of medical meanings (biological and social) and re-analysed, so that "irrelevant" input from the patient may be excluded and the story of the disease constructed'.

The doctor–patient relationship sometimes entails the discussion of difficult topics or the deliverance of difficult news. The conventions for the discussion of these topics and the deliverance of such news often differ across cultures (e.g. Cordella & Spike 2008; Cordella & Musgrave 2009; Zayts & Schnurr 2011). For instance, Cordella and Musgrave (2009) investigated the performance of international medical graduates (IMGs) in the Australian context. They focused on the enactment of empathy in the deliverance of a bowel cancer diagnosis in a simulated consultation. They noted variation in how the mostly Asian IMGs delivered the news in terms of word selection, sequence organisation and patient focus. In a few cases, this led to patients' view that the IMGs had poor communication skills. For instance, patients (actors in this case) believed some IMGs did not adequately initiate or sustain reassurance patterns. Furthermore, from patients' perspectives, some IMGs were not attentive enough to the patients' words. This led the IMGs to not respond with the appropriate amount of empathy when delivering difficult news (Cordella & Musgrave 2009).

Zayts and Schnurr (2011) show how laughter may be used to mitigate the discussion of difficult topics in a Hong Kong medical context. They investigate how medical providers use laughter in prenatal genetic counselling to assist patients make decisions. Notably, Zayts and Schnurr draw on conversation analytical techniques in approaching interactions (see Chapter 5). They show that medical practitioners use laughter to 'overcome patient resistance' and to help themselves deal with tough patient questions (Zayts & Schnurr 2011, p. 1). For instance, in the following exchange, a medical practitioner uses laughter to resist a patient's refusal of further information:

(MP = medical provider; P = patient)

1	P:		I want to continue (pregnancy).
2	MP:		You want to continue. Mm, or, would you like to have
3			more information on amniocentesis?
4	P:		((shakes her head throughout the utterance)) No (it's
5			not – it's not) [(necessary)].
6	MP:	→	[You d(h)on't] wa(h)nt [hah hah hah
7		→	hah < hah]
8	P:	→	[heh heh huh huh
9		→	huh] I'm s(h)o(h) –
10	MP:	→	Yo(h)u don't w(h)ant.
11	P:	→	I don't wa(h)nt t(h)o.

(Zayts & Schnurr 2011, p. 11)

The laughter in line 6 enables the medical practitioner to respond to and arguably to overcome the patient's resistance to further information

(Zayts & Schnurr 2011). It is worth noting that Zayts and Schnurr do not present this as a distinctly Hong Kong way of using laughter. However, it does show how laughter may be used in the medical context to mitigate difficult topics or difficult news. Furthermore, considered alongside other discussions of laughter and humour in this book, it shows how laughter may be mobilised for a variety of conversational goals across contexts and cultures.

The issue of differences in cultural expectations of communication, and of expectations about medical encounters in general, as well as the inherent asymmetrical knowledge–power relationship between doctors and patients, thus makes intercultural medical encounters particularly complex. Since the diagnosis and subsequent decision-making about treatment rely so heavily on input from the patient, any difficulties in gathering information may undermine the process significantly.

10.5   LEGAL CONTEXTS

Much of the work of the legal profession also involves the gathering of information from clients and witnesses, and relies heavily on questions and answers. Furthermore, as with medical encounters, the legal context often includes the discussion of difficult topics and the deliverance of difficult news. It is thus crucial that legal practitioners are aware of the complexities involved in information gathering in general, and particular issues involved in intercultural contexts. Poor communication between legal practitioners and the public may result in injustice and inefficiencies (Gibbons 2001). Those less proficient in English or from different cultures particularly run the risk of being disadvantaged in the legal system (Gibbons 2001).

Ethnic minorities, asylum seekers, the deaf and limited English profi-cient populations are among those disadvantaged by the Anglo legal system. The legal system can be complex and includes many face-threatening acts (e.g. adversarial questioning, overruling) (Charnok 2009; Archer 2011). Furthermore, legal professionals have been shown to engage in unscrupu-lous behaviours in interviews. For instance, deaf defendants have obligingly and trustingly signed documents placed in front of them by police officers (Vernon et al. 2001). These documents have sometimes led the deaf inad-vertently to acknowledge guilt or processes they did not fully understand. Furthermore, in the US context, defendants with limited English have been interrogated by police officers with limited Spanish (Berk-Seligson 2009). This has led to problems due to linguistic misunderstandings but also because the roles of interpreter and interrogator should not be blurred (Berk-Seligson 2009). As noted in Chapter 9, the interpreter should be impartial and aim for pragmatic equivalence.

Intercultural differences come to bear on individuals' participation in the legal process. For instance, Jacquemet (2011), drawing on Gumperz's work above, outlines reasons for communicative breakdowns in asylum seeker interviews in Europe. Jacquemet (2011, p. 482) writes:

> One of the most problematic issues in the asylum process is the determination of the asylum seeker's credibility. In making this determination, state officials routinely rely on their own indigenous understanding of the factors that establish credibility, an understanding that asylum seekers do not necessarily share.

This can lead officials to erroneously label confusing aspects of an asylum seeker's narrative as problematic and in the asylum seeker context this can be a death sentence. For instance, in the following exchange, an asylum seeker encounters difficulty with an official who doesn't understand the asylum seeker's address:

Belgian Asylum Courts

AS = woman, Sierra Leone, prob. Njala; O = woman, Belgian

O:	ok . . . your address in Sierra Leone
AS:	Puba
O:	Puba . . . no street name
AS:	Puba
O:	that is the city hen . . . Puba
AS:	<<unintelligible>
O:	what is it . . .
AS:	I don't understand . . . au that
O:	Puba . . . is the city or the village?
AS:	it's a VILLAge
O:	yes . . . and the name of the street . . .
AS:	what?
O:	name of the street
AS:	Puba
O:	ALSO Puba?
AS:	the name of the street
O:	Yes . . . your street has no name

(based on Jacquemet 2011, p. 486)

A Belgian interviewer from an urban European context might find it difficult to comprehend a lack of street address. For instance, Bohmer and Shuman (2007, cited in Jacquemet 2011) note that a US judge found an Afghani asylum seeker's story non-credible because the asylum seeker said his brother was in a prison hospital but could not provide the hospital's name. Bohmer and Shuman note that in Afghanistan a hospital's name is not as common knowledge as it is in the United States.

Focusing on particular cultural groups, Indigenous Australians are often disadvantaged in the Anglo-Australian court system because of differing communication norms. Pauwels, D'Argaville and Eades (1992) observe that although Aboriginal people use direct questions in routine situations, such as to find out who a person is related to, or where they come from, in situations where Aboriginal people want to find out significant information they do not use direct questions. In Aboriginal interactions, information is sought as part of a two-way exchange. Hinting, volunteering information for confirmation or denial, silence, and waiting until people are ready to give information, are all central to Aboriginal ways of seeking any substantial information. It is important not to rush people or put them on the spot, and not to invade their personal privacy with direct questions about substantial issues.

Pauwels, D'Argaville and Eades (1992, pp. 103–4) provide the following fictionalised series of examples, drawn from a number of actual cases, that contrast the way an Aboriginal English speaker gives information about the time of an event, in courtroom questioning, and in answer to investigation by an Aboriginal Field Officer. They point out that it would be a mistake to conclude that the speaker is vague or uncertain about the timing of the event in question. He is able to give much precise information relevant to this, in his own terms, relating the incident to other events that happened on the same morning. On the other hand, his courtroom evidence, which is tied down to clock times, may give the false impression that the speaker is unsure about the event, or inconsistent, or an unreliable witness.

EXAMPLE 1

Examination-in-chief: Defence Counsel (DC), Aboriginal witness (A)

DC: What time did this happen?
A: I don't know ... I know we's working ...
DC: Well, what time was it?
A: About 10 o'clock.

EXAMPLE 2

Cross-examination: Public Prosecutor (PP), Aboriginal witness (A)

PP: When did this happen?
A: It was in the morning sometime . . .
PP: Was it late in the morning?
A: Yeah, pretty late.
PP: Say, 11.30?
A: Yeah, 11.30.

EXAMPLE 3

Investigation: Aboriginal Field Officer (FO), Aboriginal witness (A)

FO: When that thing you talking about happened?
A: I don't know . . . I know we's working . . . morning, or afternoon . . . I don't really know.
FO: You fellas already had 'smoko'?
A: Well, we have smoko already, then old Aunt Bessie come
down – she was lookin' for that cousin belong to what's-'is-
name, used to live up there along the riverbank before. She
stopped for a while, then she went up to the hospital – that
cousin might be there, eh? – then we's working again a bit
more. Then that's when the boolimun [policeman] came,
like I'm telling you.
FO: Them school kids, they already came back for lunch?
A: No, boolimun come before that.

Indigenous Australian participation in the Anglo-Australian legal system
is among the most well-studied intercultural legal contexts. This is largely
because of the rich body of work conducted by Australian linguist Diane
Eades (e.g. Eades 1992, 1993, 2000, 2004, 2006, 2012).[1] For example,
Eades (2000) examines the reaction of Aboriginal witnesses in a New
South Wales country town to various types of questions, and shows that
even though several of these witnesses are able, to their advantage, to use
yes/no questions as an invitation to tell an explanatory narrative, such
leeway seems to be restricted to the provision of evidence that the defence

---

[1] Spanish speakers' participation in the US American system is well studied, too. This is in part
because of the vast body of work conducted by Susan Berk-Seligson.

lawyer or the judge feels is relevant. In cases in which these narratives relate family relationships and other aspects of contemporary Aboriginal social organisation that seem less relevant to the same officers of the court, they tend to restrict the Aboriginal witness' answers, effectively 'silencing' that part of the witness' testimony.

10.6   SUMMARY

In this chapter we have seen a variety of features of intercultural communication drawing on research conducted in actual intercultural professional and workplace contexts. We reviewed a number of studies to emerge from Melbourne in the 1990s. These studies often tested and revised some of the core theoretical concepts of intercultural communication (e.g. Grice's maxims, Speech Act Theory). We also introduced more contemporary approaches to workplace discourse, paying particular attention to the Community of Practice concept. This enabled a review of workplace communication in business, medical and legal contexts. In sum, this research further enhances our understanding of the nature of intercultural communication, which ultimately constitutes a basis for intercultural competence. The global workplace is increasingly an intercultural workplace. This chapter has sought to show how a variety of theoretical concepts introduced in this book could be mobilised to understand the global and intercultural workplace.

10.7   REVIEW

1. **Key terms**
    Communication conventions, cultural expectations/assumptions, norms, norm discrepancy, follow-up interviews, information gathering, question and answer sequences, asymmetric power, communication breakdown, miscommunication, negotiation of meaning (from Chapter 3, positive and negative politeness).
2. **Key ideas**
    Having read this chapter you should:
    a. understand the importance of expectations and norms in relation to communication in general, and intercultural communication in particular
    b. appreciate the potential for communication failure in such contexts, and be able to identify some of the causes of communication breakdown

    c. be able to use an understanding of these issues for the purpose of smooth intercultural interaction.

3. **Focus questions**

    a. Positive and negative politeness strategies of French and Australian co-workers

    Consider the examples of positive and negative politeness provided by Béal in the research reported above and identify which strategies you might use in a similar context. Are you more inclined to use positive or negative politeness strategies?

    b. The importance of norms in understanding intercultural communication

    Much of the material in this chapter provides examples of miscommunication that has occurred in intercultural communication, often due to differences in what we call cultural norms or cultural expectations. One of the problems with differences in cultural norms or expectations is that the speaker is usually unaware that there is a particular expectation or norm involved. Speakers usually regard their own communication style as 'sensible' and 'appropriate'. In view of this, do you think that either of the terms or 'cultural norm' or 'cultural expectation' is more suitable than the other? (You need to consider what is meant by 'expectation' in this context.)

    c. Questions and answers in contexts of asymmetrical power

    In the speech acts table in the Appendix, Searle (1969) outlines a number of conditions for the speech act question. Consider in what way the conditions identified by Searle may be helpful in understanding why people in positions of relatively little power, such as patients in the medical context and witnesses in the legal context, often have difficulty answering the questions that are put to them.

4. **Research analysis**

    Indigenous Australian witnesses in the courtroom

    Which of the utterances provided by the Aboriginal witnesses in the scenarios above would contribute to a conclusion that Aboriginal people are uncooperative in the courtroom? Discuss.

5. **Research exercise**

    The research reported in this chapter is all based on authentic intercultural communication data.

    a. What do you think are the reasons that there is more cross-cultural research (where two cultures are compared) than intercultural research (where speakers from different cultures are engaged in some activity)?

b. Check a recent research journal on intercultural communication, or intercultural pragmatics, and determine whether or not this is the case for the research reported in the journal you choose.

SUGGESTED FURTHER READING

Gumperz and Clyne provide foundational work for modern study of workplace communication. Gumperz, in particular, has shown how a sophisticated analysis of naturally occurring speech can highlight intercultural miscommunications and contribute to their avoidance. In more recent years, Holmes and colleagues have conducted a phenomenal project on language in the workplace in New Zealand. The Language in the Workplace Project (LWP) has yielded a rich body of work on intercultural communication. Furthermore, it has provided innovative means for approaching the study of workplace communication. Cordella and colleagues have recently provided excellent and sophisticated accounts of intercultural communication in medical contexts. Eades' work on Indigenous Australians in the legal process complements (and informs) Hale's and Berk-Seligson's (introduced in the previous chapter). In any case, all three authors illustrate how minority groups may be disadvantaged within the mainstream legal process.

Clyne, M. 1994 *Inter-cultural Communication at Work: Cultural Values in Discourse*. Cambridge: Cambridge University Press.

Cordella, M. & Musgrave, S. 2009 'Oral communication skills of international medical graduates: Assessing empathy in discourse'. *Communication and Medicine*, vol. 6, no. 2, pp. 129–42.

Eades, D. 2012 'Communication with Aboriginal speakers of English in the legal process'. *Australian Journal of Linguistics*, vol. 32, no. 4, pp. 473–89.

Gumperz, J. 1982 *Discourse Strategies*. Cambridge: Cambridge University Press.

Holmes, J., Marra, M. & Schnurr, S. 2008 'Impoliteness and ethnicity: Māori and Pākehā discourse in New Zealand workplaces'. *Journal of Politeness Research*, vol. 4, pp. 193–219.

Holmes, J. & Stubbe, M. 2005 '"Feminine" workplaces: stereotype and reality'. In Holmes J. & Meyerhoff M. (eds) *The Handbook of Language and Gender*. Malden, MA: Blackwell, pp. 573–99.

Schnurr, S., Marra, M. & Holmes, J. 2008 'Impoliteness as a means of contesting power in the workplace. In Bousfield D. & Locher M. (eds) *Impoliteness in Language: Studies with Power in Theory and Practice*. Berlin: Mouton De Gruyter, pp. 211–30.

Victoria University of Wellington, School of Linguistics and Applied Language Studies 2014 'The Language in the Workplace Project' <www.victoria.ac.nz/lals/centres-and-institutes/language-in-the-workplace> (accessed 12 May 2014).

11 Successful intercultural communication

11.1 INTRODUCTION

THIS BOOK has sought to provide a sophisticated but accessible discussion of intercultural communication. In Chapter 1, we noted that an understanding of intercultural communication is critically related to an understanding of context. The spoken and written word may be interpreted differentially depending on context. At its most basic level, a spoken or written text may be understood in terms of its contextual felicity. In other words, we noted, drawing on Roberts (2006, p. 199), contextual felicity refers to 'the aptness of an utterance' in 'expressing a proposition that one could take to be reasonable and relevant in light of the context'. Much of Chapters 2–4 were dedicated to aspects of contextual felicity. Yet, we also presented context as something that could be updated and repaired (i.e. contextual update). With this in mind, much of Chapters 5–8 were dedicated to the nuanced, structured and co-constructed nature of social life through the spoken and written word. Chapters 9–10 extended the discussion of contextual felicity and contextual update into the professional realm.

This final chapter examines the implications of the theoretical and professional knowledge of intercultural communication. The reader might consider this his or her call to action. We explore a series of studies and projects that take as their starting point the idea that successful intercultural communication is something that can be achieved. Otherwise, this book and others like it would be pointless. This chapter shows that individuals engaged in intercultural communication can draw on creative discourse strategies to circumvent some aspects of potential miscommunication. As noted in Chapter 9, a human being is capable of establishing a communicative 'bridgehead' with another human being even if the two individuals do not share a linguistic system (e.g. a Westerner encountering a tribesman in Papua New Guinea). In sum, to repeat an assertion made in Chapter 9, 'there is a broad background of shared beliefs and understandings common to us all by virtue of being a human person' (Foley 1997, p. 173).

We begin this chapter by discussing how individuals may work (and indeed have worked) towards successful intercultural communication. We then provide an overview of how institutions and major institutional projects have taken steps to achieve intercultural communication. We next introduce a series of strategies a speaker may employ to achieve intercultural communication in a context. Among other things, we revisit the notion of communication accommodation (see Chapter 1) as well as introduce Sharifian's notion of conceptual renegotiation (Sharifian 2008). We lastly reflect on the reader's role in achieving successful intercultural communication and how this may lead to a safer, healthier and inclusive society. Our focus remains throughout this chapter, as it has in the book on the whole, the role language and language variation play in an increasingly global world.

11.2 INDIVIDUALS AND INTERCULTURAL COMMUNICATION

Numerous books, papers and articles have discussed what it means to achieve successful intercultural communication. This has varyingly been discussed in terms of cultural intelligence (e.g. Earley, Ang & Tan 2006) and intercultural (communication) competence (e.g. Lustig & Koester 2010). **Cultural intelligence**, emerging from international business communication, refers to 'a manager's ability to adapt to new cultural environments' (Earley, Ang & Tan 2006, p. vii). The notion of cultural intelligence highlights that social and emotional intelligence in one's home country does not necessarily translate into cultural intelligence abroad (Earley, Ang & Tan 2006). Cultural, social and emotional intelligence are linked but certainly not inextricably.

However, it is the label 'intercultural (communication) competence' that is most often used to describe a person's ability to achieve successful intercultural communication (e.g. Redmond 2000; Arasaratnam & Banerjee 2011; Holmes & O'Neil 2012). Intercultural competence in the broader sense (i.e. without the parenthetical 'communication') is defined varyingly and inconsistently (Holmes & O'Neil 2012). In short, as Holmes and O'Neil (2012, p. 708, quoting Rathje 2007) write, there is a 'dizzying amount of material [on the subject and] . . . the lack of any unity in the definition of the term'. Yet, focusing on the notion of **intercultural communication competence (ICC)**, Arasaratnam and Banerjee (2011) provide a definition that overlaps with our context-focused approach to intercultural communication. **ICC**, they note, 'has to do with effectiveness (ability to accomplish one's goals) and appropriateness (to exhibit expected and accepted behaviour in context) in intercultural situations'.

Chapters 2–4 of this book have dealt with appropriateness in line with the notion of contextual felicity (Roberts 2006). We have argued that appropriateness may be linked to such concepts as schema, face and politeness. Effectiveness may be linked to the notion of contextual update (Roberts 2006). Ultimately, effectiveness, whether in role, translation or discourse, may only be achieved through co-constructed social action. This requires the ability to co-construct conversational interactions or written work with others. This was indeed the focus of Chapters 5–8 of this book. This led us to explore appropriateness (contextual felicity) and effectiveness (contextual update) in professional contexts in Chapters 9–10.

Intercultural (communication) competence is influenced by any number of factors. For instance, Redmond (2000), drawing on Hofstede's dimensions (see Chapter 1), has linked one's ability to achieve successful intercultural communication to cultural distance. Redmond (2000) examined international students at US American universities. He found that the greater the cultural difference between the students' home culture and the US American culture, the less well students were able to achieve intercultural competence. Numerous studies have shown how intercultural (communication) competence may be achieved, among other things, through cultural knowledge and awareness (e.g. Lustig & Koester 2010), by acknowledging reluctance and fear (e.g. Holmes & O'Neil 2012), through intercultural encounters (e.g. Weigl 2009; Yashima 2010) and by foregrounding and questioning stereotypes (e.g. Holmes & O'Neil 2012). These factors are dealt with in numerous general introductory texts on intercultural communication (e.g. Martin & Nakayama 2004; Lustig & Koester 2010; Samovar et al. 2013; Sorrells 2013).

Returning to the linguistic focus of this book, it is ultimately up to the individual to achieve successful intercultural communication and ICC. This ability ultimately emerges from the individual's motivations, willingness and ability to accommodate to an interlocutor in the intercultural context. Thus, for the individual, at the onset, Communication Accommodation Theory (first introduced in Chapter 1) provides a powerful explanatory device for the motivation and facilitation of intercultural communication. Giles (1977, p. 322), from the perspective of language and social psychology, observes that successful communicators are often motivated to adjust their speech (verbal and non-verbal) to accommodate to the conventions of others, as a means of expressing positive values, attitudes and intentions towards them.

Giles' **Communication Accommodation Theory (CAT)** examines the social motivation for speakers to accommodate to the language conventions of the addressee, including factors such as individual and group identity, and whether the speaker is a member of a dominant or subordinate group (see also Gallois et al. 1988 and articles in Giles & Robinson 1990). In a general sense, CAT proposes that speakers converge towards the speech of a listener to increase intimacy or diverge from the listener's speech to decrease intimacy (Giles & Powesland 1975). This behaviour is driven by a speaker's desire to appear more attractive and promote communicative efficiency (Coupland 2007).

Coupland et al. (1988) extended CAT by incorporating the notion of conversational needs into the model. This focus on the other's interpretive competence (ability to understand) leads to a set of interpretability strategies that include decreasing diversity of vocabulary or simplifying syntax, and modifying pitch, loudness and tempo; and to discourse management strategies that include topic choice (maintaining topic coherence and thematic development), sharing topic selection and sharing management of turn-taking. We return to Coupland et al.'s approach to CAT in section 11.4 below, where we outline the direct strategies an individual may use to facilitate intercultural communication.

11.3   INSTITUTIONS AND INTERCULTURAL COMMUNICATION

Linguistic and cultural knowledge have historically been viewed as 'soft skills' in institutions and have been marginalised in favour of 'hard skills' such as mathematics and accountancy (Ainsworth 2012). However, businesses, governments and non-governmental organisations are increasingly seeing the value of intercultural training. This increased interest has resulted from institutions' financial losses as well as increased global competition. With regard to loss, the attrition rates of US Americans sent to overseas assignments can be staggering. For instance, Caudron (1991, cited in Ferraro 2002; see also Rost-Roth 2007) notes attrition rates of up to 68 per cent for Americans sent to Saudi Arabia, 36 per cent for those sent to Japan and 27 per cent for those sent to Brussels. The financial losses incurred through such attrition can also be staggering. Rost-Roth (2007) notes that insufficient preparation of employees for overseas assignments can lead to losses of US$50 000–$150 000 in individual cases and several tens of millions for companies with hundreds of overseas employees.

Businesses also face increasing competition from globalisation and some cultures have shown a greater interest in attaining intercultural (communication) competence than others. For example, Professor Howard Perlmutter of the Wharton School of Business has famously pointed out: 'If you have a joint venture with a Japanese company, they'll send 24 people here to learn everything you know, and you'll send one person there to tell them everything you know...' (Kupfer 1988, p. 58, cited in Ferraro 2002). At least some Anglo business leaders have taken notice of how such practices put them at a disadvantage in international business. For instance, a recent statement by the Business Council of Australia (2009) noted: 'Australia's future depends not only on our economic success but on our ability to solve fundamental global problems. Understanding the languages and cultures of our nearest neighbours is critical to this effort.' Thus, many institutions have turned their attention to intercultural training and assessment. Notably, language remains a 'soft skill' in the eyes of many employers but these same employers have shown a 'keen interest in "cultural awareness"' (see Prechtl & Lund 2007, p. 467). Prechtl and Lund (2007, p. 467) write: 'Employers identified a need for a better understanding of ways of working with colleagues, suppliers, customers, suppliers, customers, etc. in other countries but had difficulty articulating the concept.' This has led a number of institutions to create projects and schemes for providing such training. A number of professional organisations have been set up throughout the world. For instance, the Society for Intercultural Training, Education and Research (SIETAR) was set up in the United States in 1974 (Rost-Roth 2007). Branches of SIETAR were subsequently set up in Europe in the 1990s. The Commission of the European Community also funded a major intercultural training project, known as the INCA project (Prechtl & Lund 2007). The INCA project provided both training and assessment criteria for intercultural competence. It emerged in response to requests from engineering companies with multi-ethnic teams.

The means through which such training is provided varies. Rost-Roth (2007) notes that role-playing and simulations are the classic methods when it comes to intercultural training. A number of books have also been published that provide the opportunity for individual, self- or other-guided reflective study. For instance, Pan, Scollon and Scollon (2002) draw on their long and rich investigations of intercultural communication in penning such a book. Pan, Scollon and Scollon (2002) firstly compare and contrast US American business contexts with a series of Asian contexts (e.g. Japanese, Hong Kong Chinese, Beijing Chinese), and then provide a rich appendix of self-reflective exercises. Major long-term research projects conducted by universities also lead to the creation of a rich body of training materials. For instance, the University of Warwick's GlobalPAD (Global **P**rofessional and **A**cademic **D**evelopment) program provides a rich body of free and for-pay materials for academic and intercultural training. The same is true of the long-running Language in the Workplace Project (LWP) conducted at Victoria University of Wellington, New Zealand. LWP research is justifiably well cited in this book.

Training materials generally cover a wide range of topics, but often include some aspect of speech acts and some component that compares and contrasts the home culture with another relevant culture. For instance, Rost-Roth (2007), drawing on Müller-Jacquier (2000), suggests discussion of the following as part of an intercultural training program:

1. lexical and social meaning
2. speech acts
3. conversational organisation and conventions of discourse sequence
4. taboo subjects
5. cultural similarities and differences across several cultures in order to understand the two in question
6. register differences
7. paraverbal communication.

Suffice to say that a well-organised training program meets the needs of the requesting institution while at the same time addressing critical points of intercultural communication (many of which have been introduced by this book).

11.4   STRATEGIES FOR INTERCULTURAL COMMUNICATION

Strategies for intercultural communication seem to be motivated by a shared responsibility for making meaning in a mutually challenging context. Participants do not seem to be motivated to accommodate to each other's conventions, but rather they are using discourse strategies in a creative way that seems to be mutually useful in the language context in which they find themselves. In this way, the communicative strategies proposed here very much take their cues from Coupland et al.'s conversational extensions to CAT. There are many such strategies for reducing miscommunication. This section firstly introduces Sharifian's notion of cultural conceptualisations before outlining some successful strategies for intercultural communication, mostly emerging from the work of Bowe and Neil.

CULTURAL CONCEPTUALISATIONS

By way of conclusion to this book, we will turn to research that provides insight into the nature of the interaction between culture and cognition, and the way in which cultural conceptualisations are integrative and thus amenable to reinterpretation. This research comes from the tradition of cognitive linguistics and draws upon the connectionist models (e.g. Rumelhart et al. 1986).

Sharifian (2004, 2005, 2008) provides a model of the complex processes that relate cultural cognition, conceptualisation and language (see Chapter 3 on cultural schemas). The multifaceted nature of the relationship between cultural cognition, conceptualisation and language provides an explanation of how individuals can respond to the challenges of intercultural communication.

Sharifian (2008) explains that research on cultural cognition draws on the fields of cognitive psychology, cognitive linguistics, cultural linguistics and cognitive anthropology. He draws on Sperber and Hirschfeld's (1999, p. cxv) characterisation of the relationship between culture and cognitive activity:

> The study of culture is of relevance to cognitive sciences for two major reasons. The first is that the very existence of culture, for an essential part, is both an effect and a manifestation of human cognitive abilities. The second reason is that the human societies of today culturally frame every aspect of human life, and, in particular, of cognitive activity.

It is the observation that culture is both an 'effect and a manifestation of human cognitive abilities' that seems most relevant to our discussion here.

Sharifian (2004, pp.120 ff.) draws a distinction between cognition at the level of the individual, or what may be termed psychological cognition, and cognition at the level of the cultural group, or what may be termed cultural cognition. He suggests that cultural knowledge is the collective knowledge of the members of a cultural group: not just the knowledge shared by members of a cultural group, but rather 'a pool of knowledge that is represented in a distributed fashion across the minds in a cultural group' (Sharifian 2004, p. 121). In other words, although aspects of the knowledge can be seen to be distributed across the entire group, not all members of the group necessarily command each aspect. Sharifian (2008, p. 109) further presents an integrative view of cognition as a 'system that emerges from the interactions between members of a cultural group'. He suggests that 'Members of a cultural group negotiate and renegotiate their emergent cultural cognition across time and space' (2008, p. 109).

It would seem that it is the emergent and distributed nature of cultural cognition, as defined by Sharifian (2008), that provides the means by which individuals can adapt the conceptualisations of their immediate culture to negotiate new interpretations and expand their own conceptual understanding through the study of, and engagement in, intercultural communication.

REPETITION AND ELABORATION

Using similar methodology to that developed by Clyne (1994), Bowe (1994) examined discourse between migrant workers in the automotive industry. This study, conducted mainly on the factory floor, used tape-recorded samples of communication between supervisors and operators who were almost all immigrants to Australia. Spoken communication between supervisors and operators typically involves messages about health and safety in the factory, productivity, quality control, training and staff organisation, as well as general communication of a more personal nature that functions to maintain rapport. In many cases, supervisors are carrying out tasks originating from production meetings and quality control reports.

This research found that there was a considerable difference in the style of discourse adopted by supervisors who had an Anglo-Australian background and those who were migrants from a non-English-speaking background.[1] A prominent feature of the English discourse of non-English-speaking migrants was the use of repetition (with relevant intonation) in place of the more minimal responses such as *mmm* and *uh-huh* (see Chapter 5). Such use of repetition ensures not only that the listener is attending to what is being said, but that the propositions on which the feedback is based are able to be checked.

---

[1] The term 'migrant' is used in Australia to refer to the many people who have taken up permanent residence in Australia and have the right to take up citizenship. Their situation is quite different from the large numbers of immigrant workers who are temporary residents in many countries of the world.

In cases where the proposition was correctly restated, the repetition functions as the appropriate response, that is, agreement, assent, query and so on. In cases where the proposition was misunderstood, the response in the form of repetition can expose the source of the misunderstanding and the proposition can be corrected. The data that was collected from the shop floor contained numerous examples of repetition of several kinds (Bowe 1995), some of which are presented here.

a. **Repetition as a means of acknowledging receipt of information**

In this example, Sombat, a Laotian group leader, informs his Tongan team member that his long service leave application has been approved. The team member repeats *approved* followed by *yes, okay* in acknowledgment of having received the information.

> Sombat: Tupou ++ your application for + long service leave + has been approved
> Tupou: ↑Ah
> Sombat: It's [approved]
> Tupou: **[Approved] yes [okay]**
> Sombat: [Yes] ++ eight weeks you're going for +
> Tupou: Thank you

b. **Repetition as a means of confirming information**

In this example, Frank, the Italian group leader, reminds his Serbian team leader, Stefan, that there will be a safety check on Thursday. Stefan reiterates *Thursday* to show he is aware of the arrangement.

> Frank: We have to do something about it + the other part over there ++ and no forget we + on **Thursday** we have safety check
> Stefan: **Thursday [yeah]**
> Frank: [Yeah] otherwise we have nothing xxxxx

c. **Repetition as an expression of solidarity**

In this example, there is a problem in the paint shop which seems to be occurring infrequently. Sometimes the cars come through with defects, while on other occasions there are no faults at all. The Greek team member, Panteli, explains this to his Vietnamese team leader, Alfred, by saying that (the cars are) *sometime alright, sometime no good*. Alfred repeats the utterance *sometime alright, sometime no good* to indicate that he is listening and taking notice.

Alfred:	How job the paint shop ++ what you think the job the paint shop
Panteli:	Where
Alfred:	In the paint shop + job come ↑okay +3+ ↑why
Panteli:	\<I don't know xxxxx xxxxx xxxxx \<**sometime alright sometime no good**
Alfred:	**Sometime alright sometime no good** + what the ↑problem + ↑roof + or frame or
Panteli:	xxxxx xxxxx xxxxx frame
Alfred:	xxxxx ↑frame + xxxxx frame
Panteli:	xxxxx like that like this
Alfred:	Like frame frame buff cut or ↑something

In a similar conversation between two native speakers of English, a more minimal response such as *aha* or *mmm* would have been more likely. However, the use of repetition accomplishes the same function while providing opportunities for picking up misunderstandings.

d. Repetition as a means of confirming the speaker's hypothesis
In the following example, Spiro, a Greek team leader, and Alfonso, an Italian team leader, discuss forthcoming soccer finals. There is some confusion as to which teams will be playing and when the matches will be held. Alfonso is talking about which teams will play *tomorrow night*. Spiro asks about *Wollongong* and Alfonso replies that this team has to play too. Spiro then clarifies *tomorrow too*. Alfonso's repetition of *tomorrow too* confirms Spiro's hypothesis.

Spiro:	Juventus play tonight
Alfonso:	[No tomorrow]
Spiro:	[xxxxx]
Alfonso:	Tomorrow night
Spiro:	Er Wollongong who with er xxxxx no play ↑anymore
Alfonso:	Yeah they have to play too
Spiro:	**Tomorrow too**
Alfonso:	**Tomorrow too** and ah Sunday

Spiro: Hellas Marconi
Alfonso: Marconi

e. Repetition as a means of answering a negative question

In the following example, we see Marco, an Italian team leader, speaking to his Lebanese team member, Hassan. Hassan wants to check that Jim, another team member, is not coming in to work. Marco's reply, *yeah Jimmy no in today*, is in fact a repetition of the relevant details of Hassan's utterance with the addition of the word *no* to negate the proposition. However, Marco has prefaced the reply with the affirmative *yeah* to indicate agreement with Hassan. Had Marco simply replied *no* without any additional information, this may have resulted in misunderstanding because of the fact that in some languages *no* in this context would indicate disagreement with the foregoing proposition, meaning that Jimmy was in fact going to come in to work.

Hassan: What ↑**Jim. not coming today**
Marco: Yeah Jimmy no in today ++ now +
            I wanna you ...

f. Repetition as a query

In the following conversation, Colin, an Anglo-Australian team leader, uses repetition (with rising intonation) as a means of requesting confirmation of what he thought he heard. Ian, a Sri Lankan (Burgher) team leader, asks Colin to get him some plastic tape. Colin queries *plastic tape* and Ian repeats the key words of his initial utterance, *yeah sure, plastic plastic*, as a way of letting Colin know that he has correctly understood the directive. The use of repetition as a query is a strategy often used by Anglo-Australians and speakers more generally.

Ian: My best buddy friend + er ++ would you be
            able to **get me some plastic + tape** please
Colin: **Plastic ↑tape**
Ian: Yeah sure + plastic plastic

g. Repetition as a means of acknowledging the correction of a wrong hypothesis

This example is from a conversation between Ian, the Sri Lankan (Burgher) team leader, and Toby, an Afghan team member. Ian

asks Toby whether his niece was born in Afghanistan. Toby replies
Pakistan and Ian repeats this as a way of acknowledging the
correction.

> Ian: but she was born in Australia [↑wasn't she]
> Toby: [no no]
> Ian: [in Afghanistan]
> Toby: [xxxxx **Pakistan**]
> Ian: **Pakistan** ++

h. **Repetition as a means of framing a question**

In the following example, Van, a Vietnamese team leader, informs
his Italian group leader, Frank, that he may be leaving early on
Friday. He says *maybe maybe Friday I go home early*. In response to
this, Frank wants to know the reason Van will be leaving earlier
than usual. Instead of simply asking *why* he also repeats the
important details of Van's utterance *you go home early on Friday*,
then adds the interrogative *why*.

> Van: Hey Frank +2+
> Frank: What +2+
> Van: Maybe maybe **Friday** ++ **I go home early** ++
> Frank: **You go home early on** ↑**Friday** ↑**why** +
> Van: Because . . .

By employing a repetitive discourse strategy, communication
breakdown can be avoided. In the example above, Frank makes
it clear to Van what his interrogative question *why* actually refers
to by repeating the important details of Van's utterance, that is,
the details Frank wishes to know more about.

i. **Routine repetition exposing miscommunication**

In the following example, Sammy, a Laotian panel beater, tells
Tim, a Cambodian team leader, how many years he has been
working at Rising Sun Motors. Tim repeats the number of years
(with upward intonation), indicating surprise as well. It turns out
that he had misheard the number, and because he had repeated
what he thought he had heard, the miscommunication was able
to be corrected.

> Sammy: After after xxxxx after um + this year is **sixteen**
>   ++

Tim:	↑**Sixty**
Sammy:	<**Sixteen**
Tim:	**One six**
Sammy:	[**Oh one six**]
Tim:	[Alright] +

This research has shown that a prominent feature of the English discourse of factory workers from non-English-speaking backgrounds is the use of repetition for a range of discourse functions, including agreement, assent, affirmation and acknowledgment. These are precisely the types of functions for which researchers such as Duncan (1973, 1974), Sacks, Schegloff and Jefferson (1974), Schegloff (1982) and Levinson (1983) have identified the use of minimal responses such as *mmm* and *uh-huh*. The use of repetition (with relevant intonation) rather than more minimal responses such as *mmm* and *uh-huh* is a creative strategy to ensure that intercultural communication occurs in an unambiguous way, despite different cultural expectations and the difficulties of having to use a second language with limited grammatical competence.

TURN-SHARING AS COLLABORATION

In her research Neil (1996, p. 97) reports that collaborative strategies are a significant feature of the intercultural communication of hospital ancillary staff from non-English-speaking backgrounds using English as a lingua franca in a Melbourne hospital:

> In intercultural communication, the need for both speakers' participation is heightened if the interaction is going to proceed smoothly and be optimally effective. Speakers must take an active, joint responsibility for constructing and sustaining talk which is mutually comprehensible. In this way, joint text production in intercultural discourse has the social function of engaging speakers equally in successfully producing meaning.

Neil illustrates that turn-sharing is a significant feature of the joint discourse production of her subjects.

Building on the work of Sacks (1967–8), Lerner (1991) and others, Neil (1996, p. 98) distinguishes between turn completions that are *pre-emptions*, usually the initiative of the interlocutor, and those that result after *petering out* on the part of the speaker, which can act as a tacit invitation to the interlocutor to complete the turn. In the first case, one speaker offers an anticipatory completion of a turn, which was begun by the other speaker.

By contrast, in the latter case, the interlocutor's completion is more likely to be invited by the speaker when words fail and his or her turn begins to peter out.

Neil (1996, p. 104) provides the following example of 'pre-emptive' turn-sharing between Hien, a Vietnamese woman who speaks Cantonese at home, and her supervisor, Juana, whose first language is Tagalog.

> Hien: You go to the dentist for, for ~~ (0)
> Juana: (0) Private? yeah
> Hien: Yeah, how much? one [twenty!]

Neil suggests that Juana's contextual knowledge of the conversation and her familiarity with her interlocutor make the nature of Hien's question predictable for Juana. She therefore latches onto Hien's *for* ~~, marked by a level tone, which prompts Juana to realise that Hien is searching for the next word and to pre-empt this word. Juana's use of question intonation may indicate that this is a suggestion being offered, not a definitive statement.

The following is an example provided by Neil (1996, p. 107) of an utterance begun by Theona being completed by her conversation partner, Juana, because Theona's first utterance *peters out*.

> Theona: I don't know! too many <XplaceX what's it called? I forgot where they test the –
> Juana: Oh yeah, they test th+e ~~
> Theona: Yeah
> Juana: The <XglucoseX>
> Theona: (0) Yeah, them or another place. (0)

Neil explains that Theona has used the routine formula *what's it called?* to signal that she is struggling for a word. Inherent in this formulation is the invitation for Juana to intercept with the right word. But rather than pausing to await Juana's response, Theona continues with the turn. The additional information supplied by *I forgot where they test the* – makes it easier for her interlocutor to identify the word she means. The petering out also sets the scene for Juana's turn completion; Theona's utterance peters out at the point in her turn where the word must be supplied.

Neil argues (1996, p. 120) that contrary to the view articulated by Zuengler (1989) that finishing another's statement is a dominating move, collaborative productions, or utterance completions, are an indication of the solidarity and close social organisation that enable workers from language backgrounds other than English to communicate successfully using English as a lingua franca. Neil's 1996 monograph provides a well-documented inventory of collaborative strategies found in her data, including several different turn-sharing strategies, the collaborative use of repetition, the collaborative use of paraphrase, clarification strategies and the use of information questions for topic development.

11.5 SUMMARY

Depending on an individual's exposure and experience as a communicator in intercultural contexts, they may be at a different stage in the development of an awareness of the ways in which sociocultural conventions shape language use. In the early stages, individuals may approach intercultural communication through the ethnocentric prism of their own immediate culture and misread the intentions of their intercultural communication partners. We have seen the potential for this in the research on cross-cultural comparisons of a number of perspectives, particularly the research on cross-cultural realisations of speech acts (Blum-Kulka, House & Kasper 1989). Much of the research on intercultural communication in the workplace shows that conventions of a speaker's language and cultural background do influence many speakers engaged in intercultural interaction, regardless of whether the encounters are of relatively short duration or whether the interaction is part of a full-time job.

At the start of this book, we noted that human beings have at their disposal an infinitely complex and creative symbolic system: language. The richness of language use that allows speakers to conventionally code meaning in non-literal ways means that the job of negotiating language meaning is an ongoing one, even for speakers who share the same language and culture. We hope that the presentation in this book of the many processes involved in intercultural communication will not only enable readers to communicate more effectively in the intercultural world, but will also enable researchers from different disciplines to incorporate some of the perspectives presented here into their own research.

In conclusion, at the start of this book we noted that language made humans a distinctive species. However, Tomasello (1999) argues that it is not language that distinguishes human beings from other animals but, in fact, our ability to adopt and understand the perspective of the 'other'. Animals can only learn by interacting and responding with their environment. Human consciousness, on the other hand, enables us to learn about the world through others as well as to imagine what another may know or be feeling (Verhagen 2005). Moreover, it enables us to make sense of another's choices.

This book has attempted to shed light on the symbolic resources and strategic linguistic choices of the other. We hope that through this book the reader will come to analyse the linguistic behaviours of others through a prism of human behaviour rather than an ethnocentric one. In sum, to paraphrase anthropologist David Kilcullen, the things that annoy us about other cultures are not US American, Chinese or Spanish behaviours (see Berreby 2007). They are human behaviours within US American, Chinese or Spanish socio-cultural contexts.

11.6   REVIEW

1. **Key terms**
   Common-ground collaborative discourse strategies, repetition, accommodation, turn-sharing, pre-emption, cultural schemas, cultural cognition, conceptualisation, conceptual renegotiation.

2. **Key ideas**
   Having read this chapter you should:
   a. be aware of some of the ways in which speakers can engage in collaborative discourse strategies to minimise potential misunderstanding in intercultural contexts
   b. be aware of the process of accommodation and its potential role in intercultural communication
   c. be able to consider cognitive aspects of intercultural communication such as conceptual renegotiation.

3. **Focus questions**
   a. Collaborative discourse strategies
      (i) In what kinds of communicative contexts might you have used collaborative discourse strategies such as turn-sharing, turn completion, repetition and paraphrase?
      (ii) What was your motivation?
   b. Accommodation
      (i) In what kinds of communicative contexts have you used language accommodation?
      (ii) What was your motivation?

4. **Research analysis**
   Consider the data in section 11.4 and decide whether, in a parallel conversation, it would seem more natural for you, as a fluent speaker of English, to use minimal responses such as *mmm* and *uh-huh* instead

of the repetition used by the speakers with minimal English skills in each of the example dialogues.

5. **Research exercise**

Until relatively recently, many English speakers used to offer a Christian prayer to mark the beginning of a meal, known as *grace*. It was usually offered by the head of the household, typically a male, and was an important part of the social context of family life. This would be an example of what cognitive linguists such as Sharifian refer to as a cultural schema. More recently this practice has fallen out of use, leaving a bit of a vacuum. Australian English speakers tend to adopt expressions from other languages, such as the French *bon appetit* to fulfil this function. Conduct a survey among your classmates, or friends and acquaintances, and find out whether they have a conventional way of beginning a meal, who performs it and what cultural ideas and values attach to it.

SUGGESTED FURTHER READING

Cultural intelligence, and intercultural (communication) competence have emerged as fields of study in their own right. Earley, Ang and Tan introduce cultural intelligence and Lustig and Koester provide an overview of intercultural (communication) competence. There are a growing number of training programs for intercultural communication. Rost-Roth presents a brilliant overview of how organisations approach intercultural training. In recent years, as noted above, research at the University of Warwick and Victoria University of Wellington, New Zealand, has led to the creation of a number of free and for-pay intercultural training programs. Many of these programs are set out on the respective institutions' websites. Lastly, much of this book has focused on relativist and constructivist approaches to intercultural communication. Sharifian's rich body of work provides a wonderful overview of more cognitive perspectives.

Earley, P. C., Ang, S. & Tan, J. 2006 *CQ: Developing Cultural Intelligence at Work*. Stanford, CA: Stanford University Press.

Lustig, M. & Koester, J. 2010 *Intercultural Competence: Interpersonal Communication Across Cultures*. 6th edn. Boston, MA: Pearson.

Rost-Roth, M. 2007 'Intercultural training'. In Kotthoff, H. & Spencer-Oatey, H. (eds) *Handbook of Intercultural Communication*. Berlin: Mouton de Gruyter, pp. 491–518.

Sharifian, F. 2008 'Distributed, emergent cultural cognition, conceptualisation and language'. In Frank, R. M., Dirvan, R., Ziemke, T. & Bernárdez, E. (eds) *Body, Language and Mind (vol. 2): Sociocultural Situatedness*. Berlin/New York: Mouton de Gruyter, pp. 109–36.

244 COMMUNICATION ACROSS CULTURES

University of Warwick GlobalPAD (**G**lobal **P**rofessional and **A**cademic **D**evelopment) <www2.warwick.ac.uk/fac/soc/al/globalpad/> (accessed 12 May 2014).

Victoria University of Wellington, School of Linguistics and Applied Language Studies 2014 'The Language in the Workplace Project' <www.victoria.ac.nz/lals/centres-and-institutes/language-in-the-workplace> (accessed 12 May 2014).

Appendix: Speech acts

Types of rule	Request	Assert (state that)	Question
Propositional content	Future act *A* of *H*.	Any proposition *P*.	Any proposition or propositional function.
Preparatory	1. *H* is able to do *A*. *S* believes *H* is able to do *A*. 2. It is not obvious to both *S* and *H* that *H* will do *A* in the normal course of events of his own accord.	1. *S* has evidence reasons, etc.) for the truth of *P*. 2. It is not obvious to both *S* and *H* that *H* knows (does not need to be reminded of, etc.) *P*.	1. *S* does not know 'the answer', i.e., does not know if the proposition is true, or, in the case of the propositional function, does not know the information needed to complete the proposition truly (but see comment below). 2. It is not obvious to both *S* and *H* that *H* will provide the information at that time without being asked.
Sincerity	*S* wants *H* to do *A*.	*S* believes *P*.	*S* wants this information.
Essential	Counts as an attempt to get *H* to do *A*.	Counts as an undertaking to the effect that *P* represents an actual state of affairs.	Counts as an attempt to elicit this information from *H*.
Comment	*Order* and *command* have the additional preparatory rule that *S* must be in a position of authority over *H*. *Command* probably does not have the 'pragmatic' condition requiring non-obviousness. Futhermore, in both, the authority relationship infects the essential condition because the utterance counts as an attempt to get *H* to do *A* virtue of the authority *of S* over *H*.	Unlike argue, these do not seem to be essentially tied to attempting to convince. Thus 'I am simply stating that *P* and not attempting to convince you' is acceptable, but 'I am arguing that *P* and not attempting to convince you' sounds inconsistent.	There are two kinds of questions, (a) real questions, (b) exam questions. In real questions *S* wants to know (find out) the answer; in exam questions, *S* wants to know if *H* knows.

(Searle 1969, pp. 66–7)

Thank (for)	Advise	Warn	Greet	Congratulate
Past act *A* done *by H*.	Future act *A* of *H*.	Future event or state, etc., *E*.	None.	Some event, act, etc., *E*, related to *H*.
A benefits *S* and *S* believes *A* benefits *S*.	1. *S* has some reason to believe *A* will benefit *H*. 2. It is not obvious to both *S* and *H* that *H* will do *A* in the normal course of events.	1. *S* has reason to believe *E will* occur and is not in *H's* interest. 2. It is not obvious to both *S* and *H* that *E* will occur.	*S* has just encountered (or been introduced to, etc.) *H*.	*E* is in *H's* interest and *S* believes *E is* in *H's* interest.
S feels grateful or appreciative for *A*.	*S* believes *A* will benefit *H*.	*S* believes *E is* not in *H's* best interest.	None.	*S* is pleased at *E*.
Counts as an expression of gratitude or appreciation.	Counts as an undertaking to the effect that *A* is in *H's* best interest.	Counts as an undertaking to the effect that *E* is not in *H's* best interest.	Counts as courteous recognition of *H* by *S*.	Counts as an expression of pleasure at *E*.
Sincerity and essential rules overlap. Thanking is just expressing gratitude in a way that, e.g. promising is not just expressing an intention.	Contrary to what one might suppose advice is not a species of requesting. It is interesting to compare 'advise' with 'urge', 'advocate' and 'recommend'. Advising you is not trying to get you to do something in the sense that requesting is. Advising is more like telling you what is best for you.	Warning is like advising, rather than requesting. It is not, I think, necessarily an attempt to get you to take evasive action. Notice that the above account is of categorical not hypothetical warnings. Most warnings are probably hypothetical: 'If you do not do X then Y will occur.'		'Congratulate' is similar to 'thank' in that it is an expression of its sincerity condition.

References

Adegbija, E. 1989 'A comparative study of politeness phenomena in Nigerian English, Yoruba and Ogori'. *Multilingua*, vol. 8, no. 1, pp. 57–80.

Adler, P., Adler, P. & Fontana, A. 1987 'Everyday life sociology'. *Annual Review of Sociology*, vol. 13, pp. 217–35.

Adrefiza & Jones, J. 2013 'Investigating apology response strategies in Australian English and Bahasa Indonesia: Gender and cultural perspectives'. *Australian Review of Applied Linguistics*, vol. 36, no. 1, pp. 71–101.

Agha, A. 1998 'Stereotypes and registers of honorific language'. *Language in Society*, vol. 27, pp. 151–93.

  2007 *Language and Social Relations*. Cambridge: Cambridge University Press.

Ainsworth, J. 2012 'Integrating methods and strategies from language teaching and business studies in languages for specific business purposes courses'. *Global Advances in Business Communication*, vol. 1, no. 1, pp. 1–24.

Albert, S. & Kessler, S. 1976 'Processes for ending social encounters: The conceptual archaeology'. *Journal for the Theory of Social Behaviour*, vol. 6, pp. 147–70.

  1978 'Ending social encounters'. *Journal of Experimental Social Psychology*, vol. 14, pp. 541–53.

Al-Gahtani, S. & Roever, C. 2013 'Proficiency and sequential organization of L2 requests'. *Applied Linguistics*, vol. 33, no. 11, pp. 42–65.

Alim, H. S. 2006 *Roc the Mic Right: The Language of Hip Hop Culture*. New York: Routledge.

Alim, H. S., Ibrahim, A. & Pennycook, A. (eds) 2009 *Global Linguistic Flows: Hip Hop Cultures, Youth Identities, and the Politics of Language*. New York: Routledge.

Allan, K. 1986 *Linguistic Meaning*, 2 vols. London: Routledge & Kegan Paul.

  1991 'Cooperative principle'. In Bright, W. (ed.) *Oxford International Encyclopedia of Linguistics*. New York: Oxford University Press.

Amin-Zaki, A. 1995 'Religious and cultural considerations in translating Shakespeare into Arabic'. In Dingwaney, A. & Maier, C. (eds) *Between Languages and Cultures: Translation and Cross-Cultural Texts*. Pittsburgh, PA: University of Pittsburgh Press, pp. 223–44.

Angermeyer, P. 2005 'Who is you? Polite forms of address and ambiguous roles in court reporting'. *Target*, vol. 17, no. 2, pp. 203–26.

Angouri, J. 2010 '"If we know about culture it will be easier to work with one another": Developing skills for handling corporate meetings with multinational participation'. *Language and Intercultural Communication*, vol. 10, no. 3, pp. 206–24.

Angouri, J. & Marra, M. 2011 '"OK one last thing for today then": Constructing identities in coroporate identities in corporate meeting talk'. In Angouri, J. & Marra, M. (eds) *Constructing Identities at Work*. London: Palgrave, pp. 85–102.

Arasaratnam, L. & Banerjee, S. 2011 'Sensation seeking and intercultural communication competence: A model test'. *International Journal of Intercultural Relations*, vol. 35, pp. 226–33.

Archer, D. 2011 'Cross-examining lawyers, facework and the adversarial courtroom'. *Journal of Pragmatics*, vol. 43, pp. 3216–30.

Archer, D. & Grundy, P. 2011 'Introduction'. In Archer, D. & Grundy, P. (eds) *The Pragmatics Reader*. London & New York: Routledge, pp. 1–10.

Atawneh, A. & Sridhar, S. 1993 'Arabic-English bilinguals and the directive speech act'. *World Englishes*, vol. 12, no. 3, pp. 279–97.

Auer, P. 1998 'Introduction to chapter 7'. In Auer, P. (ed.) *Code-Switching in Conversation: Language, Interaction and Identity*. London: Routledge, pp. 151–5.

Austin, J. L. 1962 *How to Do Things with Words*. Oxford: Oxford University Press.

1970 *Philosophical Papers*. Oxford: Clarendon Press.

Backhaus, P. 2009 'Politeness in institutional elderly care in Japan'. *Journal of Politeness Research*, vol. 5, pp. 53–71.

Bader, J. 2002 *Schriftlichkeit und Mündlichkeit in der Chat-Kommunikation*, Networx Nr. 29 <www.mediensprache.net/networx/networx-29.pdf> (accessed 8 April 2014).

Bailey, B. 2001 'Communication of respect in interethnic service encounters'. In Duranti, A (ed.) *Linguistic Anthropology: A Reader*. Malden, MA: Blackwell, pp. 119–46.

Bakhtin, M. 1981 *The Dialogic Imagination*. Austin: University of Texas Press.

1986 *Speech Genres and Other Late Essays*. Austin: University of Texas Press.

Bardovi-Harlig, K. & Hartford, B. 1993 'Refining the DCTs: Comparing open questionnaires and dialogue and completion tests'. In Bouton, L. & Kachru, Y. (eds) *Pragmatics and Language Learning, Monograph 4*. Urbana-Champaign, IL: University of Illinois, Division of English as an International Language, pp. 237–645.

Bargiela-Chiappini, F. & Harris, S. J. 1996 'Requests and status in business correspondence'. *Journal of Pragmatics*, vol. 28, pp. 635–62.

Bargiela, F., Boz, B. C., Gokzadze, L., Hamza, A., Mills, S. & Rukhadze, N. 2002 'Ethnocentrism, politeness and naming strategies'. *Working Papers on the Web*, vol. 3, pp. 1–17, <www.shu.ac.uk/wpw/politeness/bargiela.htm> (site no longer active).

Bassnett, S. 1998 'Translating across cultures'. In Hunston, S. (ed.) *Language at Work: Selected Papers from the Annual Meeting of the British Association for Applied Linguistics*. Clevedon: Multilingual Matters, pp. 72–85.

Bateson, G. 1980 *Naven*, London: Wildwood House.

Bauman, R. & Briggs, C. 2003 *Voices of Modernity: Language Ideologies and the Politics of Inequality*. New York: Cambridge University Press.

Bayraktaroğlu, A. & Sifianou, M. 2012 'The iron fist in a velvet glove: How politeness can contribute to impoliteness'. *Journal of Politeness Research*, vol. 8, pp. 143–60.

Bays, H. 1998 'Framing and face in internet exchanges: A socio-cognitive approach'. *Linguistik Online*, vol. 1, pp. 1–20, <www.linguistik-online.de/bays.htm> (accessed 7 January 2007).

Béal, C. 1990 'It's all in the asking: A perspective on problems of cross-cultural communication between native speakers of French and native speakers of Australian English in the workplace'. *Australian Review of Applied Linguistics*, vol. 7, pp. 16–32.

1992 'Did you have a good weekend? Or why is there no such thing as a simple question in cross-cultural encounters?' *Australian Review of Applied Linguistics*, vol. 15, no. 1, pp. 23–52.

Beale, P. 1990 'And so Nobby called to Smudger . . . nicknames associated with individual surnames'. *Lore and Language*, vol. 9, no. 1, pp. 3–18.

Beebe, L. & Cummings M. 1996 'Natural speech act data versus written questionnaire data: How data collection method affects speech act performance'. In Gass, S. & Neu, J. (eds) *Speech Acts Across Cultures*, Berlin, Mouton de Gruyter, pp. 65–86.

Bell, N. & Attardo, S. 2010 'Failed humor: Issues in non-native speakers' appreciation and understanding of humor'. *Intercultural Pragmatics*, vol. 7, no. 3, pp. 423–47.

Bella, S. 2012 'Pragmatic development in a foreign language: A study of Greek FL requests'. *Journal of Pragmatics*, vol. 44, pp. 1917–47.

Belz, J. 2003 'Linguistic perspectives on the development of intercultural competence in telecollaboration'. *Language Learning and Technology*, vol. 7, no. 2, pp. 68–117.

Bennett, A. 2011 *Academic Writing in Portugal. Discourses in Conflict*. Coimbra: Universidade de Coimbra.

Berk-Seligson, S. 1988 'The impact of politeness in witness testimony: The influence of the court interpreter'. *Multilingua*, vol. 7, no. 4, pp. 411–40.

2001 'The role of register in the bilingual courtroom'. In Oaks, D. (ed.) *Linguistics at Work: A Reader of Applications*. Cambridge, MA: Heinle & Heinle Publishing, pp. 597–609.

2009 *Coerced Confessions: The Discourse of Bilingual Police Interrogations*. Berlin: Mouton de Gruyter.

Berreby, D. 2007 'The zombie concept of identity' In Brockman J. (ed.) *What are You Optimistic About?* London: Simon & Schuster, pp. 88–91.

Bhathia, V. K. 1993 *Analyzing Genre: Language Use in Professional Settings*. London: Longman.

2004 *Worlds of Discourse: A Genre Based View*. London: Continuum.

Bialystok, E. 1993 'Symbolic representation and attentional control in pragmatic competence'. In Kasper, G. & Blum-Kulka, S. (eds) *Interlanguage Pragmatics*. Oxford: Oxford University Press, pp. 43–63.

Biber, D., Leech, G., Conrad, S. & Finegan, E. 1999 *Longman Grammar of Spoken and Written English*. Harlow: Pearson.

Blommaert, J. 2010 *Sociolinguistics of Globalization*. Cambridge: Cambridge University Press.

Blommaert, J. & Rampton, B. 2011 'Language and superdiversity: A position paper'. *Diversities*, vol. 13, no. 2, pp. 1–21.

Blum-Kulka, S. 1987 'Indirectness and politeness in requests: Same or different?' *Journal of Pragmatics*, vol. 11, pp. 131–46.

1989 'Playing it safe: The role of conventionality in indirectness'. In Blum-Kulka, S., House, J. & Kasper, G. (eds) *Cross-Cultural Pragmatics: Requests and Apologies*. Norwood, New Jersey: Ablex, pp. 27–70.

Blum-Kulka, S. & House, J. 1989 'Cross-cultural and situational variation in requesting behavior'. In Blum-Kulka, S., House, J. & Kasper, G. (eds) *Cross-Cultural Pragmatics: Requests and Apologies*. Norwood, New Jersey: Ablex, pp. 123–54.

Blum-Kulka, S., House, J. & Kasper, G. (eds) 1989 *Cross-Cultural Pragmatics: Requests and Apologies.* Norwood, New Jersey: Ablex.

Blum-Kulka, S. & Olshtain, E. 1984 'Requests and apologies: A cross-cultural study of speech act realisation patterns'. *Applied Linguistics*, vol. 5, no. 3, pp. 176–213.

Bohmer, C. & Shuman, A. 2007 *Rejecting Refugees: Political Asylum in the 21st Century.* London: Routledge.

de Boinod, A. 2007 *Toujours Tingo.* London: Penguin.

Bolden, G. 2012 'Across languages and cultures: Brokering problems of understanding in conversational repair. *Language in Society*, vol. 41, no. 1, pp. 97–121.

Bousfield, D. 2008 'Impoliteness in the struggle for power'. In Bousfield, D. & Locher, M. (eds) *Impoliteness in Language: Studies on its Interplay with Power in Theory and Practice.* Berlin: Mouton de Gruyter, pp. 127–54.

Bousfield, D. & Locher, M. 2008 (eds) *Impoliteness in Language: Studies on its Interplay with Power in Theory and Practice.* Berlin: Mouton de Gruyter.

Bowe, H. 1994 'Developing successful communication with recently arrived migrants in industry'. Research paper submitted to the DEET National Priority Reserve Fund.

1995 'The elaboration of repetition as a creative discourse strategy in the multilingual workforce'. Paper read at the Australian Linguistics Conference, Canberra.

Bowe, H. & Martin, K. 2007 *Communication Across Cultures: Mutual Understanding in a Global World.* 1st edn. Cambridge: Cambridge University Press.

Bowe, H. & Zhang, M. 2001 'Travel agency advertisements in Chinese newspapers'. Lecture given as part of LIN3160, *International Cultural Interaction.* Monash University, Berwick.

Brabant, M., Watson, B. & Gallois, C. 2007 'Psychological perspectives: Social psychology, language, and intercultural communication'. In Kotthoff, H. & Spencer-Oatey, H. (eds) *Handbook of Intercultural Communication.* Berlin: Walter de Gruyter, pp. 55–75.

Braun, F. 1988 *Terms of Address: Problems of Patterns and Usage in Various Languages and Cultures.* Mouton de Gruyter, Berlin.

Broder, J. 2007 'Familiar fallback for officials: "Mistakes were made". *New York Times*, March 14, 2007.

Brown, B. & Crawford, P. 2009 'Politeness strategies in question formulation in a UK telephone advisory service'. *Journal of Politeness Research*, vol. 5, pp. 73–91.

Brown, R. & Ford, M. 1961 'Address in American English'. *Journal of Abnormal and Social Psychology*, vol. 67, pp. 375–85.

Brown, R. & Gilman, A. 1960 'The pronouns of power and solidarity'. In Sebeok, T. A. (ed.) *Style in Language.* New York: Technology Press of MIT, pp. 253–76.

Brown, P. & Levinson, S. 1978 'Universals in language usage: Politeness phenomena'. In Goody, E. (ed.) *Questions and Politeness.* Cambridge: Cambridge University Press, pp. 56–289.

1987 *Politeness: Some Universals in Language Usage.* Cambridge: Cambridge University Press.

Brumark, A. 2006 'Non-observance of Gricean maxims in family dinner table conversation'. *Journal of Pragmatics*, vol. 38, pp. 1206–38.

Bucher, H. 2002 'The power of the audience: Interculturality, interactivity and trust in internet-communication – theory, research design and empirical results'. In Sudweeks, F. & Ess, C. (eds) *Proceedings, Cultural Attitudes Towards Technology and Communication.* Australia: Murdoch University, pp. 3–14.

Bucholtz, M. 2009 'From stance to style: Gender, interaction, and indexicality in Mexican immigrant youth slang'. In Jaffe, A. (ed.) *Stance: Sociolinguistic Perspectives*. New York: Oxford, pp. 146–90.

Bungarten, T. (ed.) 1981 *Wissenschaftssprache*. Munich: Fink.

Burdelski, M. 2013 'Socializing children to honorifics in Japanese: Identity and stance in interaction'. *Multilingua*, vol. 32, no. 2, pp. 247–73.

Burridge, K. & Florey, M. 2002 '"Yeah-no He's a good kid": A discourse analysis of Yeah-no in Australian English'. *Australian Journal of Linguistics*, vol. 22, no. 2, pp. 149–71.

Business Council of Australia 2009 'Statement of the Business Alliance for Asia Literacy'. Business Council of Australia, Melbourne.

Butler, J. 1990 *Gender Trouble: Feminism and the Subversion of Identity*. New York: Routledge.

Caldwell-Harris, C., Kronrod, A. & Yang, J. 2013 'Do more, say less: Saying "I love you" in Chinese and American cultures'. *Intercultural Pragmatics*, vol. 10, no. 1, pp. 41–69.

Cameron, D. 2000 'Styling the worker: Gender and the commodification of language in the globalized service economy'. *Journal of Sociolinguistics*, vol. 4, pp. 323–47.

2009 'Sex/gender, language and the new biologism'. *Applied Linguistics*, vol. 31, no. 2, pp. 173–92.

Cameron, J. 1996 *Titanic: A Screenplay*. Twentieth Century Fox.

Canagarajah, S. 2013 'Reconstructing heritage language: Resolving dilemmas in language maintenance for Sri Lankan Tamil migrants'. *International Journal of the Sociology of Language*, vol. 222, pp. 131–54.

Cardon, P. 2008 'A critique of Hall's contexting model: A meta-analysis of literature on intercultural business and technical communication'. *Journal of Business and Technical Communication*, vol. 22, pp. 399–428.

Cargile, A. & Bolkan, S. 2013 'Mitigating inter- and intra-group ethnocentrism: Comparing the effects of culture knowledge, exposure, and uncertainty intolerance'. *International Journal of Intercultural Relations*, vol. 37, no. 3, pp. 345–53.

Caudron, S. 1991 'Training ensures success overseas'. *Personnel Journal*, December, pp. 27–30.

Charnok, R. 2009 'Overruling as a speech act: Performativity and normative discourse'. *Journal of Pragmatics*, vol. 41, pp. 401–26.

Chen, R., He, L. & Hu, C. 2013 'Chinese requests: In comparison to American and Japanese requests and with reference to the "East-West divide"'. *Journal of Pragmatics*, vol. 55, pp. 140–61.

Cherry, C. 1996 'What is communication?' In Corner, C. & Hawthorn, J. (eds) *Communication Studies: An Introductory Reader*. 2nd edn. London: Edward Arnold, pp. 10–14.

Chiang, S. 2011 'Pursuing a response in office hour interactions between US college students and international teaching assistants'. *Journal of Pragmatics*, vol. 43, pp. 3316–30.

Christopherson, K. 2007 'The positive and negative implications of anonymity in internet social interactions: "On the Internet, nobody knows you're a dog"'. *Computers in Human Behaviour*, vol. 23, pp. 3038–56.

Clark, H. 1996 *Using Language*. Cambridge: Cambridge University Press.

Clark, H. & French, J. 1981 'Telephone goodbyes'. *Language in Society*, vol. 10, no. 1, pp. 1–19.

Clift, R. 1999 'Irony in conversation'. *Language in Society*, vol. 28, no. 4, pp. 523–53.

2012 'Identifying action: Laughter in non-humorous reported speech'. *Journal of Pragmatics*, vol. 44, pp. 1303–12.

Clyne, M. 1980 'Writing, testing and culture'. *The Secondary Teacher*, vol. 11, pp. 13–6.

1987 'Cultural differences in the organisation of academic discourse'. *Journal of Pragmatics*, vol. 11, pp. 211–47.

1991a 'The sociocultural dimension: The dilemma of the German-speaking scholar'. In Schröder, H. (ed.) *Subject-Oriented Texts*. Berlin: De Gruyter, pp. 49–67.

1991b 'Trying to do things with letters: letters of request and complaint in the university domain'. In *Linguistics in the Service of Society: Essays in Honour of Susan Kaldor*. Perth: Institute of Applied Language Studies, Edith Cowan University.

(ed.) 1992 *Pluricentric Languages*. Berlin: Mouton de Gruyter.

1994 *Inter-cultural Communication at Work: Cultural Values in Discourse*. Cambridge: Cambridge University Press.

Clyne, M. & Platt, J. 1990 'The role of language in cross-cultural communication'. In *Proceedings of the Conference on Cross-Cultural Communication in the Health Profession*. National Centre for Community Languages in the Professions, Melbourne: Monash University, pp. 38–55.

Coates, J. 2004 *Women, Men, and Language*. London: Pearson Longman.

Cohen, A. & Olshtain, E. 1981 'Developing a measure of sociocultural competence: The case of apology'. *Language Learning*, vol. 31, no. 1, pp. 113–34.

Cole, P. 2004 'Cultural competence now mainstream medicine'. *Postgraduate Medicine*, vol. 116, no. 6.

Connor, U. 2003 'Changing currents in contrastive rhetoric: Implications for teaching and research' In Knoll B. (ed.) *Exploring Dynamics of Language Writing*. New York: Cambridge University Press, pp. 218–41.

2008 'Mapping multidimensional aspects of research: Reaching to intercultural rhetoric' in Connor U., Nagelhout E. & Rozycki, W. (eds) *Contrastive Rhetoric: Reaching to Intercultural Rhetoric*. Amsterdam: John Benjamins.

2011 *Intercultural Rhetoric in Second Language Writing*. Ann Arbor: University of Michigan Press.

Connor, U. & Kaplan, R. (eds) 1987 *Writing Across Cultures*. Reading, Mass.: Addison-Wesley.

Connor, U., Nagelhout, E. & Rozycki, W. (eds) 2008 *Contrastive Rhetoric: Reaching to Intercultural Rhetoric*. Amsterdam: John Benjamins.

Cook, H. 2013 'A scientist or a salesman? Identity construction through referent honorifics on a Japanese shopping channel program'. *Multilingua*, vol. 32, no. 2, pp. 177–202.

Cordella, M. 1990 'Spanish speakers apologizing in English: A cross-cultural pragmatic study'. *Australian Review of Applied Linguistics*, vol. 14, pp. 115–38.

2004 *The Dynamic Consultation: A Discourse Analytical Study of Doctor–patient Communication*. Amsterdam: Benjamins.

2012 'Negotiating religious beliefs in a medical setting'. *Journal of Religion and Medicine*, vol. 51, pp. 837–53.

Cordella, M. & Musgrave, S. 2009 'Oral communication skills of international medical graduates: Assessing empathy in discourse'. *Communication and Medicine*, vol. 6, no. 2, pp. 129–42.

Cordella, M. & Spike, N. 2008 'Working toward a better communication between international medical graduates and their patients in Victoria'. *Health Issues*, vol. 96, pp. 28–9.

Cortese G. & Duszak A. (eds), *Identity, Community, Discourse: English in Intercultural Settings*. Frankfurt: Peter Lang, pp 269–93.

Coupland, J. 2000 *Small Talk*. London: Longman.

Coupland, N. 2001 'Language, situation, and the relational self: Theorizing dialect-style in sociolinguistics'. In Eckert, P. & Rickford, J. (eds) *Style and Sociolinguistic Variation*. Cambridge: Cambridge University Press, pp. 185–210.

2007 *Style: Language Variation and Identity*. Cambridge: Cambridge University Press.

Coupland, N. & Bishop, H. 2007 'Ideologised values for British accents'. *Journal of Sociolinguistics*. vol. 10, no. 5, pp. 74–103.

Coupland, N., Coupland, J., Giles, H. & Henwood, K. 1988 'Accommodating the elderly: Invoking and extending a theory'. *Language in Society*, vol. 17, pp. 1–41.

Coxhead, A. 2000 'A new Academic Word List'. *TESOL Quarterly*, vol. 38, no.4, pp. 663–88.

Crystal, D. 2006 *Language and the Internet*. 2nd edn. Cambridge: Cambridge University Press.

Crystal, D. 2010 *The Cambridge Encyclopedia of Language*. 3rd edn. Cambridge: Cambridge University Press.

Culpeper, J. 2005 'Impoliteness and entertainment in the television quiz show: "The Weakest Link"'. *Journal of Politeness Research*, vol. 1, pp. 35–72.

2008 'Reflections on impoliteness, relational work and power'. In Bousfield, D. & Locher, M. (eds) *Impoliteness in Language*. Berlin: Mouton de Gruyter, pp. 17–44.

2011a *Impoliteness: Using Language to Cause Offence*. Cambridge: Cambridge University Press.

2011b 'Politeness and impoliteness'. In Aijmer, K. & Anderson, G. (eds) *Pragmatics of Society*. Berlin: Mouton de Gruyter, pp. 391–436.

Culpeper, J., Marti, L., Mei, M., Nevala, M. & Schauer, G. 2010 'Cross-cultural variation in the perception of impoliteness: A study of impoliteness events reported by students in English, China, Finland, German and Turkey'. *Intercultural Pragmatics*, vol. 7, no. 4, pp. 597–624.

Cutler, C. 1999 '"Keepin' it real": White hip-hoppers' discourses of language, race, and authenticity'. *Journal of Linguistic Anthropology*, vol. 13, no. 2, pp. 211–33.

Cutrone, P. 2005 'A case study examining backchannels in conversations between Japanese–British dyads'. *Multilingua*, vol. 24, pp. 237–74.

Daun, Å 2004 [1984] 'Swedishness as an obstacle in cross-cultural interaction'. In Kiesling, S. & Paulston, C. (eds) *Intercultural Discourse and Communication: The Essential Readings*. Boston, MA: Wiley Blackwell, pp. 150–63.

Davidson, A. I. 1986 'Archaeology, genealogy and ethics'. In Hoy, D. C. (ed.) *Foucault: A Critical Reader*. Oxford: Basil Blackwell, pp. 221–33.

Davidson, B. 2000 'The interpreter as institutional gatekeeper: The social-linguistic role of interpreters in Spanish–English medical discourse'. *Journal of Sociolinguistics*, vol. 4, no. 3, pp. 379–405.

Davies, C. 2004 'Developing awareness of crosscultural pragmatics: The case of American/German sociable interaction'. *Multilingua*, vol. 23, no. 3, pp. 207–31.

Deacon, T. 1997 *The Symbolic Species: The Co-evolution of Language and the Brain*. New York: Norton.

Demente, B. 1988 *Korean Etiquette and Ethics in Business*. Lincolnwood, Ill.: NTC Business Books.

1989 *Chinese Etiquette and Ethics in Business.* Lincolnwood, Ill.: NTC Business Books.

Djenar, D. 2008 'Which self? Pronominal choice, modernity, and self-categorizations'. *International Journal for the Sociology of Language*, vol. 189, pp. 31–54.

Doi, T. 1973 *The Anatomy of Dependence.* J. Bester (trans.), Tokyo: Kodansha.

Dorfman, P., Howell, J., Hibino, S., Lee, J., Tate, U. & Bautista, A. 1997 'Leadership in Western and Asian countries: Commonalities and differences in effective leadership processes across cultures. *Leadership Quarterly*, vol. 8, no. 3, pp. 233–74.

Drew, P. 1998 'Complaints about transgressions and misconduct'. *Research on Language and Social Interaction*, vol. 31, nos 3/4, pp. 295–325.

Drew, P. & Heritage, J. (eds) 1992 *Talk at Work: Interaction in Institutional Settings.* Cambridge: Cambridge University Press.

Drew, P. & Walker, T. 2009 'Going too far: Complaining, escalating and disaffiliation'. *Journal of Pragmatics*, vol. 41, pp. 2400–14.

Duncan, S. 1973 'Towards a grammar for dyadic conversation'. *Semiotica*, vol. 9, pp. 29–46.

1974 'On the structure of speaker interaction during speaking turns'. *Language in Society*, vol. 2, pp. 161–80.

Duranti, A. 1988 'Intentions, language and social action in a Samoan context'. *Journal of Pragmatics*, vol. 12, pp. 13–33.

2001 'Linguistic anthropology: History, ideas and issues'. In Duranti, A (ed.) *Linguistic Anthropology: A Reader*. Malden, MA: Blackwell, pp. 1–38.

Duranti, A. & Goodwin, C. 1992 'Rethinking context: An introduction'. In Duranti, A. & Goodwin, C. (eds) *Rethinking Context: Language as an Interactive Phenomenon.* Cambridge: Cambridge University Press, pp. 1–42.

Duszak, A. 2005 'Between styles and values: An academic community in transition'. In Cortese, G. & Duszak, A. (eds), *Identity, Community, Discourse: English in Intercultural Settings.* Frankfurt: Peter Lang, pp. 269–93.

Eades, D. 1992 *Aboriginal English and the Law: Communicating with Aboriginal English Speaking Clients: A Handbook for Legal Practitioners.* Brisbane: Queensland Law Society.

1993 'The case for Condren: Aboriginal English, pragmatics and the law'. *Journal of Pragmatics*, vol. 20, no. 2, pp. 141–62.

2000 'I don't think it's an answer to the question: Silencing Aboriginal witnesses in court'. *Language in Society*, vol. 29, pp. 161–95.

2004 'Understanding Aboriginal English in the legal system: A critical sociolinguistics approach'. *Applied Linguistics*, vol. 25, no. 4, pp. 491–512.

2006 'Lexical struggle in court: Aboriginal Australians versus the state'. *Journal of Sociolinguistics*. vol. 10, no. 2, pp. 153–80.

2007 'Understanding Aboriginal silence in legal contexts'. In Kotthoff, H. & Spencer-Oatey, H. (eds) *Handbook of Intercultural Communication*. Berlin: Mouton de Gruyter, pp. 285–302.

2012 'Communication with Aboriginal speakers of English in the legal process'. *Australian Journal of Linguistics*, vol. 32, no. 4, pp. 473–89.

Earley, P. C., Ang, S. & Tan, J. 2006 *CQ: Developing Cultural Intelligence at Work*. Stanford, CA: Stanford University Press.

Eckert, P. & McConnell-Ginet, S. 1992 'Think practically and look locally: Language and gender in community-based practice'. *Annual Review of Anthropology*, vol. 21, pp. 461–90.

Eckert, P. & Rickford, J. 2001 (eds) *Style and Sociolinguistic Variation*. Cambridge: Cambridge University Press.

Edwards, D. 2005 'Moaning, whinging and laughing: The subjective side of complaints'. *Discourse Studies*, vol. 7, no. 1, pp. 5–29.

Eelen, G. 2001 *A Critique of Politeness Theories*. Manchester: St Jerome.

Eggington, W. 1987 'Written academic discourse in Korean'. In Connor, U. & Kaplan, R. B. (eds) *Writing Across Cultures*. Reading: Addison-Wesley, pp. 153–68.

El-Dash, L. G. & Busnardo, J. 2001 'Perceived in-group and out-group stereotypes among Brazilian foreign language students'. *International Journal of Applied Linguistics*, vol. 11, no. 2, pp. 224–37.

Englebretson, R. 2007 'Grammatical resources for social purposes: Some aspects of stancetaking in colloquial Indonesian conversation'. In Englebretson, R. (ed.) *Stancetaking in Discourse*. Amsterdam: John Benjamins, pp. 69–110.

Errington, J. 1985a *Language and Social Change in Java: Linguistic Reflexes of Modernisation in a Traditional Royal Polity*. Ohio: Ohio University Press.

1985b 'On the nature of the sociolinguistic sign: Describing the Javanese speech levels'. In Mertz, E. (ed.) *Semiotic Mediation: Sociocultural and Psychological Perspectives*. London: Academic Press, pp. 287–310.

1988 *Structure and Style in Javanese: A Semiotic View of Linguistic Etiquette*. Philadelphia: University of Pennsylvania Press.

Fairclough, N. 1989 *Language and Power*. Harlow: Longman Group.

1992 *Discourse and Social Change*. Cambridge, UK: Polity Press.

2000 *New Labour, New Language*. London: Routledge.

Fairclough, N. & Wodak, R. 1997 'Critical discourse analysis'. In van Dijk, T. A. (ed.) *Discourse as Social Interaction*. London: Sage Publications, pp. 258–84.

Ferguson, C. 1976 'The structure and use of politeness formulas'. *Language in Society*, vol. 5, pp. 137–51.

Ferraro, G. 2002 *The Cultural Dimension of International Business*. 4th edn. Upper Saddle River, NJ: Prentice Hall.

Firth, A. (ed.) 1995 *The Discourse of Negotiation: Studies of Language in the Workplace*. Oxford: Pergamon.

Fløttum, K. (ed.) 2008 *Language and Discipline Perspectives on Academic Discourse*. Cambridge: Cambridge Scholars Publishing.

2010 'Linguistically marked cultural identity in research articles'. In Garzone, G. & Archibald, J. (eds) *Discourse, Identities and Roles in Specialized Communication*. Bern: Peter Lang, pp. 267–80.

2012 'Variation of stance and voice across cultures'. In Hyland, K. & Sancho Guinda, C. (eds) *Stance and Voice in Written Academic Genres*. Basingstoke; New York: Palgrave Macmillan, pp. 218–31.

Fløttum, K., Dahl, T., Kinn, T., Gjesdal, A. M. and Vold, E. T. 2008 'Cultural identities and academic voices'. In Fløttum, K. (ed.) *Language and Discipline Perspectives on Academic Discourse*. Cambridge: Cambridge Scholars Publishing.

Flowerdew, L. 2004 'The argument for using English specialized corpora to understand academic and professional language'. In Connor, U. & Upton, T. (eds) *Discourse in the Professions: Perspectives from Corpus Linguistics*. Amsterdam: John Benjamins, pp. 11–33.

2012 'Corpus based discourse analysis'. In Gee, J. P. & Handford, M. (eds) *The Routledge Handbook of Discourse Analysis*. New York: Routledge, pp. 174–87.

2013 *Discourse in English Language Education*. Hoboken, NJ: Taylor & Francis.

Foley, W. 1997 *Anthropological Linguistics: An Introduction*. Malden, MA: Blackwell.

Forbes, K. & Cordella, M. 1999 'The role of gender in Chilean argumentative discourse'. *International Review of Applied Linguistics in Language Teaching*, vol. 37, no. 4, pp. 277–89.

Forman, R. 2011 'Humorous language play in a Thai EFL classroom'. *Applied Lingusitics*, vol. 32, no. 5, pp. 541–65.

Foucault, M. 1963 [1973] *The Birth of the Clinic: An Archaeology of Medical Perception*. New York: Vintage Books.

1978 *The History of Sexuality: Volume 1: An Introduction*. Hurley R. (trans.), Harmondsworth: Penguin Books.

1980 *Power/Knowledge: Selected Interviews and Other Writings, 1972–1977*. New York: Pantheon.

Fraser, B. 1990 'Perspectives on politeness'. *Journal of Pragmatics*, vol. 14, pp. 219–36.

Gallois, C., Franklyn-Stokes, A., Giles, H. & Coupland, N. 1988 'Communication accommodation in intercultural encounters'. In Kim, Y. Y. & Gudykunst, W. B. (eds) *Theories in Intercultural Communication*. Newbury Park: Sage Publications, pp. 157–85.

Gaudio, R. 2003 'Coffeetalk: Starbucks and the commercialization of casual conversation'. *Language in Society*, vol. 32, no. 5, pp. 659–91.

Gavioli, L. 1995 'Turn-initial versus turn-final laughter: Two techniques for initial remedy in English/Italian bookshop service encounters'. *Discourse Processes*, vol. 19, pp. 369–84.

Gee, J. 1999, 2005 *An Introduction to Discourse Analysis: Theory and Method*. London: Routledge.

Geertz, C. 1960 *The Religion of Java*. Glencoe, IL: Free Press.

1973 *The Interpretation of Cultures: Selected Essays*. New York: Basic.

1976 'Linguistic etiquette'. In Pride, J. B. & Holmes, J. (eds) *Sociolinguistics*. New Hampshire: Penguin Books, pp. 167–79.

Gentile, A. 1991 'Working with professional interpreters'. In Pauwels, A. (ed.) *Cross-cultural Communication in Medical Encounters*. Melbourne: Monash University, Community Languages in the Professions Unit, Language and Society Centre, pp. 26–48.

Geyer, N. 2013 'Discernment and variation: The action-oriented use of Japanese honorifics. *Multilingua*, vol. 32, no. 2, pp. 155–76.

Giannoni, D. 2008 'Medical writing at the pheriphery: The case of Italian journal editorials'. *Journal of English for Academic Purposes*, vol. 7, no. 2, pp. 97–107.

Gibbons, J. 2001 'Revising the language of New South Wales police procedures: Applied linguistics in action'. *Applied Linguistics*, vol. 22, no. 4, pp. 439–69.

Giddens, A. 1982 *Profiles and Critiques in Social Theory*. London: Macmillan.

1993 *New Rules of Sociological Method*, 2nd edn. Cambridge: Polity Press.

Giles, H. 1977 *Language, Ethnicity and Intergroup Relations*. London: Academic Press.

Giles, H. & Powesland, P. 1975 *Speech Style and Social Evaluation*. London: Academic Press.

Giles, H. & Robinson, W. P. 1990 (eds) *Handbook of Language and Social Psychology*. Chichester: John Wiley & Sons.

Givón, T. (ed.) 1983 *Topic and Continuity in Discourse: A Quantitative Cross-Language Study*. Amsterdam: Benjamins.

Goddard, C. 1989 'Issues in natural semantic metalanguage'. *Quaderni di Semantica*, vol. 10, no. 1, pp. 51–64.

2005 'The lexical semantics of culture'. *Language Sciences*, no. 27, pp. 51–73.

2012 '"Early interactions" in Australian English, American English, and English English: Cultural differences and cultural scripts'. *Journal of Pragmatics*, vol. 44, pp. 1038–50.

Goddard, D. 1977 'Same setting, different norms: Phone call beginnings in France and in the United States'. *Language in Society*, vol. 6, pp. 209–19.

Goffman, E. 1955 'On facework: An analysis of ritual elements in social interaction'. *Psychiatry*, vol. 18, pp. 213–31.

1959 *The Presentation of Self in Everyday Life*. Doubleday, New York.

1967 *Interaction Ritual: Essays in Face to Face Behavior*. Doubleday, New York.

1971 *Relations in Public*. New York: Basic Books.

1974 *Frame Analysis*. Harper Collins, New York.

González-Lloret, M. 2011 'Conversation analysis of computer-mediated communication'. *CALICO Journal*, vol. 28, no. 2, pp. 308–25.

Goodwin, M. 2005 'The relevance of ethnicity, class, and gender in children's peer negotiations'. In Holmes, J. & Meyerhoff, M. (eds) *The Handbook of Language and Gender*. Malden, MA: Blackwell, pp. 229–51.

Gottlieb, N. 2006 'Book review: Fushimi, N., Matsuzawa, K., Kurokawa, N., Yamanaka, T., Oikawa, K., Noguchi, K. 2002 "Okama" wa sabetsu ka: Shūkan Kinyōbi no *Sabetsu Hyōgen* Jiken [Does "okama" have discriminatory connotations? The discriminating expression case in the weekly magazine *Shūkan Kinyōbi*]'. *Intersections: Gender, History and Culture in the Asian Context*, issue 12 <http://intersections.anu.edu.au/issue12/gotlieb_review.html> (accessed 14 May 2014).

Graham, S. 2009 'Hospitalk: Politeness and hierarchical structures in interdisciplinary discharge rounds'. *Journal of Politeness Research*, vol. 5, pp. 11–31.

Grainger, K. 2011 '"First order" and "second order" politeness: institutional and intercultural contexts'. In Linguistic Politeness Research Group (eds) *Discursive Approaches to Politeness*. Berlin: Mouton de Gruyter, pp. 167–88.

Grainger, K., Mills, S. & Sibanda, M. 2010 '"Just tell us what to do": Southern African face and its relevance to intercultural communication'. *Journal of Pragmatics*, vol. 42, no. 8, pp. 2158–71.

Grice, H. P. 1975 'Logic and conversation'. In Cole, P. & Morgan, J. (eds) *Syntax and Semantics 3: Speech Acts*. New York: Academic Press.

1989 *Studies in the Way of Words*. Cambridge, MA: Harvard University Press.

Gudykunst, W. B. 1995 'Anxiety/Uncertainty management (AUM) theory to intercultural adjustment training'. In Wiseman, R. (ed.) *Intercultural Communication Theory*. Thousand Oaks, CA: Sage, pp. 8–58.

2001 *Asian American Ethnicity and Communication*. Thousand Oaks, CA: Sage, pp. 8–58.

Gumperz, J. 1982 *Discourse Strategies*. Cambridge: Cambridge University Press.

1992 'Contextualisation and understanding'. In Duranti, A. & Goodwin, C. (eds) *Rethinking Context: Language as an Interactive Phenomenon*. Cambridge: Cambridge University Press, pp. 229–52.

1996 'The linguistic and cultural relativity of inference'. In Gumperz, J. & Levinson, S. (eds) *Rethinking Linguistic Relativity*. Cambridge: Cambridge University Press, pp. 374–406.

2004 [1982] 'Interethnic communication'. In Kiesling, S. & Paulston, C. (eds) *Intercultural Discourse and Communication: The Essential Readings*. Boston, MA: Wiley Blackwell, pp. 33–44.

Gumperz, J. & Hymes, D. (eds) 1972 *Directions in Sociolinguistics: The Ethnography of Communication*. New York: Holt, Rinehart and Winston.

Gumperz, J., Jupp, T. & Roberts, C. 1979 *Crosstalk*. Videotape. London: National Centre for Industrial Language Training.

Haffner, L. 1992 'Translation is not enough: Interpreting in a medical setting in "cross cultural medicine – a decade later"'. Special issue, *Western Journal of Medicine*, vol. 157, pp. 255–9.

2012 'Legal context'. In Jackson, J. (ed.) *The Routledge Handbook of Language and Intercultural Communication*. London: Routledge, pp. 523–36.

Haines, R. & Mann, J. 2011 'A new perspective on de-individuation via computer-mediated communication'. *European Journal of Information Sytsems*, vol. 20, pp. 156–67.

Hale, S. 2004 *The Discourse of Court Reporting. Discourse Practices of the Law, the Witness and the Interpreter*. Amsterdam: Benjamins.

Hall, E. 1959 *The Silent Language*. New York: Fawcett.

1966 *The Hidden Dimension*. Garden City, NJ: Doubleday.

1976 *Beyond Culture*. Garden City; NY: Anchor Books.

Hall, S. 1995 'Fantasy, identity, politics'. In Carter, E., Donald, J. & Squires, J. (eds) *Cultural Remix: Theories of Politics and the Popular*. London: Lawrence & Wishart, pp. 63–9.

1997 *Representation: Cultural Representation and Signifying Practices*. London: Sage.

Harkins, J. 1990 'Shame and shyness in the Aboriginal classroom: A case for practical semantics'. *Australian Journal of Linguistics*, vol. 10, pp. 293–306.

Harris, S. 2001 'Being politically impolite: Extending politeness theory to adversarial political discourse'. *Discourse and Society*, vol. 12, no. 4, pp. 451–72.

Harrison, S. 2003 'Computer-mediated interaction: using discourse maps to represent multi-party, multi-topic asynchronous discussions'. In Sarangi, S. & van Leeuwen, T. (eds) *Applied Linguistics and Communities of Practice*. London: Continuum, pp. 60–80.

Hassall, T. 2013 'Beyond strategy choice: A reply to Al-Gahtani and Roever'. *Applied Linguistics*, vol. 34, no. 4, pp. 501–6.

Hastings, S. Musambira, G. & Ayoub, R. 2011 'Revisiting Edward T. Hall's work on Arabs and olfaction: An update with implications for intercultural communication scholarship'. *Journal of Intercultural Communication Research*, vol. 40, no. 1, pp. 3–20.

Hatfield, H. & Hahn, J. 2011 'What Korean apologies require of politeness theory'. *Journal of Pragmatics*, vol. 43, pp. 1303–17.

Hatim, B. 2001 *Teaching and Researching Translation*. Essex, UK: Pearson Education.

Haugh, M. & Bousfield, D. 2012 'Mock impoliteness, jocular mockery and jocular abuse in Australian and British English'. *Journal of Pragmatics*, vol. 44, pp. 1099–114.

Heller, M. 1988 'Strategic ambiguity: Codeswitching in the management of conflict'. In Heller, M. (ed.) *Codeswitching: Anthropological and Sociolinguistic Perspectives*. Mouton: Berlin, pp. 77–96.

2010 'The commodification of language'. *Annual Review of Anthropology*, vol. 39, pp. 101–14.

2013 'In Memorium: John Gumperz (1922–2013)'. *Journal of Sociolinguistics*, vol. 17, no. 3, pp. 394–9.

Hellerman, J. & Cole, E. 2008 'Practices for social interaction in the language-learning classroom: Disengagements from dyadic task interaction'. *Applied Linguistics*, vol. 30, no. 2, pp. 186–215.

Henry, A. & Ho, D. 2010 'The act of complaining in Brunei – then and now'. *Journal of Pragmatics*, vol. 42, pp. 840–55.

Herring, S. 2005 'Gender and power in on-line communication'. In Holmes, J. & Meyerhoff, M. (eds) *The Handbook of Language and Gender*. Malden, MA: Blackwell, pp. 202–28.

Hess-Lüttich, E. W. B. & Wilde, E. 2003 'Der Chat als Textsorte und/oder als Dialogsorte?' *Linguistik Online*, vol. 13, no. 1, pp. 161–80 <www.linguistik-online.de/13_01/hessLuettichWilde.pdf> (accessed 7 April 2014).

Heydon, G. 2005 *The Language of Police Interviewing: A Critical Analysis*. New York: Palgrave Macmillan.

Hill, J. & Irvine, J. 1993 'Introduction'. In Hill, J. & Irvine, J. (eds) *Responsibility and Evidence in Oral Discourse*. Cambridge: Cambridge University Press.

Hinds, J. 1980 'Japanese expository prose'. *Papers in Linguistics: International Journal of Human Communication*, vol. 13, no. 1, pp. 117–58.

Hofstede, G. 1980 *Culture's Consequences: International Differences in Work-Related Values*. Beverly Hills, California: Sage Publications.

1983 'Dimensions of national cultures in fifty countries and three regions'. In Deregowski, J. B. & Dziurawiec, S. & Annis, R. C. (eds) *Explications in Cross-Cultural Psychology*. Netherlands: Swets & Zeitlinger, pp. 335–55.

1998 'Think locally, act globally: Cultural constraints in personnel management'. *Management International Review*, special issue, vol. 38, no. 2, pp. 7–26.

2010 *Cultures and Organizations: Software of the Mind*. 2nd edn. New York: McGraw-Hill.

2013 'Dimensions' <www.geert-hofstede.com/dimensions> (accessed 5 December 2013).

Hofstede, G. & Hofstede, G. J. 2013 'Dimensions of national cultures' <www.geerthofstede.com/dimensions-of-national-cultures> (accessed 5 December 2013).

Holmes, J. 1995 *Women, Men and Politeness*. London: Longman.

2005 '"Leadership talk: How do leaders "do mentoring", and is gender relevant?' *Journal of Pragmatics*, vol. 37, pp. 1779–800.

2006 'Sharing a laugh: Pragmatic aspects of humor and gender in the workplace'. *Journal of Pragmatics*, vol. 38, pp. 26–50.

Holmes, J. & Marra, M. 2004 'Relational practice in the workplace: Women's talk or gendered discourse?' *Language in Society*, vol. 33, no. 3, pp. 377–98.

Holmes, J., Marra, M. & Schnurr, S. 2008 'Impoliteness and ethnicity: Māori and Pākehā discourse in New Zealand workplaces'. *Journal of Politeness Research*, vol. 4, pp. 193–219.

Holmes, J. & Stubbe, M. 2005 '"Feminine" workplaces: stereotype and reality'. In Holmes, J. & Meyerhoff, M. (eds) *The Handbook of Language and Gender*. Malden, MA: Blackwell, pp. 573–99.

Holmes, P. & O'Neil, G. 2012 'Developing and evaluating intercultural competence: Ethnographies of intercultural encounters'. *International Journal of Intercultural Relations*, vol. 36, pp. 707–18.

Holt, E. 2010 'The last laugh: Shared laughter and topic termination'. *Journal of Pragmatics*, vol. 42, pp. 1513–25.

Holtgraves, T. 2005 'The production and perception of speech acts'. *Journal of Pragmatics*, vol. 37, pp. 2024–43.

Horn, L. 2006 'Implicature'. In Horn, L. & Ward, G. (eds) *The Handbook of Pragmatics*. Malden, MA: Blackwell, pp. 53–73.

House, J. 2010 'Impoliteness in Germany: Intercultural encounters in everyday and institutional talk'. *Intercultural Pragmatics*, vol. 7, no. 4, pp. 561–95.

House, J. & Kasper, G. 1981 'Politeness markers in English and German'. In Coulmas, F. (ed.) *Conversational Routines*. The Hague: Mouton, pp. 157–85.

Hvoslef, E. 2001 'The social use of personal names among the Kyrgyz'. *Contemporary South Asia*, vol. 20, no. 1, pp. 85–95.

Hyland, K. 2000 *Disciplinary Discourses: Social Interactions in Academic Writing*. London: Longman.

2004 *Disciplinary Discourses: Social interactions in Academic Writing*. Ann Arbor: University of Michigan Press.

2005 *Metadiscourse: Exploring Interaction in Writing*. London: Continuum.

2008 'As can be seen: Lexical bundles and disciplinary variation'. *English for Specific Purposes*, vol. 27, pp. 4–21.

2009 *Academic Discourse: English in a Global Context*. London, Continuum.

Hyland K. & Sancho Guinda C. (eds) 2012 *Stance and Voice in Written Academic Genres*. Basingstoke; New York: Palgrave Macmillan pp 218–31.

Hyland, K. & Tse, P. 2005 'Hooking the reader: A corpus study of evaluative that in abstracts'. *English for Specific Purposes*, vol. 24, pp. 12–39.

Hymes, D. 1972 'Models of the interaction of language and social life'. In Gumperz, J. & Hymes, D. (eds) *The Ethnography of Communication*. New York: Holt, Rinehart & Winston, pp. 35–71.

1974 *Foundations of Sociolinguistics: An Ethnographic Approach*. Philadelphia: University of Pennsylvania Press.

Ide, S. 1989 'Formal forms and discernment: Two neglected aspects of universals of linguistic politeness'. *Multilingua*, vol. 8, nos. 2/3, pp. 223–38.

Intachakra, S. 2012 'Politeness motivated by the "heart" and "binary" rationality in Thai culture'. *Journal of Pragmatics*, vol. 44, pp. 619–35.

Jacquemet, M. 2011 'Crosstalk 2.0: Asylum and communicative breakdowns'. *Text and Talk*, vol. 31, no. 4, pp. 475–97.

Jary, M. 1998 'Relevance theory and the communication of politeness'. *Journal of Pragmatics*, vol. 30, no. 1, pp. 1–19.

Jaworski, A. & Thurlow, C. 2009 'Taking an elitist stance: Ideology and the discursive production of social distinction'. In Jaffe, A. (ed.) *Stance: Sociolinguistics Perspectives*. New York: Oxford University Press.

Johansson, S. 1998 'On the role of corpora in cross-linguistic research'. In Johansson, S. & Oksefjell, S. (eds) *Corpora and Cross-Linguistic Research: Theory, Method, and Case Studies*. Amsterdam: Rodopi, pp. 1–24.

Joseph, J. 2006 *Language and Politics*. Edinburgh: Edinburgh University Press.

Kachru, Y. 1988 'Writers in Hindi and English'. In Purves, A. (ed.) *Writing across Languages and Cultures*. Newbury Park: Sage, pp. 109–37.

de Kadt, E. 1998 'The concept of face and its applicability to the Zulu language'. *Journal of Pragmatics*, vol. 29, pp. 173–91.

Kageyama, T. & Tomori, I. 1976 'Japanese whimperatives'. *Papers in Japanese Linguistics*, vol. 4, pp. 13–53.

Kaplan, R. B. 1966 'Cultural thought patterns in intercultural education'. *Language Learning*, vol. 16, no. 1, pp. 1–20.

1972 Cultural thought patterns in inter-cultural education. In Croft, K. (ed.) *Readings in English as a Second Language*. Cambridge, Mass.: Winthrop, pp. 246–62.

1988 'Contrastive rhetoric and second language learning: notes toward a theory of contrastive rhetoric'. In Purves, A. (ed.) *Writing across Languages and Cultures*. Newbury Park: Sage, pp. 275–304.

Kartomihardjo, S. 1981 *Ethnography of Communicative Codes in East Java* (vol. D/39). Canberra: The Department of Linguistics, Research School of Pacific Studies, The Australian National University.

Kasper, G. 2006 'Speech acts in interaction: Towards discursive pragmatics'. In Bardovi-Harlig, K., Félix-Brasdefer, J. & Omar, A. (eds) *Pragmatics and Language Learning*. National Foreign Language Resource Center, University of Hawaii, pp. 281–314.

Kasper, G. & Blum-Kulka, S. (eds) 1993 *Interlanguage Pragmatics*. Oxford: Oxford University Press.

Katriel, T. 1986 'Talking straight: Dugri speech in Israeli Sabra culture'. Cambridge: Cambridge University Press.

Kecskes, I. 2013a 'Focus on the speaker: An introduction'. *Journal of Pragmatics*, vol. 48, pp. 1–3.

2013b *Intercultural Pragmatics*. Oxford: Oxford University Press.

Keeler, W. 1990 'Speaking of gender in Java'. In Atkinson, J. & Errington, S. (eds) *Power and Difference: Gender in Island Southeast Asia*. Stanford, CA: Stanford University Press, pp. 127–52.

2001 *Javanese: A Cultural Approach*. Athens: Ohio University for International Studies.

Kendon, A. 1990 *Conducting Interaction: Patterns of Behavior in Focused Encounters*. Cambridge: Cambridge University Press.

Kiesling, S. 1997 'Power and the language of men'. In Johnson, S. & Meinhof, U. (eds) *Language and Masculinity*. Oxford: Blackwell.

2004 'Dude' *American Speech*, vol. 79, no. 3, pp. 281–305.

2009 'Style as stance: Stance as the explanation for patterns of sociolinguistic variation'. In Jaffe, A. (ed.) *Stance: Sociolinguistic Perspectives*. New York: Oxford, pp. 171–94.

Kim, Y. Y. 1977 'Communication patterns of foreign immigrants in the process of acculturation'. *Human Communication Research*, vol. 41, pp. 66–76.

1988 *Cross-Cultural Adaptation: Current Approaches*. Newbury Park, CA: Sage.

King, J. 2011 'Silence in the second language classrooms of Japanese universities'. *Applied Linguistics*, vol. 34, no. 3, pp. 325–43.

Kirkpatrick, A 1991 'Information sequencing in mandarin letters of request'. *Anthropological Linguistics*, vol. 33, no. 2, pp. 183–203.

Kitalong, K. & Kitalong, T. 2000 'Complicating the tourist gaze: Literacy and the Internet as catalysts for articulating a postcolonial Palauan identity'. In Hawisher, G. & Selfe, C. (eds) *Global Literacies and the World-Wide Web*. London: Routledge, pp. 1–18.

Kjaerbeck, S. 1998 'The organization of discourse units in Mexican and Danish business negotiations'. *Journal of Pragmatics*, vol. 30, pp. 347–62.

de Klerk, V. & Bosch, B. 1997 'The sound patterns of English surnames'. *Language Sciences*, vol. 19, no. 4, pp. 289–301.

Klopf, D. & McCroskey, J. 2007 *Intercultural Communication Encounters*. Boston, MA: Pearson.

Knapp, M. L., Hart, R. P., Friedrich, G. W. & Shulman, G. M. 1973 'The rhetoric of goodbye: Verbal and nonverbal correlates of human leave-taking'. *Speech Monographs*, vol. 40, pp. 182–98.

Koentjaraningrat, R. M. 1989 *Javanese Culture*. Singapore: Oxford University Press.

Koyama, T. 1992 *Japan: A Handbook in Intercultural Communication*. Sydney: Macquarie University Press.

Kretzenbacher, H. L. 2005 'Hier im großen internetz, wo sich alle dududuzen [Internet discourse politeness and German address]'. Paper given at the Third International Conference on Language Variation in Europe (IClaVE), Amsterdam, pp. 1–15.

Kupfer, A. 1988 'How to be a global manager'. *Fortune*, March, pp. 52–8.

Kuppens, A. 2009 'English in advertising: Generic intertextuality in a globalizing media environment'. *Applied Linguistics*, vol. 31, no. 1, pp. 115–35.

Kurniasih, Y. 2006 'Gender, class and language preferences: A case study in Yogyakarta'. In Allan, K. (ed.) *Selected Papers from the 2005 Conference of the Australian Linguistic Society*. Clayton, Australia: Monash University Press.

Labov, W. 1972a *Language in the Inner City*. Philadelphia: Pennsylvania University Press.
1972b *Sociolinguistic Patterns*. Philadelphia: Pennsylvania University Press.

Ladegaard, H. 2011 '"Doing power" at work: Responding to male and female management styles in a global business corporation'. *Journal of Pragmatics*, vol. 43, pp. 4–19.
2012 'Rudeness as a discursive strategy in leadership discourse: Culture, power and gender in a Hong Kong workplace'. *Journal of Pragmatics*, vol. 44, pp. 1661–79.

Lakoff, R. 1973 'The logic of politeness: Or, p's and q's'. In Corum C., Smith-Stark, sT. C. & Weiser, A. (eds) *Papers from the Ninth Regional Meeting of the Chicago Linguistic Society*. Chicago Linguistic Society, pp. 292–305.
1975 *Language and Woman's Place*. New York: Harper & Row.
1979 'Stylistic strategies within a grammar of style'. In Orasanu J., Slater, M. K. & Adler, L. L. (eds) *Language, Sex and Gender*. Annals of the New York Academy of Sciences, pp. 53–80.
2005 'Language, gender, and politics: Putting "women" and "power" in the same sentence'. In Holmes, J. & Meyerhoff, M. (eds) *The Handbook of Language and Gender*. Malden, MA: Blackwell, pp. 161–78.

Lamiani, G. 2008 'Letter to the Editor: Cultural competency in healthcare: Learning across boundaries'. *Patient Education and Counseling*, vol. 73, pp. 396–97.

Larson, M. 1984 *Meaning-Based Translation: A Guide to Cross-Language Equivalence*. Lanham, MD: University Press of America.

Lea, M. & Spears, R. 1991 'Computer-mediated communication, de-individuation and group decisionmaking'. *International Journal of Man-Machine Studies*, vol. 39, pp. 283–301.

Leanza, Y. 2007 'Roles of community interpreters in paediatrics as seen by interpreters, physicians and researchers'. In Pöchhackert F. & Shlesinger M. (eds) *Healthcare Interpreting*. Amsterdam: Benjamins, pp. 11–34.

Lebra, T. S. 1976 *Japanese Culture and Behaviour: Selected Readings*. rev. edn. Honolulu: University Press of Hawaii.

Lee, J. 2009 'Interpreting inexplicit language during courtroom examination'. *Applied Linguistics*, vol. 30, no. 1, pp. 93–114.

Lee, J. & Pinker, S. 2010 'Rationales for indirect speech: The theory of the strategic speaker'. *Psychological Review*, vol. 117, no. 3, pp. 785–807.

Leech, G. 1983 *Principles of Pragmatics*. New York: Longman.

2007 'Politeness: Is there an East–West divide?' *Journal of Politeness Research: Language, Behaviour, Culture*, vol. 3, no. 2, pp. 167–206.

Lerner, G. 1991 'On the syntax of sentences-in-progress'. *Language in Society*, vol. 20, pp. 441–58.

Leung, E. & Gibbons, J. 2009 'Interpreting Cantonese utterance-final particles in bilingual courtroom discourse'. *Interpreting*, vol. 11, no. 2, pp. 190–215.

Levinson, S. C. 1983 *Pragmatics*. Cambridge: Cambridge University Press.

1985 'What's special about conversational inference?' Paper presented to the British Psychological Society Annual Meeting, Swansea, April 1985.

1992 'Activity types and language'. In Drew, P. & Heritage, J. (eds) *Talk at Work: Interaction in Institutional Settings*. Cambridge: Cambridge University Press, pp. 66–100.

Liddicoat, A. 2009 'Communication as culturally contexted practice: A view from inter-cultural communication'. *Australian Journal of Linguistics*, vol. 29, no. 1, pp. 115–33.

Lieberman, M. 2013 'Passive blindness in the NYRB [New York Review of Books]' *Language Log* <http://languagelog.ldc.upenn.edu/nll/?p=9375> (accessed 8 April 2014).

Lingard, L. 2013 'Language matters: towards an understanding of silence and humour in medical education'. *Medical Education*, vol. 47, pp. 40–8.

Liu, S. 2011 'An experimental study of the classification and recognition of Chinese speech acts'. *Journal of Pragmatics*, vol. 43, pp. 1801–17.

Li Wei 1998 'The 'why' and 'how' questions in the analysis of conversational code-switching'. In Auer, P. (ed.) *Code-Switching in Conversation: Language, Interaction and Identity*. London & New York: Routledge, pp. 156–79.

Locher, M. 2006 'Polite behaviour within relational work: The discursive approach to politeness'. *Multilingua*, vol. 25, pp. 249–67.

Locher, M. & Watts, R. 2005 'Politeness theory and relational work'. *Journal of Politeness Research*, vol. 1, no. 1, pp. 9–33.

Loftus, E. 2001 'Language and memories in the judicial system'. In Oaks, D. (ed.) *Linguistics at Work: A Reader of Applications*. Cambridge, MA: Heinle & Heinle Publishing, pp. 3–12.

Loven, K. 2008 *Watching Si Doel: Television, Language, and Cultural Identity in Contemporary Indonesia*. Hawaii: University of Hawaii Press.

Lustig, M. & Koester, J. 2010 *Intercultural Competence: Interpersonal Communication Across Cultures*. 6th edn. Boston, MA: Pearson.

Makoni, S. & Pennycook. A. 2007 'Disinventing and reconstituting languages'. In Makoni S. & Pennycook A. (eds) *Disinventing and Reconstituting Languages*. Clevedon, UK: Multilingual Matters, pp. 1–41.

Manns, H. 2011 'Stance, style and identity in Java'. PhD thesis, Monash University, Melbourne.

2012 'First-person pronominal variation, stance and identity in Indonesia'. *Australian Journal of Linguistics*, vol. 32, no. 4, pp. 435–56.

(n.d.) 'Stance and identity in the expanding circle', unpublished paper.

Mao, Lu Ming, R. 1994 'Beyond politeness theory: "Face" revisited and renewed'. *Journal of Pragmatics*, vol. 21, pp. 451–86.

Márquez-Reiter, R. 2005 'Complaint calls to a caregiver service company: The case of desahogo'. *Intercultural Pragmatics*, vol. 2, no. 4, pp. 481–514.

2013 'The dynamics of complaining in a Latin American for-profit commercial setting'. *Journal of Pragmatics*, vol. 57, pp. 231–47.

Marriott, H. 1990 'Intercultural business negotiations: The problem of norm discrepancy'. *Australian Review of Applied Linguistics*, Series S, vol. 7, pp. 33–65.

1997 'Australian–Japanese business interaction: Some features of language and cultural contact'. In Bargiela-Chiappini, F. & Harris, S. (eds) *The Languages of Business: An International Perspective*. Edinburgh: Edinburgh University Press, pp. 49–71.

Martin, E. 2007 '"Frenglish" for sale: multilingual discourses for addressing today's global consumer'. *World Englishes*, vol. 26, no. 2, pp. 170–88.

Martin, J. & Nakayama, T. 2004 *International Communication in Contexts*. 3rd edn. Boston: McGraw Hill.

Matsumoto, Y. 1988 'Reexamination of the universality of face: Politeness phenomena in Japanese'. *Journal of Pragmatics*, vol. 12, pp. 403–26.

1989 'Politeness and conversational universals: Observations from Japanese'. *Multilingua*, vol. 8, pp. 207–21.

Matthiessen, C. 1995 *Lexicographical Cartography: English Systems*. Tokyo: International Language Sciences Publishers.

Mauranen, A. 1993 *Cultural Differences in Academic Rhetoric*. Frankfurt am Main: Peter Lang.

2005 'English as a lingua franca – an unknown language?' In Cortese G. & Duszak A. (eds), *Identity, Community, Discourse: English in Intercultural Settings*. Frankfurt: Peter Lang, pp. 269–93.

Mauranen, A., Pérez-Llantada, C. & Swales, J. 2010 'Academic Englishes – a standardized knowledge?' In Kirkpatrick, A. (ed.) *The Routledge Handbook of World Englishes*. London: Routledge, pp. 634–52.

Mauss, M. 1974 *Oeuvres 2*. Paris: Editions de Minuit.

McConvell, P. 1988 'MIX-IM-UP: Aboriginal codeswitching, old and new'. In Heller, M. (ed.) *Codeswitching: Anthropological and Sociolinguistic Perspectives*. Mouton: Berlin, pp. 97–150.

Macfadyen, L., Roche, J. & Doff, S. 2004 *Communicating across Cultures in Cyberspace*. Münster: Lit Verlag.

Meeuwesen, L., van den Brink-Muinen, A. & Hofstede, G. 2009 'Can dimensions of national culture predict cross-national differences in medical communication?' *Patient and Education Counseling*, vol. 75, pp. 58–66.

Meier, A. J. 1995a 'Defining politeness: Universality in appropriateness'. *Language Sciences*, vol. 17, no. 4, pp. 345–56.

1995b 'Passages of politeness'. *Journal of Pragmatics*, vol. 24, pp. 38–192.

Mendoza-Denton, N. 2007 *Homegirls: Language and Cultural Practice among Latina Youth Gangs*. Malden, MA: Blackwell.

Merrison, A., Wilson, J., Davies, B. & Haugh, M. 2012 'Getting stuff done: Comparing e-mail requests from students in higher education in Britain and Australia'. *Journal of Pragmatics*, vol. 44, pp. 1077–98.

Migdadi, F. Badarneh, B. & Momani, M. 2012 'Public complaints and complaint responses in calls to a Jordanian radio phone-in program'. *Applied Linguistics*, vol. 33, no. 1, pp. 321–41.

Miller, D. & Slater, D. 2001 *The Internet: An Ethnographic Approach*. Paris: Berg Publishers.

Mills, S. 2003 *Gender and Politeness*. Cambridge: Cambridge University Press.

Mitchell-Kernan, C. 2001 'Signifying and marking: Two Afro-American speech acts'. In Duranti, A (ed.) *Linguistic Anthropology: A Reader*. Malden, MA: Blackwell, pp. 151–64.

Mitzutani, O. & Mitzutani, N. 1987 *How to Be Polite in Japanese*. Tokyo: Japan Times.

Moreno, M. 2002 'The address system in the Spanish of the Golden Age'. *Journal of Pragmatics*, vol. 34, no. 1, pp. 15–47.

Morgan, M. 2010 'The presentation of indirectness and power in everyday life'. *Journal of Pragmatics*, vol. 42, pp. 283–91.

Mugford, G. 2013 'Foreign-language users confronting anti-normative politeness in a Mexican university'. *Intercultural Pragmatics*, vol. 10, no. 1, pp. 101–30.

Mühlhäusler, P. 1996 *Linguistic Ecology: Language Change and Linguistic Imperialism in the Pacific Region*. London: Routledge.

Mullany, L. 2004 'Gender, politeness and institutional power roles: Humour as a tactic to gain compliance in workplace business meetings'. *Multilingua*, vol. 23, pp. 13–37.

2008 '"Stop hassling me!" Impoliteness, power and gender identity in the professional workplace. In Bousfield, D. & Locher, M. (eds) *Impoliteness in Language: Studies with Power in Theory and Practice*. Berlin: Mouton De Gruyter, pp. 231–54.

Müller-Jacquier, B. 2000 'Linguistic awareness of cultures: Grundlagen eines Trainingsmoduls'. In Boslten, J. (ed) *Studien zur sozialen Unternehmenskommunikation*. Leipzig: Popp, pp. 20–49.

Munday, J. 2001 *Introducing Translation Studies: Theories and Applications*. London and New York: Routledge.

Murillo, A. 1989 'Do translated ads sell?' In Hammand, D. (ed.) *Coming of Age*. 30th Annual Conference ATA. Washington DC. Medford, NJ: Learned Information.

Myers-Scotton, C. 1993 *Social Motivations for Codeswitching*. Oxford: Clarendon Press.

2006 *Multiple Voices: An Introduction to Bilingualism*. Malden, MA: Blackwell.

Neil, D. 1996 *Collaboration in Intercultural Discourse: Examples from a Multicultural Workplace*. Frankfurt am Main: Peter Lang.

Neustypný, J. V. 1985 'Language norms in Australian–Japanese contact situations'. In Clyne, M. (ed.) *Australia, Meeting Place of Languages*. Canberra: Pacific Linguistics, pp. 161–70.

Nguyên, C. 1991 'Barriers to communication between Vietnamese and non-Vietnamese'. *Journal of Vietnamese Studies*, vol. 1, no. 4, pp. 40–5.

Nida, E. & Taber, C. 1974 *The Theory and Practice of Translation*. Leiden: E. J. Brill.

Noor, R. 2001 'Contrastive rhetoric in expository prose: Approaches and achievements'. *Journal of Pragmatics*, vol. 33, no. 2, pp. 255–69.

Nureddeen, F. 2008 'Cross cultural pragmatics: Apology strategies in Sudanese Arabic'. *Journal of Pragmatics*, vol. 40, pp. 279–306.

Ochs, E. 1992 'Indexing gender'. In Duranti, A. & Goodwin, C. (eds) *Rethinking Context: Language as an Interactive Phenomenon*. Cambridge: Cambridge University Press, pp. 335–58.

Ogiermann, E. 2009 'Politeness and in-directness across cultures: A comparison of English, German, Polish and Russian requests'. *Journal of Politeness Research*, vol. 5, pp. 189–216.

O'Hanlon, R. 2006 'Australian hip hop: A sociolinguistic investigation'. *Australian Journal of Linguistics*, vol. 26, no. 2, pp. 193–209.

Olshtain, E. & Cohen, A. 1983 'Apology: A speech-act set'. In Wolfson, N. & Judd, E. (eds) *Sociolinguistics and Language Acquisition*. Rowley, Massachusetts: Newbury House, pp. 18–36.

Onorato, R. & Turner, J. 2002 'Challenging the primacy of the personal self: The case for depersonalized self-conception'. In Kashimi Y., Foddy M. & Platow M. (eds) *Self and Identity: Personal, Social, and Symbolic*. Mahwah, NJ: Lawrence Erlbaum Associates, pp. 145–78.

O'Neil, F. 2011 'From language classroom to clinical context: The role of language and culture in communication for nurses using English as a second language: A thematic analysis'. *International Journal of Nursing Studies*, vol. 48, pp. 1120–28.

Otsuji, E. & Pennycook, A. 2010 'Metrolingualism: Fixity, fluidity and language in flux'. *International Journal of Multilingualism*, vol. 7, no. 3, pp. 240–54.

Oxford English Dictionary 2013a 'come' <www.oed.com> (accessed 5 December 2013) 2013b 'you' <www.oed.com> (accessed 5 December 2013)

Pan, Y. 2011 'Cantonese politeness in the interview setting'. *Journal of Asian Pacific Communication*, vol. 21, no. 1, pp. 10–33.

Pan, Y., Scollon, S. & Scollon, R. 2002 *Professional Communication in International Settings*. Malden, MA: Blackwell.

Pandharipande, R. 1983 'Contrastive studies of English and Marathi'. *Annual Review of Applied Linguistics*, vol. 3, pp. 118–36.

Paramasivam, S. 2011 'Rapport management in air traffic control in Malaysian aviation discourse'. *Journal of Asian Pacific Communication*, vol. 21, no. 1, pp. 77–96.

Park, H. Lee, H. & Song, J. 2005 '"I am sorry to send you SPAM": Cross-cultural differences in the use of apologies in email advertising in Korea and the US'. *Human Communication Research*, vol. 31, no. 3, pp. 365–98.

Pauwels, A. 2011 'Vale Michael Clyne'. *Journal of Sociolinguistics*, vol. 15, no. 1, pp. 122–3.

Pauwels, A., D'Argaville, M. & Eades, D. 1992 'Problems and issues of cross-cultural communication in legal settings'. In Pauwels, A. (ed.) *Cross-Cultural Communication in Legal Settings*. Language and Society Centre, National Languages and Literacy Institute of Australia, Melbourne: Monash University, pp. 77–105.

Pavlidou, T. 1991 'Universality and relativity in cross-cultural politeness research'. Paper delivered at the International Conference on Contrastive Linguistics, Innsbruck, Austria, May 1991.

Pennycook, A. 2001 *Critical Applied Linguistics: A Critical Introduction*. London: Lawrence Erlbaum Associates.
2003 'Global Englishes, Rip Slyme and performativity'. *Journal of Sociolinguistics*, vol. 7, no. 4, pp. 513–33.

Peirce, C. 1991 *Peirce on Signs: Writings on Semiotic*. Chapel Hill: UNC Press.

Pérez-Llantada, C. 2012 *Scientific Discourse and the Rhetoric of Globalization: The Impact of Culture and Language*. London, New York: Continuum.

Phillips, S. 2004 [1983] 'A comparison of Indian and Anglo communicative behaviour in classroom situations'. In Kiesling, S. & Paulston, C. (eds) *Intercultural Discourse and Communication: The Essential Readings*. Boston, MA: Wiley Blackwell, pp. 291–303.

Phiri, J., Dietsch, E. & Bonner, A. 2010 Cultural safety and its importance for Australian midwifery practice'. *Collegian*, vol. 17, pp. 105–11.

Pinker, S. 2011 'Discussion note: Indirect speech, politeness, deniability, and relationship negotiation: Comment on Marina Terkourafi's "The Puzzle of Indirect Speech"'. *Journal of Pragmatics*, 48, pp. 2866–8.

Pinto, D. 2011a 'Are Americans insincere? Interactional style and politeness in everyday America'. *Journal of Politeness Research*, vol. 7, pp. 215–38.

2011b 'Passing greetings and interactional style: A cross-cultural study of American English and Peninsular Spanish'. *Multilingua*, vol. 27, pp. 371–88.

Pomerantz, A. 1984 'Agreeing and disagreeing with assessments: Some features of preferred/dispreferred turn shapes'. In Atkinson, J. M. & Heritage, J. (eds) *Structures of Social Action*. Cambridge: Cambridge University Press, pp. 57–101.

Precht, K. 1998 'A cross-cultural comparison of letters of recommendation'. *English for Specific Purposes*, vol. 17, no. 3, pp. 241–65.

Prechtl, E. & Lund, A. 2007 'Intercultural competence and assessment: Perspectives from the INCA Project'. In Kotthoff, H. & Spender-Oatey, H. (eds) *Handbook of Intercultural Communication*. Berlin: Mouton de Gruyter, pp. 467–90.

Rampton, B. 1995 *Crossing: Language and Ethnicity among Adolescents*. Singapore: Longman.

1998 'Language crossing and the redefinition of reality'. In Auer, P. (ed.) *Code-Switching in Conversation: Language, Interaction and Identity*. London & New York: Routledge, pp. 290–317.

Redmond, M. 2000 'Cultural distance as a mediating factor between stress and intercultural competence'. *International Journal of Intercultural Relations*, vol. 24, pp. 151–9.

Rees-Miller, J. 2011 'Compliments revisited: Contemporary compliments and gender'. *Journal of Pragmatics*, vol. 43, pp. 2673–88.

Rendle-Short, J. 2009 'The address term mate in Australian English: Is it still a masculine term?' *Australian Journal of Linguistics*, vol. 29, no. 2, pp. 245–68.

Rickford, J. & McNair-Knox, F. 1994 'Addressee- and topic-influenced style-shift: A quantitative sociolinguistic study'. In Finegan, E. & Biber, D. (eds) *Sociolinguistic Perspectives on Register*. New York & Oxford: Oxford University Press, pp. 235–76.

Ricks, D. A. 1983 *Big Business Blunders: Mistakes in Multinational Marketing*. Homewood, Ill.: Dow-Jones Irwin.

Roberts, C. 2006 'Context in dynamic interpretation'. In Horn, L. & Ward, G. (eds) *The Handbook of Pragmatics*. Malden, MA: Blackwell, pp. 197–220.

Rogerson-Revell, P. 2007 'Humour in business: A double-edged sword: A study of humour and style shifting in intercultural business meetings'. *Journal of Pragmatics*, vol. 39, pp. 4–28.

2011 'Chairing international business meetings: Investigating humour and leadership style in the workplace'. In Angouri, J. & Marra, M. (eds) *Constructing Identities at Work*. London: Palgrave, pp. 61–84.

Rosaldo, M. 1982 'The things we do with words: Ilongot speech acts and speech act theory in philosophy'. *Language in Society*, vol. 1, no. 2, pp. 203–37.

Rost-Roth, M. 2007 'Intercultural training'. In Kotthoff, H. & Spencer-Oatey, H. (eds) *Handbook of Intercultural Communication*. Berlin: Mouton de Gruyter, pp. 491–518.

Rumelhart, D. E., Smolensky, P., McClelland, J. L. & Hinton, G. E. 1986 'Schemata and sequential thought processes in PDP models'. In McClelland, J. L., Rumelhart, D. E. & the PDP Research Group (eds) *Parallel Distributed Processing: Explorations in the Microstructure of Cognition, vol. 2, Psychological and Biological Models*. Cambridge, Massachusetts: MIT Press, pp. 7–57.

Ryan, C. 2013 *Language Use in the United States: 2011. American Community Survey Reports*. US Department of Commerce. <www.census.gov/prod/2013pubs/acs-22. pdf> (accessed 5 December 2013).

Sacks, H. 1967–8 *Lectures on Conversation*, 2 vols (ed. G. Jefferson 1992). Cambridge, Massachusetts: Blackwell Publishers.

1992 *Lectures on Conversation, I–II* (ed. G. Jefferson). Oxford: Blackwell Publishers.

Sacks, H., Schegloff, E. A. & Jefferson, G. 1974 'A simplest systematic for the organization of turn-taking in conversations'. *Language*, vol. 59, pp. 941–2.

Sadock, J. 2006 'Speech acts'. In Horn, L. & Ward, G. (eds) *The Handbook of Pragmatics*. Malden, MA: Blackwell, pp. 53–72.

Saito, J. 2011 'Managing confrontational situations'. *Journal of Pragmatics*, vol. 43, pp. 1689–706.

Samovar, L., Porter, R., McDaniel, E. & Roy, C. 2013 *Communication Between Cultures*. 8th edn. Boston: Wadsworth Cengage.

Sánchez-Muñoz, A 2013 'Who soy yo? The creative use of "Spanglish" to express hybrid identity in Chicana/o heritage language learners of Spanish'. *Hispania*, vol. 96, no. 3, pp. 440–1.

Sanders, R. 2013 'The duality of speaker meaning: What makes self-repair, insincerity, and sarcasm possible'. *Journal of Pragmatics*, 48, pp. 112–22.

Sarangi, S. 1996 'Conflation of institutional and cultural stereotyping in Asian migrants' discourse'. *Discourse and Society*, vol. 7, pp. 359–87.

Sarangi, S. & Roberts, C. (eds) 1999 *Talk, Work and Institutional Order: Discourse in Medical, Mediation and Management Settings*. Berlin: Mouton de Gruyter.

Saville-Troike, M. 2003 *The Ethnography of Communication*. Oxford: Basil Blackwell.

Schegloff, E. A. 1968 'Sequencing in conversational openings'. In Gumperz, J. & Hymes, D. (eds) *Directions in Sociolinguistics: The Ethnography of Communication*. New York: Holt, Rinehart & Winston, pp. 346–80.

1982 'Discourse as an interactional achievement: Some uses of "Uh huh" and other things that come between sentences'. In Tannen, D. (ed.) *Analyzing Discourse: Text and Talk*. Georgetown University Round Table in Languages and Linguistics 1981, Washington DC: Georgetown University Press.

Schegloff, E. A. & Sacks, H. 1973 'Opening up closings'. *Semiotica*, vol. 8, pp. 289–327.

Schiano, D. 1997 'Convergent methodologies in cyber-psychology: A case study, Behavior Research Methods'. *Instruments and Computers*, vol. 29, no. 2, pp. 270–3.

Schilling-Estes, N. 2004 'Investigating stylistic variation'. In Chambers, J. K., Trudgill, P. & Schilling-Estes, N. (eds) *The Handbook of Language Variation and Change*. Oxford: Blackwell, pp. 375–401.

Schnurr, S. 2009a 'Constructing leader identities through teasing at work'. *Journal of Pragmatics*, vol. 41, pp. 1125–38.

2009b *Leadership Discourse at Work: Interactions of Humour, Gender and Workplace Culture*. London: Palgrave.

Schnurr, S. & Chan, A. 2011 'When laughter is not enough. Responding to teasing and self- denigrating humour at work'. *Journal of Pragmatics*, vol. 43, pp. 20–35.

Schnurr, S., Marra, M. & Holmes, J. 2007 'Being (im)polite in New Zealand workplaces: Māori and Pākehā leaders'. *Journal of Pragmatics*, vol. 39, pp. 712–29.

2008 'Impoliteness as a means of contesting power in the workplace. In Bousfield, D. & Locher, M. (eds) *Impoliteness in Language: Studies with Power in Theory and Practice*. Berlin: Mouton De Gruyter, pp. 211–30.

Schnurr, S. & Zayts, O. 2011 'Be(com)ing a leader: A case study of co-constructing professional identities at work'. In Angouri, J. & Marra, M. (eds) *Constructing Identities at Work*. London: Palgrave, pp. 40–60.

Schourup, L. 2011 'The discourse marker now: A relevance theoretic-approach'. *Journal of Pragmatics*, vol. 43, pp. 2110–29.

Schouten, B. & Meeuwesen, L. 2006 'Cultural differences in medical communication: A review of the literature'. *Patient Education and Counseling*, vol. 64, pp. 21–34.

Schouten, B., Meeuwesen, L., Tromp, F. & Harmsen, H. 2007 'Cultural diversity in patient participation: The influence of patients' characteristics and doctors' communicative behaviour'. *Patient Education and Counselling*, vol. 67, nos. 1/2, pp. 214–23.

Schulze, M. 1999 'Substitution of paraverbal and nonverbal cues in the written medium of IRC'. In Naumann B. (ed.) *Dialogue Analysis and the Mass Media. Proceedings of the International Conference in Erlangen*, 2–3 April 1998, Niemeyer (Beiträge zur Dialogforschung 20), Tübingen, pp. 65–82.

Scollon, R. Scollon, S. & Jones, R. 2012 *Intercultural Communication: A Discourse Approach*. 3rd edn. Malden, MA: Blackwell.

Searle, J. R. 1969 *Speech Acts: An Essay in the Philosophy of Language*. Cambridge: Cambridge University Press.

1975 'Indirect speech acts'. In Cole, P. & Morgan, J. (eds) *Syntax and Semantics 3 (Speech Acts)*. New York: Academic Press, pp. 59–82.

1979 *Expression and Meaning: Studies in the Theory of Speech Acts*. Cambridge: Cambridge University Press.

1995 *The Construction of Social Reality*. New York: Free Press.

Shariati, M. & Chamani, F. 2010 'Apology strategies in Persian'. *Journal of Pragmatics*, vol. 42, pp. 1689–99.

Sharifian, F. 2004 'Cultural schemas and intercultural communication: A study of Persian'. In Leigh, J. & Loo, E. (eds) *Outer Limits: A Reader in Communication Across Cultures*. Melbourne: Language Australia, pp. 119–30.

2005 'The Persian cultural schema of shekasteh-nafsi: A study of complement responses in Persian and Anglo-Australian speakers'. *Pragmatics and Cognition*, vol. 13, no. 2, pp. 337–61.

2006 'A cultural-conceptual approach and world Englishes: The case of Aboriginal English'. *World Englishes*, vol. 25, no. 1, pp. 11–22.

2008 'Distributed, emergent cultural cognition, conceptualisation and language'. In Frank, R. M., Dirvan, R., Ziemke, T. & Bernárdez, E. (eds) *Body, Language and Mind (vol. 2): Sociocultural Situatedness.* Berlin/New York: Mouton de Gruyter, pp. 109–36.

Shoaps, R. 2009 'Moral irony and moral personhood in Sakapultek discourse and culture'. In Jaffe, A. (ed.) *Stance: Sociolinguistic Perspectives.* Oxford: Oxford University Press, pp. 92–118.

Shum, W. & Lee, C. 2013 '(Im)politeness and disagreement in two Hong Kong Internet discussion forums'. *Journal of Pragmatics,* vol. 50, pp. 52–83.

Sidnell, J. 2010 *Conversation Analysis: An Introduction.* John Wiley & Sons.

Siegel, J. 1986 *Solo in the New Order: Language and Hierarchy in an Indonesian City.* Princeton: Princeton University Press.

Sifianou, M. 1989 'On the telephone again! Differences in telephone behaviour: England versus Greece'. *Language in Society,* vol. 18, pp. 527–44.

2012 'Disagreements, face and politeness'. *Journal of Pragmatics,* vol. 44, pp. 1554–65.

Silverstein, S. 2010 '"Direct" and "indirect" communicative acts in semiotic perspective'. *Journal of Pragmatics,* vol. 42, pp. 337–53.

Smith, R. 1983 *Japanese Society: Tradition, Self, and the Social Order.* Cambridge: Cambridge University Press.

Sorrells, K. 2013 *Intercultural Communication: Globalization and Social Justice.* Thousand Oaks: Sage.

Spencer-Oatey, H. 2005 '(Im)Politeness, face and perceptions of rapport: Unpacking their bases and interrelationships'. *Journal of Politeness Research,* vol. 1, pp. 95–119.

2008 'Face, (im)politeness and rapport'. In Spencer-Oatey, H. (ed.) *Culturally Speaking: Culture, Communication and Politeness Theory.* 2nd edn. London: Continuum, pp. 11–47.

Spencer-Oatey, H. & Xing, J. 2003 'Managing rapport in intercultural business interactions: A comparison of two Chinese–British welcome meetings'. *Journal of Intercultural Studies,* vol. 24, no. 1, pp. 33–46.

Sperber, D. & Hirschfeld, L. 1999 'Culture, cognition and evolution'. In Wilson, R. & Kiel, F. (eds) *MIT Encyclopedia of the Cognitive Sciences.* Cambridge, Massachusetts: MIT Press, pp. cxi–cxxxii.

Sperber, D. & Wilson, D. 1986 *Relevance.* London: Routledge & Kegan Paul.

St Andre, J. 2013 'How the Chinese lost "face"'. *Journal of Pragmatics,* vol. 55, pp. 68–85.

Starks, D., Taylor-Leech, K. & Willoughby, L. 2012 'Nicknames in Australian secondary schools: Insights into nicknames and adolescent views of self'. *Names,* vol. 60, no. 3, pp. 135–49.

Sugimoto, N. 1998 'Norms of apology depicted in US American and Japanese literature on manners and etiquette'. *International Journal of Intercultural Relations,* vol. 22, no. 3, pp. 251–76.

Sugimoto, T. & Levine, J. 2000 'Multiple literacies and multimedia: a comparison of Japanese and American uses of the Internet'. In Hawisher G. & Selfe C. (eds) *Global Literacies and the World-Wide Web.* London: Routledge.

Sumner, W. 1906 *Folkways: A Study of the Sociological Importance of Usages, Manners, Customs, Mores, and Morals.* Boston: Ginn and Company.

Sun, H. 2012 'Shifting practices and emerging patterns: Telephone service encounters in Shanghai'. *Language in Society,* vol. 41, pp. 417–47.

Suszczyńska, M. 1999 'Apologizing in English, Polish and Hungarian: Different languages, different strategies'. *Journal of Pragmatics,* vol. 31, pp. 1053–65.

Suurmond, J. & Seeleman, C. 2006 'Shared decision-making in an intercultural context: Barriers in the interaction between physicians and immigrant patients'. *Patient Education and Counseling*, vol. 60, pp. 253–9.

Suzuki, T. 1976 'Language and behavior in Japan: The conceptualization of personal relations'. *Japan Quarterly*, vol. 23, no. 3, pp. 255–66.

Svartvik, J. & Quirk, R. (eds) 1980 *A Corpus of English Conversation*. Lund: Gleerup.

Swales, J. M. 1990 *Genre Analysis: English in Academic and Research Settings*. Cambridge: Cambridge University Press.

2004 *Research Genres: Exploration and Applications*. Cambridge: Cambridge University Press.

Tajfel, H. 1982 *Social Identity and Intergroup Relations*. Cambridge: Cambridge University Press.

Takahashi, T. & Beebe, L. M. 1993 'Cross-linguistic influence in the speech act of correction'. In Kasper, G. & Blum-Kulka, S. (eds) *Interlanguage Pragmatics*. Oxford: Oxford University Press, pp. 138–57.

Takemata, K. 1976 *Genkō Shippitsu Nyūmon [An Introduction to Writing Manuscripts]*. Tokyo: Natsume-sha.

Tannen, D. 1981 'Indirectness in discourse: Ethnicity as conversational style'. *Discourse Processes*, vol. 4, pp. 221–38.

1990 *You Just Don't Understand: Women and Men in Conversation*. New York: Harper Collins.

1994 *Talking from 9 to 5: How Women's and Men's Conversational Styles Affect Who Gets Heard, Who Gets Credit, and What Gets Done at Work*. New York: Avon Books.

2004 [1981] 'New York Jewish conversational style'. In Kiesling, S. & Paulston, C. (eds) *Intercultural Discourse and Communication: The Essential Readings*. Boston, MA: Wiley Blackwell, pp. 135–49.

2011 'John Gumperz: an appreciation'. *Text and Talk*, vol. 31, no. 4, pp. 499–502.

Teo, P. 2000 'Racism in the news: A critical discourse analysis of news reporting in two Australian newspapers'. *Discourse and Society*, vol. 11, no. 1, pp. 7–49.

Thomas, S. 1998 'Translation as intercultural conflict'. In Hunston, S. (ed.) *Language at Work: Selected Papers from the Annual Meeting of the British Association for Applied Linguistics*. Clevedon: Multilingual Matters, pp. 98–108.

Thurlow, C. & Jaworski, A. 2003 'Communicating a global reach: Inflight magazines as a globalising genre in tourism'. *Journal of Sociolinguistics*, vol. 7, no. 4, pp. 581–608.

Ting-Toomey, S. & Chung, L. 2005 *Understanding Intercultural Communication*. Los Angeles: Roxbury.

Tomasello, M. 1999 *The Cultural Origins of Human Cognition*. Cambridge: Cambridge University Press.

Trosborg, A. (ed.) 1994 *Interlanguage Pragmatics: Requests, Complaints and Apologies* (Studies in Anthropological Linguistics 7). Berlin/New York: Mouton de Gruyter.

Tulviste, T. Mizera, L. & De Geer, B. 2011 '"There is nothing bad in being talkative": Meanings of talkativeness in Estonian and Swedish adolescents'. *Journal of Pragmatics*, vol. 43, pp. 1603–9.

Turner J. & Hiraga, M. 2012 'Researching intercultural communication in a UK higher education context'. In Jin, L. & Cortazzi, M. (eds) *Researching Intercultural Learning: Investigations in Language and Education.* Houndmills: Palgrave Macmillan.

Tylor, E. B. 1871 *Primitive Culture: Researches into the Development of Mythology, Philosophy, Religion, Art, and Custom, Volume I.* London: John Murray, Albemarle Street.

Usami, M. 2002 *Discourse Politeness in Japanese Conversation: Some Implications for a Universal Theory of Politeness.* Tokyo: Hitsuji Shobo.

Van Dijk, T. 1987 *Communicating Racism: Ethnic Prejudice in Thought and Talk.* Newbury Park, California: Sage Publications.

1996 'Discourse, power and access'. In Caldas-Coulthard, C. R. & Coulthard M. (eds) *Texts and Practices: Readings in Critical Discourse Analysis.* London: Routledge, pp. 84–104.

Vassileva, I. 2000 *Who is the Author? A Contrastive Analysis of Authorial Presence in English, German, French, Russian and Bulgarian Academic Discourse.* Sankt Augustin: Asgard Verlag.

Verhagen, A. 2005 *Constructions of Intersubjectivity: Discourse, Syntax, and Cognition.* Oxford: Oxford University Press.

Vernon, M., Raifman, L., Greenberg, S. & Monteiro, B. 2001 'Forensic pretrial police interviews of deaf suspects avoiding legal pitfalls'. *Journal of Law and Psychiatry,* vol. 24, pp. 43–59.

Victor, D. 1992 *International Business Communication* New York: Harper Collins.

Waitzkin, H. 1991 *The Politics of Medical Encounters: How Patients and Doctors Deal With Social Problems.* New Haven/London: Yale University Press.

Walker, T., Drew, P. & Local, J. 2011 'Responding indirectly'. *Journal of Pragmatics,* vol. 43, pp. 2434–51.

Wardhaugh, R. 2010 *An Introduction to Sociolinguistics.* 6th edn. West Sussex: Basil Blackwell.

Warnicke, C. & Plajert, C. 2012 'Turn-organisation in mediated phone interaction using Video Relay Service (VRS)'. *Journal of Pragmatics,* vol. 44, pp. 1313–34.

Watts, R. J. 1989 'Relevance and relational work: Linguistic politeness as politic behavior'. *Multilingua,* vol. 8, pp. 131–66.

2003 *Politeness.* Cambridge: Cambridge University Press.

Watts, R. J., Ide, S. & Ehlich, K. 1992 *Politeness in Language: Studies in its History, Theory and Practice.* Berlin/New York: Mouton de Gruyter.

Weigl, R. 2009 'Intercultural competence through cultural self-study: A strategy for adult learners'. *International Journal of Intercultural Relations,* vol. 33, pp. 346–60.

Weller, G. 1992 'Advertising: A true challenge for cross-cultural translation'. In Moore, C. N. & Lower, L. (eds) *Translation East and West: A Cross-Cultural Approach: Selected Conference Papers.* Honolulu: University of Hawaii.

West, C. 1998 'When the doctor is a "lady": Power, status and gender in physician-patient encounters'. In Coates, J. (ed.) *Language and Gender: A Reader.* Oxford: Oxford University Press, pp. 396–412.

Widdowson, H. G. 1978 *Teaching Language and Communication.* London: Oxford University Press.

Wierzbicka, A. 1972 *Semantic Primitives* (Linguistische Forschungen 22). Frankfurt: Athenäum.

1980 *Lingua Mentalis: The Semantics of Natural Language*. Sydney/New York: Academic Press.

1985 'Different cultures, different languages, different speech acts'. *Journal of Pragmatics*, vol. 9, pp. 145–78.

1991 *Cross-Cultural Pragmatics: The Semantics of Human Interaction*. Berlin: Mouton de Gruyter.

1994a 'Cognitive domains and the structure of the lexicon: The case of emotions'. In Hirschfeld, L. A. & Gelman, S. A. (eds) *Mapping the Mind: Domain Specificity in Cognition and Culture*. Cambridge: Cambridge University Press, pp. 771–97.

1994b 'Cultural scripts: A semantic approach to cultural analysis and cross- cultural communication'. In Bouton, L. & Kachru, Y. (eds) *Pragmatics and Language Learning*. Urbana-Champaign: University of Illinois, pp. 1–24.

2003 *Cross-Cultural Pragmatics: The Semantics of Human Interaction*. 2nd edn. Berlin: Mouton de Gruyter.

Wierzbicka, A. & Goddard, C. 2004 'Cultural scripts: What are they and what are they good for?' *Intercultural Pragmatics*, vol. 1, no. 2, pp. 153–66.

Willoughby, L. 2007 'You have to speak it at least: Language and identity maintenance among Australian migrant teenagers'. PhD thesis, Monash University, Melbourne.

Wilson, S. 1998 *The Means of Naming: A Social and Cultural History of Personal Naming in Western Europe*. London: OCL Press.

Wodak, R. 1996 *Disorders of Discourse*. London: Addison Wesley Longman.

Wolfowitz, C. 1991 *Language Style and Social Space: Stylistic Choice in Suriname Javanese*. Urbana and Chicago: University of Illinois Press.

Woods, N. 1988 'Talking shop: Sex and status as determinants of floor apportionment in a work setting'. In Coates, J. & Cameron, D. (eds) *Women in their Speech Communities*. London: Longman, pp. 141–57.

Woolard, K. 1988 'Codeswitching and comedy in Catalonia'. In Heller, M. (ed.) *Anthropological and Sociolinguistic Perspectives*. Mouton: Berlin, pp. 53–76.

2008 'What dat now?: Linguistic-anthropological contributions to the explanation of sociolinguistic icons and change'. *Journal of Sociolinguistics*, vol. 12, no. 4, pp. 432–52.

Wouk, F. 1998 'Solidarity in Indonesian conversation: The discourse marker kan'. *Multilingua*, vol. 17, pp. 379–406.

Wyatt, B. & Promkandorn, S. 2012 'A discourse analysis of the Thai experience of "being krengjai"'. *Intercultural Pragmatics*, vol. 9, no. 3, pp. 361–83.

Yashima, T. 2010 'The effects of international volunteer work experiences on intercultural competence of Japanese youth'. *International Journal of Intercultural Relations*, vol. 34, pp. 268–82.

Young, L. 1982 'Inscrutability revisited'. In Gumperz, J. J. (ed.) *Discourse Structures*. Cambridge: Cambridge University Press, pp. 72–84.

Yu, C. 2013 'Two interactional functions of self-mockery in everyday English conversations: A multimodal analysis'. *Journal of Pragmatics*, vol. 50, pp. 1–22.

Zayts, O. & Schnurr, S. 2011 'Laughter as medical providers' resource: Negotiating informed choice in prenatal genetic counseling'. *Research on Language and Social Interaction*, vol. 44, no. 1, pp. 1–20.

Žegarac, V. 2007 'A cognitive pragmatic perspective on communication and culture'. In Koffhoff, H. & Spencer-Oatey, H. (ed.) *Handbook of Intercultural Communication*. Berlin: Mouton de Gruyter, pp. 31–54.

2008 'Culture and communication'. In Spencer-Oatey, H. (ed.) *Culturally Speaking: Culture, Communication and Politeness Theory*. London: Continuum, pp. 48–70.

Žegarac, V. & Pennington, M. 2008 'Pragmatic transfer'. In Spencer-Oatey, H. (ed.) *Culturally Speaking: Culture, Communication and Politeness Theory*. London: Continuum, pp. 141–63.

Zuengler, J. 1989 'Performance variation in native speaker–non native speaker interactions: Ethnolinguistic differences or discourse domain?' In Gass, S., Madden, C., Preston, D. & Selinker, L. (eds) *Variation in Second Language Acquisition, Volume 1: Discourse and Pragmatics*. Cleveland: Multilingual Matters.

Index